TRABAJOS QUE QUIEREN LOS NIÑOS

¿QUÉ SIGNIFICA SER BOMBERO?

CHRISTINE HONDERS

PowerKiDS press™
New York

ROUND LAKE AREA
LIBRARY
906 HART ROAD
ROUND LAKE, IL 60073
(847) 546-7060

Published in 2020 by The Rosen Publishing Group, Inc.
29 East 21st Street, New York, NY 10010

Copyright © 2020 by The Rosen Publishing Group, Inc.

All rights reserved. No part of this book may be reproduced in any form without permission in writing from the publisher, except by a reviewer.

First Edition

Translator: Ana María García
Editor, Spanish: Natzi Vilchis
Book Design: Michael Flynn

Photo Credits: Cover, p. 1 Tyler Stableford/Stone/Getty Images; pp. 4, 6, 8, 10, 12, 14, 16, 18, 20, 22 (background) Apostrophe/Shutterstock.com; p. 5 Isaiah Shook/Shutterstock.com; p. 7 (main) sandyman/Shutterstock.com; p. 7 (inset) 7th Son Studio/Shutterstock.com; p. 9 https://commons.wikimedia.org/wiki/File:Raphael_-_Fire_in_the_Borgo.jpg; p. 11 Justin Sullivan/Getty Images; p. 13 Bruno Ismael Silva Alves/Shutterstock.com; p. 15 JRP Studio/Shutterstock.com; p. 17 potowizard/Shutterstock.com; p. 19 Rena Schild/Shutterstock.com; p. 21 Anton Havelaar/Shutterstock.com; p. 22 Jamroen Jaiman/Shutterstock.com.

Cataloging-in-Publication Data

Names: Honders, Christine.
Title: ¿Qué significa ser bombero? / Christine Honders.
Description: New York : PowerKids Press, 2020. | Series: Trabajos que quieren los niños | Includes glossary and index.
Identifiers: ISBN 9781725305830 (pbk.) | ISBN 9781725305489 (library bound) | ISBN 9781725305472 (6 pack)
Subjects: LCSH: Fire extinction—Vocational guidance—Juvenile literature. | Fire fighters—Juvenile literature.
Classification: LCC TH9119.H66 2019 | DDC 363.37023—dc23

Manufactured in the United States of America

CPSIA Compliance Information: Batch #CSPK19. For Further Information contact Rosen Publishing, New York, New York at 1-800-237-9932.

CONTENIDO

Los peligros del fuego 4
¿Cómo se produce un incendio? . . . 6
Los primeros bomberos 8
¡Al rescate! 10
El equipo de los bomberos 12
¡La seguridad es lo primero! 14
Arriesgando la vida 16
Convertirse en bombero 18
Un día en la estación
   de bomberos 20
Los héroes del vecindario 22
Glosario. 23
Índice 24
Sitios de Internet. 24

Los peligros del fuego

El fuego es increíble: nos da calor y luz, pero también puede ser peligroso. Puede arruinar casas y bosques. También puede matar gente. Cuando el fuego se convierte en un peligro, llamamos a los bomberos. El trabajo de un bombero es apagar incendios.

5

¿Cómo se produce un incendio?

El fuego necesita tres cosas para arder: **combustible**, calor y **oxígeno**. Los bomberos apagan los incendios eliminando uno de estos tres elementos. Eliminan el calor del fuego rociándolo con agua y eliminan el oxígeno utilizando **extintores**.

7

Los primeros bomberos

¡Hace dos mil años, en Roma, ya había bomberos! Si se producía un incendio, se colocaban formando una fila junto al lago o río más cercano. Se iban pasando baldes o cubetas de agua unos a otros formando una cadena. El último bombero de la fila arrojaba el agua sobre el fuego.

LEO·PP·IIII

¡Al rescate!

Cuando suena la alarma contra incendios, ¡los bomberos corren al rescate! Apagan el fuego y evitan que se propague. Además, localizan y ayudan a las personas que quedan atrapadas. Los bomberos también luchan contra los incendios forestales en los bosques. De igual forma, intervienen en otras emergencias, como los accidentes de auto.

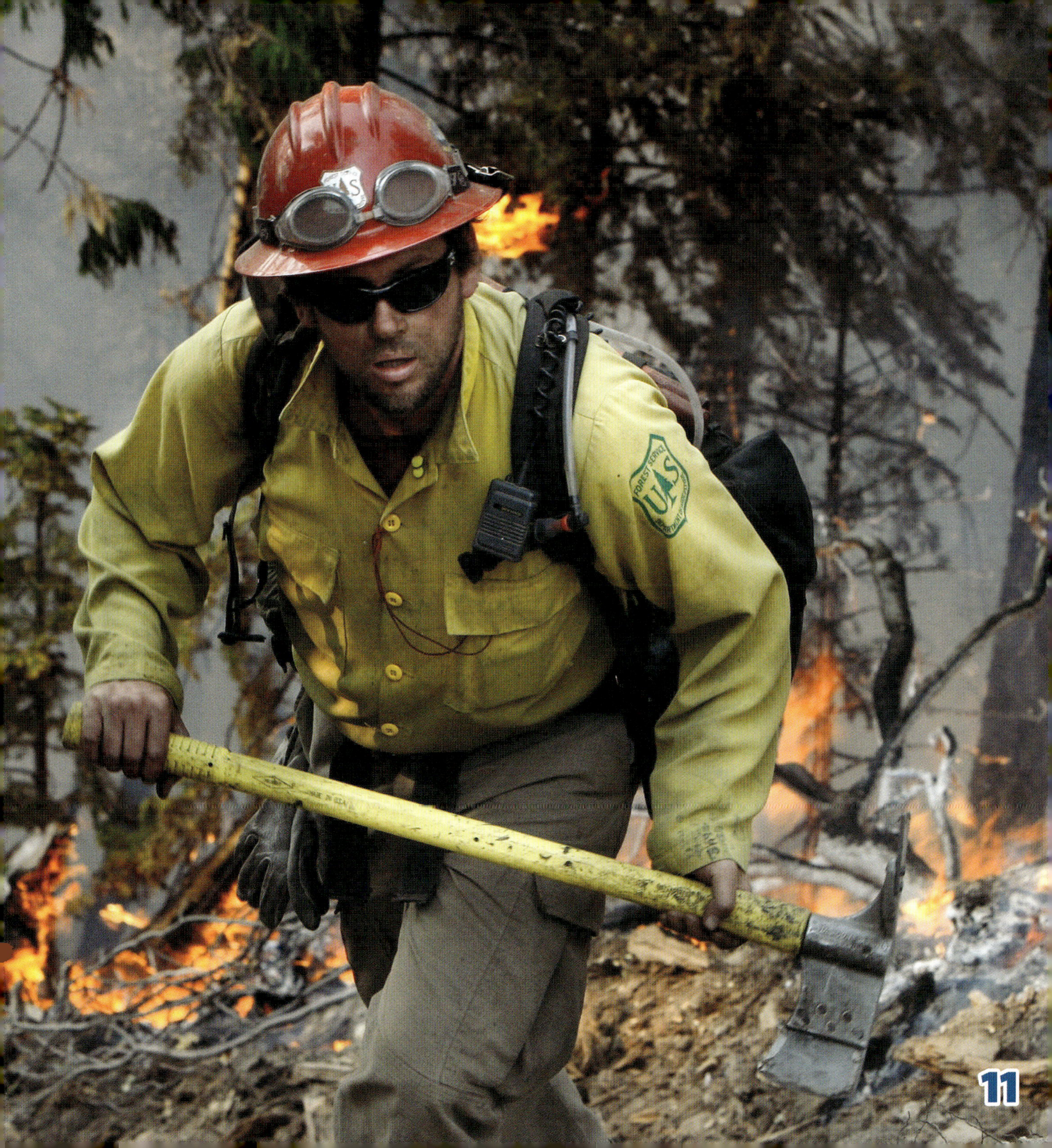
FOREST SERVICE
U.S.

El equipo de los bomberos

Los bomberos utilizan muchas herramientas. Conectan mangueras a los **hidrantes de incendio** y usan bombas de agua para alimentar las mangueras. También tienen vehículos especiales. Los camiones bomba disponen de bombas de agua y largas mangueras. Los camiones de escalera giratoria se utilizan para rescatar personas de edificios altos. Los helicópteros arrojan agua para apagar los incendios forestales.

13

¡La seguridad es lo primero!

Los bomberos usan cascos, chaquetas, guantes y botas especiales para protegerse del calor y de las llamas. También llevan máscaras con tanques de aire para poder respirar. En caso de necesitar ayuda, los bomberos utilizan **dispositivos** especiales que emiten un sonido para indicar a otros bomberos su posición.

15

Arriesgando la vida

Los bomberos arriesgan su vida constantemente. Se meten en edificios en llamas para rescatar a la gente. Algunas cosas, al quemarse, pueden ser perjudiciales para la salud de los bomberos. El humo puede causarles problemas respiratorios **de por vida**.

17

Convertirse en bombero

Para ser bombero necesitas graduarte de la escuela secundaria o *high school*. Después debes pasar tres pruebas para demostrar que estás capacitado para este trabajo. También se puede acudir a la escuela de bomberos. Algunos reciben entrenamiento en la estación de bomberos con bomberos experimentados.

19

Un día en la estación de bomberos

La mayoría de las llamadas no son por incendios, sino de personas que están enfermas o **lesionadas**. Algunos bomberos tienen formación médica para estas emergencias. También se dedican a enseñar a la gente cómo prevenir los incendios o cómo actuar en caso de encontrarse con uno.

21

Los héroes del vecindario

Los bomberos hacen su trabajo en equipo, por lo que tienen que cuidarse los unos a los otros. Hacen lo posible para mantener la seguridad del grupo. Son como una familia. Los bomberos arriesgan su vida para salvar a los demás. ¡Son los héroes de nuestro vecindario!

GLOSARIO

combustible: algo que se usa para producir calor o electricidad (como gasolina o madera).

de por vida: para siempre.

dispositivo: herramienta que realiza una cosa determinada.

extintor: herramienta que apaga el fuego rociándolo y cortando su oxígeno.

hidrante de incendio: tubería en el suelo con una salida a la que se puede conectar una manguera para rociar agua.

lesionado: que está herido o adolorido.

oxígeno: gas incoloro e insípido que se encuentra en el aire que necesitamos para respirar.

ÍNDICE

A
agua, 6, 8, 12
alarma, 10

B
bosque, 4, 10

C
calor, 4, 6, 14
camión, 12

E
estación
   de bomberos, 18, 20

H
helicóptero, 12
humo, 16

L
luz, 4

M
manguera, 12

R
rescatar, 10, 12, 16
Roma, 8

SITIOS DE INTERNET

Debido a que los enlaces de Internet cambian constantemente, PowerKids Press ha creado una lista de sitios de Internet relacionados con el tema de este libro. Este sitio se actualiza con regularidad. Por favor, utiliza este enlace para acceder a la lista:
www.powerkidslinks.com/JKW/firefighter

BRADNER LIBRARY
SCHOOLCRAFT COLLEGE
18600 HAGGERTY ROAD
LIVONIA, MICHIGAN 48152

Y0-CWO-188

JN 371 .L18 1969
Larson, Laurence Marcellus, 1868-1938.
The king's household in England before the Norman

WITHDRAWN

WITHDRAWN

BULLETIN OF THE UNIVERSITY OF WISCONSIN
NO. 100

HISTORY SERIES, VOL. 1, No. 2, PP. 55-204

THE KING'S HOUSEHOLD IN ENGLAND BEFORE THE NORMAN CONQUEST

BY

LAURENCE MARCELLUS LARSON

A THESIS SUBMITTED FOR THE DEGREE OF DOCTOR OF PHILOSOPHY
UNIVERSITY OF WISCONSIN
1902

MADISON, WISCONSIN
SEPTEMBER, 1904

Republished by
Scholarly Press, 22929 Industrial East, St. Clair Shores, Michigan 48080

JN
371
.L18
1969

Standard Book Number 403-00042-4

This edition is printed on a high-quality, acid-free paper that meets specification requirements for fine book paper referred to as "300-year" paper

PREFACE.

This study was undertaken at the suggestion of Professor Charles H. Haskins, now of Harvard University. Professor Haskins has followed the work through all its various stages, including that of proof-sheets, and to him first and most of all do I wish to express my thanks for continued assistance and generous encouragement. To Professor F. G. Hubbard I am indebted for assistance in various ways, especially on the Old English side of the work; to Professor Julius E. Olson for placing at my disposal his Norse library and otherwise helping me to secure the necessary literature; and to Professor Charles Gross of Harvard University for criticisms and suggestions after the work had reached the manuscript stage. I also owe much to the assistance of my wife, Lillian May Larson, whose hand has helped in the preparation of almost every page. Further I desire to express my appreciation of the many courtesies extended to me by the library staffs of the Wisconsin Historical Society and of the University of Wisconsin while pursuing my investigations. My thanks are also due to the authorities of Harvard University Library for the use of books not obtainable here.

LAURENCE M. LARSON.

Madison, Wis., Aug. 3, 1904.

CONTENTS.

	PAGE
ABBREVIATIONS	61

CHAPTER I.
The Problem and the Sources 63

CHAPTER II.
The Earlier *Comitatus* in England: the Gesith 76

CHAPTER III.
The Later *Comitatus* in England: the Thegn 89

CHAPTER IV.
The King's Reeve: *Praefectus Regis* 104

CHAPTER V.
The Secular Dignitaries of the Royal Household 117

CHAPTER VI.
The King's Priest. The Chancery 137

CHAPTER VII.
The Innovations of Cnut and the Danes 146

CHAPTER VIII.
The Lesser Officials and Servants of the Court 172

CHAPTER IX.
The Development of the King's Household in England and on the Continent 185

INDEX 205

ABBREVIATIONS.

A.-S. Chron.: Anglo-Saxon Chronicle. (Thorpe.) 2 vols. London, 1861.
Beow.: Beowulf.
Bibl. der ang. Poesie: Bibliothek der angelsächsischen Poesie. (Grein; later edition by Wülker.) 3 vols. Cassel, 1883–98.
Bibl. der ang. Prosa: Bibliothek der angelsächsischen Prosa. (Grein.) Cassel and Göttingen, 1872.
Cartul.: Cartularium Saxonicum. (Birch.) 3 vols. London, 1885–93.
C. H.: Stubbs, Constitutional History of England. Vol. I. Oxford, 1897. (Sixth edition.)
Conqu. of Eng.: Green, Conquest of England. New York, 1884.
C. P. B.: Corpus Poeticum Boreale. 2 vols. (Vigfusson and Powell.) Oxford, 1883.
D. R. G.: Brunner, Deutsche Rechtsgeschichte. 2 vols. Leipzic, 1887.
D. V. G.: Waitz, Deutsche Verfassungsgeschichte. 6 vols. Berlin, 1880. (Third edition.)
Eng. Hist. Rev.: English Historical Review.
Flor. Wig.: Florentii Wigorniensis Chronicon ex Chronicis. (Thorpe.) 2 vols. London, 1848–49.
Found. of Eng.: Ramsay, The Foundations of England. 2 vols. London, 1898.
H. E.: Bedae Historia Ecclesiastica. (Stevenson.) London, 1838.
Hist. des Inst. Mon.: Luchaire, Histoire des Institutions Monarchiques. 2 vols. Paris, 1891. (Second edition.)

Hist. of Eng.: Lappenberg, History of England. 2 vols. (Thorpe.) London, 1881.

Hist. York: The Historians of the Church of York and Its Archbishops. (Raine.) Vol. I. London, 1879.

K. C. D.: Codex Diplomaticus. (Kemble.) 6 vols. London, 1839-48.

N. C.: Freeman, History of the Norman Conquest of England. 6 vols. Oxford, 1873-79.

N. F. H.: Munch, Det norske Folks Historie. 6 vols. Christiania, 1852-63.

Reg. Sacr. Anglic: Stubbs, Registrum Sacrum Anglicanum. Oxford, 1858.

Sax. in Eng.: Kemble, Saxons in England. (Birch.) 2 vols. London, 1876.

S. R. D.: Scriptores Rerum Danicarum (Langebek.) 9 vols. Copenhagen, 1777-1878.

Vocab.: Anglo-Saxon and Old English Vocabularies. (Wright and Wülker.) 2 vols. London, 1884.

THE KING'S HOUSEHOLD IN ENGLAND BEFORE THE NORMAN CONQUEST.

CHAPTER I.

THE PROBLEM AND THE SOURCES.

The importance of the king's household as an element in the social and political life of a nation has always been considerable. In earlier days, as the center of culture and the home of power, the royal court exerted a directing influence that was felt to the farthest limit of the kingdom and often beyond. In the shadow of the king's house creed and custom grew to strength and maturity, dialects rose to the dignity of language and the beginnings of letters, learning and art received a sheltering care. It is not long since the final word on all political matters was spoken in the king's council-chamber; and even in these days of organic laws and parliaments the influence of the royal surroundings on the determination of state policies is not to be wholly ignored. During the middle ages, when the royal court and the central administration were practically the same thing, this influence was particularly potent. However, as government in the later centuries became more highly organized and was differentiated from the court, the importance of the palatine service naturally declined. New institutions developed and replaced the crude creations of the earlier age; still, many of these, when followed back to their origins, will be found to have historic connection with the royal court.

It is my purpose to present in the following chapters a study of the king's household in early England,—to show, as far as possible, the lines of development, the causes of changes, the sources of innovations, and the successive periods of growth. The work naturally begins with the earliest historic period of Teutonic Britain and properly closes with the passing of the Saxon dynasty. The field of research can be most conveniently divided into four sections, corresponding to the four periods of Old English history: the time before Alfred, when the country was still divided into petty kingdoms; the period from 871 to 1015, or, in a general way, the tenth century; the Danish period; and the reign of Edward the Confessor. In discussing the sources, however, no distinction need be made between those of the third and fourth periods as they are of much the same character and may be considered under one head, as eleventh century documents.

Of the sources antedating Alfred's accession the charters and the laws claim the greatest antiquity. In Kemble's collection of Anglo-Saxon charters[1] there are sixty-two documents that are referred to the seventh century. Unfortunately nearly all of these are forgeries; of the sixty-two only eleven have satisfied Kemble as to their genuineness,[2] and in all probability a closer examination would reduce this number considerably. In justice to Kemble it should be said that his criticisms generally appear so just and so conservative that one who uses his work hesitates to question his authority. Yet, I am unable to see how he could have passed the first document in his collection without at least expressing a doubt. As the charter has no signatures we have to depend wholly on the text in investigating it as to authenticity. The grant has the boundaries given in the vernacular,[3] in a sentence of good normal West-Saxon which might have been written in the tenth century. That such could have been the language of Kent in the days of Augustine is simply unthinkable. There seems to be no authentic charter before the last quarter of the seventh century. Birch, in his *Cartularium Saxonicum,* has introduced a number of documents of ecclesiastical origin which belong to the seventh century. But while these have their value it

---

[1] *Codex Diplomaticus.*
[2] Nos. 1, 12, 16, 19, 27, 32, 35, 36, 43, 47, 995. Kemble thinks the oldest document in his cartulary (dated 604) is genuine, but marks the following ten as suspicious, thus finding but one genuine charter before 676.
[3] Hic est terminus mei doni: fram suðgeate west, andlanges wealles oð norðlanan to stræte, and swa east fram stræte oð doddinghyrnan ongean bradgeat.

is not as native English sources reflecting Saxon life and institutions: they are mainly papal letters, valuable to the student of institutional history only when they presuppose English sources and conditions.[4] Furthermore, we cannot know whether we possess them in their original form. Many are from the writings of Bede and other churchmen who may or may not have copied them accurately. And if they have been summarized rather than transcribed, they are for our purposes of no more ancient authority than other statements by the transcriber.[5]

The case of the Old English laws differs somewhat from that of the charters. Their beginning is usually referred to the reign of Æthelbirht. While we cannot know whether this king issued any charters, we have good reason to believe that he mended the laws. Bede tells us that Æthelbirht, following the example of the Romans, established laws; he adds that these were in force in his own day and that they were written down in the speech of the Angles.[6] The Kentish dooms have come down to us in a manuscript of the twelfth century.[7] As this was produced more than five hundred years after the time of Æthelbirht, we have good reason to doubt whether we possess these laws in their original form. What language was used when they were first put to writing we cannot know, though Bede informs us that an Old English version existed in his day.[8] If we assume that they were originally written in the Kentish dialect, we are met by the question, to what extent was the phraseology changed when they passed into their present form? The language is archaic, but not sufficiently so to remove all doubts. The same question arises if we assume a Latin original and a later translation into Anglo-Saxon toward the close of the century. If the present version is based on such a translation the value of these laws for present purposes would be greatly reduced. Our work deals

---

[4] For ecclesiastical documents see especially the great compilation of Haddan and Stubbs: *Councils and Ecclesiastical Documents Relating to Great Britain and Ireland.* 3 vols. Oxford, 1869-78.
[5] Birch has published a number of charters that are not found in Kemble's *Codex.* Many of these are, however, of a decidedly suspicious character.
[6] *H. E.,* II, 5.
[7] Schmid, *Gesetze,* XXX.
[8] Alfred understands Bede to say that the King ordered the laws to be drawn up in the Kentish language ("and ča het on Englisc awritan") but such is not a necessary interpretation of Bede's language: "quae conscripta Anglorum sermone hactenus habentur et observantur." *H. E.,* II, 5.

largely with terms and the great problem is to fix their significance for this or that particular period. The changes that occurred in the Germanic dialects during the middle ages were of far-reaching consequence in the world of language. Many terms that suffered no external change might express several wholly different ideas in the space of a few centuries. The same lack of stability appears in the Latin of the age: almost any official or man of prominence might be called a *princeps;* and this term might again be rendered differently by a Saxon translator, *eþeling, ealdorman, eorl* and *gesiþ* being possible renderings. From a study of the probabilities of the case I conclude, that the terminology of the Kentish laws can hardly belong to a period much earlier than the close of the seventh century.[9] This conclusion especially affects the dooms of Æthelbirht. But the substance of these laws evidently belongs to a very early period and may be much older than the language of the versions that have come down to us.[10]

The narrative Latin prose of this period dates from the beginning of the eighth century. Bede's Life of Saint Cuthbert[11] is one of our earliest sources, but an anonymous life of the same saint was written a few years earlier, about the year 700.[12] The titles, character and value of Bede's works are so well known that I refrain from enumerating or discussing them at length.[13] Alongside of Bede's writings the student of early English culture would place Eddi's Life of Wilfrid,[14] a semipolemic biography from about 710. The very fact that it was written by a partisan makes it valuable, as it thus shows the active forces of culture in a stronger and clearer light.

The chroniclers and encomiasts can, as a rule, in institutional

---

[9] Schmid (*Gesetze,* XXXI) and Sievers (Paul und Braunes *Beiträge,* XII, 173–174) believe the language of Æthelbirht's laws to be such as was spoken in Kent in the days of that king.
[10] The Anglo-Saxon laws are found in the following collections:
Thorpe, *Ancient Laws and Institutes of England.* 2 vols. London, 1840.
Schmid, *Die Gesetze der Angelsachsen.* Leipzic, 1858. Cited as *Gesetze.*
Liebermann, *Die Gesetze der Angelsachsen.* Halle, 1898–99. Cited as *Gesetze.*
[11] Venerabilis Bedae *Opera* (Stevenson). London, 1841.
[12] *Ibid.,* II, 259–84.
[13] The *Historia Ecclesiastica* has been several times edited, as have Bede's other works. See Gross, *Sources and Literature of English History,* 180–81, 216. My citations are from Stevenson's edition of Bede's works published by the English Historical Society.
[14] *Hist. York,* I.

matters be regarded as speaking for their own generation only. Rarely, as when sources are quoted verbatim, can we trust them for earlier times. But when we approach the poetic memorials of the age, we meet a wholly different problem. It is usual to speak of two periods of Old English literature:[15] the Anglian, which may be said to close about the year 800, and the Saxon, beginning with Alfred's reign.[16] Scholars have, in general, come to an agreement as to which period the various works are to be assigned. The specifically Biblical poems seem to belong for the most part to the earlier age. When the earliest was produced cannot be known. Christianity came to Kent in 596, and about thirty years later it got a foothold in Northumbria; but we should not expect the poets to become immediate masters of the poetic materials of the new faith. We may reject the legend as to how Cædmon was endowed with the gift of song, but the essential facts seem reasonable. Cædmon is said to have died about 680; he became a poet in his old age. So far as we know, then, Christian poetry arose among the Angles some time during the last quarter of the seventh century. For institutional purposes we may consider it as reflecting the life of the eighth.[17]

Our most important poetic sources are, however, not Christian. There are in Old English literature a few brief poems of a lyric or heroic nature, which point to a purely Teutonic origin.[18] With these we should class, perhaps, the greater part of Beowulf.[19] These afford us glimpses of the life in camp and court; they show us the *comitatus*, not as a mere memory but as a vital fact. How far back in time these can be placed is uncertain; but it seems to me they must have been produced and have become current before Christianity became a dominant influence. At the very latest, they must be placed before the middle of the seventh century. These poems, as the bearers of the old Odinic culture, as the mem-

---

[15] On matters of date and authorship of Anglo-Saxon writings, see Wülker, *Grundriss zur Geschichte der angelsächsischen Literatur*. Leipzic, 1885. Cited as *Grundriss*.

[16] During the intervening century, the period of the viking invasions, culture in the form of literary productions was apparently extinct.

[17] The best collection of Anglo-Saxon poetry is Grein's *Bibliothek der angelsächsischen Poesie*. The most recent edition of this is by R. P. Wülker. 3 vols. Cassel, 1883-98.

[18] The poems I refer to are *Widsith, The Fight at Finnsburg, Deor's Lament, The Wanderer, The Seafarer, The Wife's Complaint*, and *The Husband's Message*. It seems likely that some of the *Riddles* are also rather ancient.

[19] My references are to Wyatt's edition of *Beowulf*. Cambridge, 1898.

ories of the age before the coming of history, should be considered as a separate group of sources. It is true, they are interpolated to some extent, but the intruding lines are usually not difficult to detect.

Intimately related to these in metrical form, in legendary foundation and in elements of reflected culture, are the Eddic poems of the North. I have used these to some extent to illustrate the institutional life of earliest England,[20] so far as we are able to know it, but it may be necessary to say a word in justification of using them for such a purpose. The study of the runic inscriptions of the North has fixed the limits of a period within which we must place the rise of the Eddas, at least in the form in which the poems have come down to us. For linguistic reasons they cannot be older than the year 800; for religious reasons their period of origin cannot pass the year 1000. Thus these poems are at least two centuries younger than the Anglian lyrics of the heroic age. It must be remembered, however, that Teutonic civilization lived on in the North as nowhere else. No Roman soldier ever trod as a conqueror north of the Baltic. Roman missionaries never came to Norway. Feudalism never got a real foothold in Scandinavia. The influence that came in with commerce, though important, could not have produced any sweeping changes. Most important was the influence that resulted from the viking raids and the consequent contact with southern peoples. But, on the whole, it can safely be said that Teutonic civilization was permitted to develop along its own lines for nearly four centuries after its growth was checked in England by Saint Augustine's mission. Thus it came to pass that the Germanic race revealed itself most clearly and fully in the pre-Christian poetry of the scalds. This expresses the life of a kindred people in much the same stage of development as the English in the seventh century, and it is the poetry not only of a kindred race but of a people with whom the Angles were in almost constant contact from the close of the eighth century or earlier.[21]

---

[20] The Old Norse poems have been collected and edited by Vigfusson and Powell in *Corpus Poeticum Boreale*. This work has convenient and fairly accurate translations of most of the poems and I have frequently quoted these in preference to the originals. The Eddic poems are in vol. I.

[21] The occurrence of the word viking in an eighth century gloss (see Sweet's *Oldest English Texts*, 84, uuicing sceadan) and still earlier in *Widsith* (ll. 59 and 80) leads me to think that the Norse incursions antedate 787, the year given in the *Chronicle* as the time when the Norsemen first visited Wessex.

In nearly all the Anglo-Saxon sources, even after the question of chronology has been disposed of as far as may be, there remains the difficulty of interpretation. The same is largely true of the Latin writings, but a careful comparison of contemporaneous works and a study of Anglo-Saxon translations in the Glossaries[22] and the works of Alfred and his associates[23] will generally enable us to fix the value of Latin expressions with comparative definiteness. But the problem in the interpretation of Old English poetry is of a different sort: how are we to determine whether a word contains the idea of an actual living institution or of a fossilized one? Germanic poetry makes great use of epithets, largely of a metaphoric character.[24] Many of them are such as would appear in the verses of any age, but some have institutional origins; in these a great deal of genuine history is bound up. When the epithet was first used, the component parts, as well as the resulting whole, doubtless represented living realities. A good example of this is the frequently used 'kenning' *eorla dryhten,* lord or leader of warriors, most likely of noble warriors. In the society described in Beowulf[25] this expression certainly had a meaning; but it is also used by the Chronicler in describing the Battle of Brunanburh in the tenth century, when both the *eorl* and the *drihten* of older days had long belonged to the past; thus while the kennings doubtless contain a good deal of hidden history, it is a history without chronology and without perspective. At times the context gives valuable assistance; but usually we must look elsewhere for light, and the question becomes one of pure linguistics.

Among the sources of this period should also be included the West Saxon laws of Ine and for some purposes those of Alfred. The former date from the early part of the eighth century; but we know them only in the form in which they were reënacted by Alfred one hundred and fifty years later. We may assume that they are in substance the laws that Ine promulgated;[26] but to

---

[22] Collected by Thomas Wright in *Anglo-Saxon and Old English Vocabularies.* Wülker's edition of these Vocabularies is the one cited in this study.
[23] See *Bibl. der ang. Prosa* (Grein); also the publications of the Early English Text Society.
[24] These were called kenningar by the Icelandic poets who carried the use of them to an absurd extent.
[25] 1050 et passim.
[26] Alfred did not reënact all of Ine's laws. The rest are not extant.

claim that the language has been in every case retained, would not be safe. Whenever the question becomes one of terminology and the use of particular phrases, these laws should be treated as belonging to the age of Alfred.[27]

From the tenth century, the true Anglo-Saxon period, we have an excellent body of sources, though they are not so good on the subject of the royal court. The reason for this is that the great mass of the literature of that day was produced in monasteries by men who were not interested in the details of court organization. If the king's household in the tenth century had also been a literary center, we should probably know more about the royal surroundings than we do. As examples of the monastic literature of that age may be mentioned the exceedingly important biographies of Saints Dunstan[28] and Oswald.[29] The Anglo-Saxon Chronicle also belongs to this class. This great source begins in Alfred's reign, and, though very important for earlier history in other respects, as a source of institutional history it cannot be trusted for the period before the reign of Alfred.[30] In addition to the Chronicle there is a large body of Old English prose, most of which may be called ecclesiastical. This comprises, among productions of less note, the works of Alfred and his assistants,[31] the Blickling Homilies,[32], the so-called Homilies of Wulfstan[33] and the writings of Ælfric,[34] the great master of Old English prose. As these are mainly translations or paraphrases they are often sources of great perplexity, as we cannot know whether the institutions they allude to are native or not. A large body of laws has come down to us from this period and also a

---

[27] Cf. Schmid, *Gesetze*, XXXVII, where a different opinion is expressed; also Steenstrup, *Danelag* (Copenhagen, 1882), 51.
[28] *Memorials of St. Dunstan* (Stubbs). London, 1874.
[29] *Hist. York*, I.
[30] The chroniclers naturally translated the language of their sources into the idiom and terminology of their own day. Hence the allusion to an institution as existing several hundred years before Alfred merely proves that it existed when the Chronicle was composed.
[31] See *Bibl. der ang. Prosa* and the publications of the Early English Text Society.
[32] Edited by Morris and published by the Early English Text Society.
[33] Wulfstan: *Sammlung der ihm zugeschriebenen Homilien* (Napier). Berlin, 1883.
[34] *Homilies of Ælfric* (Thorpe). 2 vols. London, 1844–46. Ælfric Society. *Ælfric's Lives of Saints* (Skeat). 2 vols. London, 1881–1900. Early English Text Society. *Bibl. der ang. Prosa*, III. *Angelsächsische Homilien und Heiligenleben*.

considerable number of charters. Some notable poems were produced in this age, though poetic activity was not so great in the tenth century as in the eighth. Asser's biography of Alfred[35] also belongs to this period.

Of the eleventh century sources we need consider only such as differ essentially from those of the preceding periods. The great histories that were produced soon after the Conquest, such as Florence of Worcester's *Chronicon*[36] and William of Malmesbury's *Gesta*,[37] now begin to be useful. They are, indeed, not from the Saxon period, but there can be no doubt that the authors had access to earlier sources that have since perished. Another exceedingly important source dating from Norman times is Domesday.[38] As the Survey gives the names and titles of the principal land-holders of Edward's day, we are able to determine to a great extent who the royal officials of that reign were and in what relation they stood to the king. The *Gesta Cnutonis*[39] is of particular importance for matters relating to the Danish invasion. But the sources that need to be specially noticed are the Norse poems and sagas and the early Danish histories.

Of Danish histories I have used the *Lex Castrensis* by Sveno Aggonis[40] and Saxo Grammaticus' *Gesta Danorum*.[41] Sveno's work is an account of the origin of Cnut's famous guard of housecarles, its governing laws, and the changes that had taken place in these. Sveno was the earliest Danish historian and flourished in the second half of the twelfth century. He claims merely to have translated from an earlier account in the vulgar idiom, the authorship of which he attributes to his friend and superior, the famous bishop Absalon of Lund, who obtained his information from King Cnut, the son of Waldemar I.[42] As Cnut reigned

[35] *Monumenta Historica Britannica* (Petrie), 1848. Cited as Petrie's *Monumenta*. For Asser's work see pp. 467-98. Stevenson, *Asser's Life of King Alfred*. Oxford, 1903. The credibility of Asser's biography is discussed in Plummer's *Life and Times of Alfred*. Oxford, 1902. Cited as *Alfred*.
[36] *Florentii Wigorniensis Chronicon ex Chronicis*.
[37] *Willelmi Malmisbiriensis de Gestis Regum Anglorum* (Stubbs). 2 vols. London, 1887-89.
[38] *Domesday Book*. London, 1783-1816.
[39] *Gesta Regis Cnutonis* (Pertz). Hanover, 1865.
[40] Published by Langebek in *Scriptores Rerum Danicarum*, III.
[41] Cited as *Saxo*. The references are to Holder's edition. Strassburg, 1886.
[42] There has come down to us a fragment in Middle Danish usually known as the *Witherlogh*, which may be a copy of the document from which Sveno made his translation. But the oldest extant manuscript is of the fourteenth century,

from 1182 to 1202 the bishop must have produced his summary of the guild-laws some time during the last quarter of the twelfth century.[43] Saxo's treatment of the same subject is doubtless an amplification of the same material that Sveno made use of; on important points there is no disagreement between the two accounts. But it is always necessary to distinguish between Saxo's statement of a fact and his explanation of the same; and in his ornate and somewhat pompous Latin there is a good deal of ambiguity.[44]

The distinctly Norse sources are poems and sagas. Of course the former are by far the more valuable, as there is every reason to think that they are contemporary with the events alluded to. Unfortunately we have but a few fragments of the court poetry of the eleventh century that can be used in a study of this sort. To what extent the sagas may be used for historic material is a much discussed question that cannot be fully dealt with here. All depends on the nature of the saga, the sources used, the date of composition and the time of the events recorded. The sagas dealing with events after 1100 have all the presumption in their favor; those professing to deal with earlier periods may properly be questioned. The saga is a sort of historical romance told in a terse, simple style which is peculiar to this form of literature. In a sense it is based on tradition, but not on tradition as that word is commonly understood. The Njaal's Saga furnishes abundant illustration of how carefully certain matters were committed to memory and with what precision as to form the unwritten legal documents had to be reproduced.[45] The historic sagas are generally based on scaldic verses and these are frequently quoted in the text. The scald was a professional his-

---

and, though it agrees in the main with the *Lex Castrensis,* we cannot be sure that it is a copy of Absalon's work. See Holberg, *Dansk Rigslovgivning* (Copenhagen, 1889), 22, 33. Holberg believes that aside from a few minor interpolations the Witherlogh is substantially the work of the great bishop.

[43] It is of course possible that Absalon may have written his account before Cnut became king; but Sveno's translation cannot be placed earlier than 1182, nor can it have been produced much later, as Saxo, who probably survived Sveno, is thought to have died in 1204.

[44] For further discussion of the Danish sources see chapter VII.

[45] See the *Story of Burnt Njaal* (Dasent's translation). Edinburgh, 1861. It may be objected that the Njaal's Saga is largely fictitious; but even if this be granted, the story still shows what the age demanded in the way of memorizing laws and formulas.

torian: his task was to single out the great events in the career of his patron and tell them in song at the great festivals and on other occasions.[46] The internal evidence of the sagas themselves is sufficient to show to what a great extent these verses were used in the composition. In addition we have Snorre's testimony: 'At King Harold [Fairhair's] court[47] there were scalds, and men still know their lays as well as the lays sung of the kings that Norway has had since that day. And we have trusted most to those things that are told in the songs that have been sung in the presence of the chiefs themselves or of their sons..... For it is the custom of the scalds to praise him the most in whose presence they are, but no one would dare to attribute to him deeds that he had never performed; for all who heard it would know that it was mere fable and fiction, and there would be mocking rather than praise in that.'[48]

It has been my purpose to use sagas only where they find support in documents more nearly contemporaneous and refer to institutions concerning which something might be known in the North.[49] Such an institution is the corps of house-carles, which, though in a sense peculiarly English, was Norse in spirit and perhaps also in form and origin. On the whole, however, on the subject of English institutions the sagas cannot be said to throw very much light.

Turning from the sources to the writings of modern historians, we shall find but few that present more than a superficial view of the English court. The subject is treated in nearly all the general works on English history, but the discussions are usually brief, sometimes limited to a few lines, and rarely show that the author has made an independent study of the sources.[50] The

---

[46] The list of these singers is a formidable one: Finnur Jónsson has collected the names of more than one hundred, of whom some, indeed, are mythical. Jónsson, *Den oldnorske og oldislandske Litteraturs Historie*. Copenhagen, 1894–1901. Cited as *Litteraturhistorie*.

[47] Harold ruled according to generally accepted accounts from 860 to 930.

[48] Preface to *Heimskringla*. Snorre's dates are 1178–1241.

[49] In this study I have made some use of the *Knytlingasaga* and the *Jomsvikingasaga*. These are placed among the later compilations; but as there are several versions of the latter differing materially in language, it is thought that they must all have been based on some earlier work not extant. See Jónsson, *Litteraturhistorie*, II, 664.

[50] As these works will be frequently cited in the following chapters, no page references are given at this point.

earlier writers like Palgrave[51] and Lappenberg[52] display a very uncritical use of documents, particularly of charters, and their conclusions are not to be relied on. By far the best work is that of Kemble;[53] indeed, it can hardly be said that the discussion has been advanced much since his day. Kemble's conclusions are frequently mere conjectures, but in his conjectures he often comes surprisingly near the truth. Stubbs,[54] Freeman,[55] and Green[56] apparently follow Kemble. Freeman seems to have made an extensive study of the sources on this subject, but his efforts do not always lead to results and his interpretations are often incorrect. Green has a comparatively long discussion of the king's household in Saxon times, but the whole seems more like the product of imagination than of sober study. Ramsay's treatment of the subject is more satisfactory, though meager and open to criticism on several points.[57] There are also a few writers who, though they do not discuss the general question, give valuable information on some particular phase of it. Such are the studies in Anglo-Saxon society by Earle,[58] Leo,[59] Maitland[60] and Seebohm.[61] Of great value are also the discussions of general Germanic society in the works of Brunner,[62] Müllenhoff,[63] von Maurer[64] and Waitz.[65] Some of Round's essays[66] are also useful. Plummer's Life of Alfred is particularly important for his discussion of the literature belonging to the reign of that king.

Writers on Scandinavian history, especially students of the viking age, find frequent occasions to deal with Anglo-Saxon problems. First among these should be mentioned the Norse

---

[51] *The Rise and Progress of the English Commonwealth.* London, 1832.
[52] *History of England* (Thorpe's translation). London, 1881.
[53] *Saxons in England.*
[54] *Constitutional History of England.*
[55] *Norman Conquest.*
[56] *Conquest of England.*
[57] *The Foundations of England.*
[58] *Land Charters and Saxonic Documents.* Oxford, 1888.
[59] *Rectitudines Singularum Personarum.* Halle, 1842.
[60] *Domesday Book and Beyond.* Cambridge, 1897.
[61] *The English Village Community.* London, 1884. Also *Tribal Custom in Anglo-Saxon Law.* London, 1902.
[62] *Deutsche Rechtsgeschichte.*
[63] *Deutsche Altertumskunde,* IV. Berlin, 1900.
[64] *Hofverfassung.* Erlangen, 1862.
[65] *Deutsche Verfassungsgeschichte.*
[66] *Feudal England.* London, 1895. Also his discussion of the Officers of Edward the Confessor in *Eng. Hist. Rev.,* XIX, 90–92.

historian Munch,[67] whose knowledge of the later centuries of the middle ages was so extensive that his opinions are not to be lightly disregarded. The question of Danish influence on Old English institutions has been made the subject of a series of special studies by Johannes C. H. R. Steenstrup, who views the problem from the Scandinavian side, and whose conclusions frequently differ from the opinions commonly held. In the main, however, they are sound, and Steenstrup's writings, especially his volume on the Danelaw,[68] are of great value to the student of English constitutional development.

While the effort has been to look at the royal household primarily from an English point of view, the possibility of foreign influences has been constantly kept in mind. The closing chapter is largely devoted to a comparison between the English court and related or contemporary households on the Continent. In studying the Continental courts I have made no extensive use of the sources, but have drawn for information on the works of Brunner, Keyser,[69] Luchaire,[70] Viollet[71] and Waitz. Owing to lack of space this comparison has been carried out along the more general lines only; but enough has been done, I believe, to indicate with some definiteness the position of the Old English court among its Germanic neighbors, what it owed and what it contributed to the royal households over the seas, and what it left as a heritage to its Norman successor.

---

[67] Munch's massive work, *Det norske Folks Historie*, is still the greatest source of information on Norse mediaeval history.
[68] *Danelag* (Normannerne IV).
[69] *Efterladte Skrifter.* 2 vols. Christiania, 1867.
[70] *Histoire des Institutions Monarchiques.* Paris, 1891.
[71] *Histoire des Institutions Politiques de la France.* 2 vols. Paris, 1890-98.

CHAPTER II.

THE EARLIER COMITATUS IN ENGLAND: THE GESITH.

The history of the royal household begins with the history of kingship. Between these two institutions there is an essential and intimate relation which is too obvious to need discussion. Not only do they correspond as to origin, but also as to nature and course of development. Early Teutonic kingship was primarily of a military order; first of all the king was a war-chief.[72] It is natural, then, that his immediate surroundings should partake of the same martial character. Close to the royal person stood a band of chosen warrors, bound by the most solemn pledges to defend their lord and to die with him if he fell as a hero should. This was the *comitatus*, the earliest princely household among the Teutonic peoples.[73]

This peculiarly Germanic institution seems to have reached its full development, in a military sense, as early as the times of Tacitus. Its subsequent growth was generally away from the original idea. The privilege of maintaining a *comitatus* was not limited to the king; it was shared by the *principes*,[74] at least till after the period of the migrations. Perhaps the institution is also much older than kingship. Snorre tells us that the kings 'were formerly called *drottnar*, their wives *drottningar* and their household *drott*.'[75] Analogous terms are found in other Germanic dialects with much the same significance. Parallel to the Old

---

[72] Cf. von Amira, Recht, in Paul's *Grundriss*, II, 2, 126.

[73] It is not the purpose of this chapter to present a discussion of the comitatus in general, but to trace, as far as can be done, the further development of the institution after its introduction into England. For the general subject see Brunner, *D. R. G.*, I, 136–43; Müllenhoff, *Deutsche Altertumskunde*, IV, 255 ff.; Sars, *Udsigt over den norske Historie*, I, 95 ff.; Stubbs, *C. H.*, I, 22 ff., 166, ff.; Waitz, *D. V. G.*, I, 236 ff., 371–401.

[74] Tacitus, *Germania*, 13.

[75] *Ynglingasaga*, 20.

Norse *drottinn* is the Anglo-Saxon *drihten;* both are archaic remains frequently found in poetry though seldom in prose. In both the *dominus* idea is always present;[76] but that they originally had a martial coloring appears from the meaning of related Gothic words, all of which relate to warfare.[77] We can hardly escape the conclusion that *drihten* originally meant a war-lord.

The use of such an expression as *eorla drihten*,[78] lord of earls, which often occurs in Old English poetry, might lead us to conclude that the members of the *comitatus* were once called eorls. The word *eorl,* or some related form is found in several of the Teutonic dialects, sometimes used in the sense of man,[79] sometimes signifying a royal official corresponding to the mediaeval *comes,*[80] but more frequently suggesting a member of the martial aristocracy.[81] The last meaning, warrior, is the most common in the earliest Norse sources, of which the most important for present purposes is the Lay of Righ, a poem describing early Northern society.[82] It is the poet's purpose to glorify kingship, the new Norse kingship of Harold Fairhair. To do this he describes and accounts for existing social classes of which there are three: thralls, churls and earls.[83] The oldest is Thrall (*þræl*). His fare is poor and his labor hard. Next comes Churl *(Karl),* who occupies a higher plane of culture and devotes himself to agriculture. Youngest is *Iarl.* 'His hair was yellow, his cheeks

---

[76] Christian writers frequently apply them to the Lord, perhaps because they contain the fullest idea of personal relationship. See the so-called *Cædmonic Hymn.*

[77] In Ulfila's Bible ga-drauhts is used where the English version has soldier. From the same root are drauhtinassus, drauhti-witoþ, warfare and drauhtinon, to make war.

[78] See, for example, *Beow.,* 1050.

[79] It frequently occurs with this meaning in the Old Saxon poem The *Heliand.*

[80] Thus in later Old English and Old Norse documents. See Cleasby and Vigfusson, *Icelandic Dictionary.*

[81] In the Old Northern runic inscriptions (thought to be from the seventh century) the title erilar or eirilar occurs not infrequently; it is usually in apposition to the name of the one who caused the runes to be written. Bugge translates it war-chief. See Bugge, *Norges Indskrifter* (Christiania, 1891), 100 ff.

[82] *C. P. B.,* I, 235–42. As a document for the history of culture this poem is of uncommon value and interest. Finnur Jónsson, the most recent critic of Old Norse literature, believes that it dates from about 892. *Litteraturhistorie,* 186 ff.

[83] This division into three social classes, servile, agricultural and military, appears to be common to the Germanic tribes. See Paul, *Grundriss,* II, 2, 111 ff. There are clear traces of it in Tacitus' *Germania,* especially in chapters 13, 14, 15, 24, 25, 26.

were rosy, his eyes keen as a young serpent's..... He began to brandish the linden [shield], to gallop his horse and fence with the sword. He began to waken war, to redden the field and to fell the doomed. He won lands; he ruled alone over eighteen households; he began to deal out wealth, and endow his people with treasures and costly things, with fine-ribbed steeds; he scattered rings and hewed great rings asunder [among them].'[84] To any one familiar with Old English poetry, this description of the activities of the original eorl must seem familiar both in thought and in terms. The hall, the extended domains, the steed, the arms, the delight in warfare, the *comitatus* and the ring-giving are met with repeatedly in Anglian literature.[85] And it seems clear that the lay does not describe a mere warrior, but a Tacitean *princeps*, that is, a chief who surrounded himself with a company of youths.[86]

As *eorl* is the Saxon equivalent of the Norse *iarl*, we should expect to find the significance of the two words to be the same. The evidence on this point is, however, not very satisfactory. With the word eorl that came in with the viking-raids, we have nothing to do; consequently, we are limited in our investigation to the very earliest sources, the heroic and Cædmonic poetry and the earlier legislation.

A striking peculiarity of Germanic law is the persistent use of alliterative formulas: 'sac and soc,' 'toll and team' will serve as, examples of Anglo-Saxon usage. With these may be classed the rhyming formula *eorl and ceorl*. This interesting combination appears for the first time, perhaps, in the Laws of Alfred.[87] As there used, it suggests a classification of men, though not a very substantial one; it looks more like a fossilized survival of an earlier age.[88] Evidently the earl as a living fact antedates Alfred's code. But in the earlier Kentish laws he appears as an

---

[84] Vigfusson's translation with slight changes (ll. 147–54).
[85] So striking is the similarity that some have believed it must have been produced somewhere on the "Western Islands." See *C. P. B.*, Introd., LXX; Bugge, *The Home of the Eddic Poems* (Schofield's translation), Introd., XXV.
[86] *Germania*, 13, 14.
[87] C. 4, 2.
[88] This supposition is strengthened by the fact that the same formula, 'churl's land and earl's land is found in the *Grágás*, an old Icelandic law, the extant manuscript of which must have been written soon after 1217 (Vigfusson). But Iceland never had an earl or jarl before 1259. The phrase in this case is clearly a 'fossil.' See *C. P. B.*, Introd., XL.

active reality.[89] The Laws of Æthelbirht clearly show us a double classification of freemen into earls and churls; the same is true of the dooms of Hlotar and Eadric. The earl enjoys a higher wergeld than the churl.[90] Higher protection is given to his home and his servants.[91] It is manifest that the earls of early Kent constituted a privileged class.[92]

It is also evident, as a study of the early Anglian poetry will show, that this aristocracy was of a military character. Its members lived in fortified strongholds, 'burgs,' while the common freeman had to be satisfied with a less pretentious enclosure, *edor*, about his buildings.[93] The king also lived in a *burh*.[94] Eorl is rarely used in the sense of man merely; at any rate the man is of an exalted station. But in almost every case the usage of the term suggests the *comitatus;* sometimes it is applied to the chief, sometimes to the members.[95] The patriarchs with their large households were looked on as eorls by the author of the Genesis.

[89] The earliest of these is thought to date from the beginning of the seventh century. *The Laws of Hlotar and Eadric* are usually dated ca. 685.

[90] *Laws of Hlotar and Eadric*, 1, 3. These dooms provide for the punishment of a serf (esne) who should slay a man whose wergeld was three hundred scillings, or one whose worth was only one hundred scillings. The ratio of the wergelds thus becomes one to three. In my interpretation of these chapters I follow Liebermann: Schmid and Thorpe have somewhat different renderings. Cf. Seebohm, *Tribal Custom in Anglo-Saxon Law*, 468.

[91] The honor of an earl's birel was worth twelve scillings; that of a churl's birel was valued at six. Slaughter in the earl's tun demanded a payment of twelve scillings; breaking into a 'man's' tun, half that amount. *Laws of Æthelbirht*, 13, 14, 16, 17.

[92] With regard to the classes of early Kentish society, Seebohm concludes that the ceorl stood on the same level as the later twelve-hynde-man of the Wessex laws, and that the earl consequently occupied a considerably higher plane than even the later thegn. *Tribal Custom in Anglo-Saxon Law*, 494-95.

[93] See *Laws of Æthelbirht*, 27; fines for 'edor-breaking.'

[94] *Beow.*, passim.

[95] In *Widsith*, which probably contains elements of greater antiquity than any found elsewhere in Old English poetry, eorl appears as a synonym for 'theoden' which in its most general sense means chief, but in this case appears to mean king (11-13). In *Deor's Lament*, which is also of a very early date, the word is applied to the members of the lord's following (33), but also to Weland, one of the saga-heroes alluded to (2). In the next line Weland is said to have sorrow and longing as his 'gesiths': "hæfde him to gesiþþe sorge and longaþ" (3). It is, indeed, possible that gesith here means companion merely; but it is more probable that the singer was thinking of the comitatus and the court. In the beautiful description of the ruined burg and the death of the doughty ones, the eorl is represented as 'hiding' his men in the grave. All are gone, the chief is the last survivor. *The Wanderer*, 77-84. The fair-haired queen in the riddle is the daughter of an eorl. *Riddle* LXXVIII. (No. 80 in Grein-Wülker.) In another riddle (IX), we are told that eorls live in burgs.

Especially is this true of Abraham,[96] and it must be admitted that three hundred and eighteen men make up a very respectable *comitatus*.[97] While the proof cannot be considered absolute, the evidence, such as we have it, points to the eorl as not merely a warrior but a lord of warriors in the peculiarly Teutonic sense.[98] The Norse parallels, the privileged position of the eorls in the laws, their princely position in the early poetry, the martial atmosphere surrounding the title, the fortress, the distribution of wealth—all these considerations support this conclusion.[99] Remarkable is also the ease and naturalness with which the title, after a long development away from its early Germanic significance, suddenly reappears in its original sense. With the Norse invasions of the ninth century the eorl resumes his ancient place. In the account of Alfred's wars we read of a number of eorls,[1] leaders of the enemy, Danish and Norwegian 'jarls.' But it will hardly do to call these vikings territorial barons: there is no evidence that such dignitaries existed among the Danes,[2] and in those very

---

[96] Ll. 1710, 1844, 1887.

[97] Abraham's three confederates in the famous expedition for the relief of Sodom are also called eorls in the *Genesis* (2045). Cf. *Book of Genesis*, 14 :22. Lamech was a ruler and an eorl (1228). Of Jared it is said that long afterwards he distributed gold to men: 'the eorl was noble, a pious hero, and the chief was dear to his kinsmen' (1181–83). Among other eorls the poet names Haran (1710), Lot (2086, 2444), Eber (1646) and Isaac (2766). Several other patriarchs bear the title in the *Höllenfahrt*. In *Azariah* (181) Nebuchadnezzar is called an eorl.

[98] For the subject of eorlship see Allen, *Essays and Monographs*, 293–99; Freeman, N. C., I, 55–56; Kemble, *Sax. in Eng.*, I, 135–36; Lappenberg, *Hist. of Eng.*, II, 382; Stubbs, *C. H.*, I, 86; Waitz, *D. V. G.*, I, 176–77. Nearly all these writers consider the eorls as forming an ancient hereditary nobility possessing certain valued privileges: especially is the possession of extensive lands emphasized. Lappenberg and Allen, however, deny this and hold that the eorls were officers appointed by the crown. Waitz rejects the opinion expressed above that the eorl was a leader of a comitatus. *D. V. G.*, I, 177. Cf. Leo, *Rectitudines*, 160.

[99] Cf. Leo, *Rectitudines*, 160, where a similar view is presented.

[1] *A.-S. Chron.*, 871.

[2] Allen, in his contention that the eorl was an appointive magistrate, depends largely on supposed Scandinavian analogies. "It may be assumed therefore that the eorls of Kent were identical with the Jarls of Denmark and Norway. Now, the Scandinavian Jarls were not an hereditary class of noblemen, but were officers or magistrates appointed for life or pleasure." *Essays*, 294–95 Munch and Keyser are quoted as authorities. To this it should be remarked that while such is the opinion of these writers with regard to the situation in the later middle ages, Munch, at least, holds that there was a hereditary earlship in the early viking age. N. F. H., I, 1, 111. See also Sars, *Udsigt over den norske Historie*, I, 135. As to the local government of early Denmark, all we can say is that it seems to have been in the hands of magistrates appointed by the king. Sars, *Udsigt*, I, 139.

years the 'jarls' of Norway were at home struggling for their independence against the conquering ambition of Harold Fairhair.[3] We shall have to regard the eorls of the Alfredian Chronicle as leaders of a personal following only, such chiefs as Snorre describes in another connection as 'sea-kings who controlled large forces but had no land.'[4] However, when one of these vikings settled with his followers in a certain locality, his authority would become territorial. There were such rulers in the Danelaw all through the tenth century,[5] but the eorl did not become an Anglo-Saxon official before the reign of Cnut.

While it doubtless was the privilege of the original eorl to maintain an armed following, we need not assume that all the members of this martial nobility made use of this right.[6] The sources show, and most clearly, that the development was rapidly away from the *comitatus* in its primitive form. When we enter the period of true English history, the substance has largely passed away. Tacitus observes that warfare is a condition necessary to the existence of a large following,[7] and this condition was probably present in Northumbria in the seventh and eighth centuries, but the same can hardly have been true of Kent.[8] And even beyond the Humber the fortunes of earlship must have found an early decline. As we follow the line of the sources forward, less emphasis is placed on military prowess and continuously more on wealth.[9] By the close of the seventh century the term eorl has practically disappeared from the legal sources,[10]

---

[3] The period of the consolidation of Norway is generally given as 864-74.
[4] *Ynglingasaga*, 34. Snorre adds that 'he alone was thought to have full right to be called a sea-king who never slept under sooty rafter and never drank at the corner of the hearth.'
[5] In 949 three eorls with Danish names, Urm, Uhtred and Scule, signed one of Eadred's charters. *K. C. D.*, No. 424. Apparently two other eorls, Andcal and Grim, are also among the testes.
[6] Such might be called eorlcund. In the *Laws of Æthelbirht* (75) there is mention of eorlcund widows. Fines for slaying eorlcund men are specified in the dooms of *Hlotar and Eadric* (1).
[7] *Germania*, 14.
[8] The limited area of this state and its relative freedom from invasions, except as it might be attacked by its Mercian or Saxon neighbors, could not be conducive to the continuation of such establishments.
[9] Even such an unwarlike man as Lot is called an eorl by the author of the Genesis, who probably had his possessions and his lineage in mind.
[10] The term eorlcund is used in Hlotar and Eadric's laws; but in Wihtræd's legislation, which is supposed to date from the following decade, gesithcund is used instead (c. 5). The word eorl appears rarely in the Wessex laws and then only in formulas. The eorl of the tenth and eleventh century documents

gesith and gesithcund taking its place. In the poetry of the period this change in terminology is not so noticeable. The two titles, eorl and gesith, appear side by side from the very beginning, at first rather sharply distinguished, but soon employed as practically synonymous terms.

The Anglo-Saxon word *gesiþ* originally meant a traveling companion,[11] and this significance it never wholly lost.[12] But it soon came to be used in the technical sense of member of some lord's *comitatus*. The transition is natural: the way is the warpath, the devoted companion, the gesith.[13] The term is used freely by the Anglian poets, who describe the gesiths as warriors, the companions of some mighty war-lord, living at his hall, or at least partaking of his liberality on certain great occasions.[14]

The relationship existing between the drihten or eorl and his gesiths was the highest and holiest that the Teutonic mind could imagine. It was the hero's delight in life, his hope after death. The scenes of earth were reënacted in the halls of the Anses, where the brave ones fought and Woden rewarded his followers

is, as has already been shown, a new official of Norse origin whose English history begins with the viking invasions. Cf. Stubbs, *C. H.*, I, 169.

[11] Gesið is derived from Old-Germanic sinþa, way or journey. This appears in Gothic as sinþs and in Anglo-Saxon as sið, journey, time. The Gothic ga-sinþa like the Anglo-Saxon gesið, means primarily a companion on the way. See Kluge, *Etymologisches Wörterbuch*, 113.

[12] In *Solomon and Saturn* (346-47) weeping and laughter are called each other's gesiths.

[13] Thus we have the Old High German gisindi and the Lombard gasindii. The latter composed the king's special following as appears from the *Laws of Liutprand*, LXII. Cf. Gengler, *Germanische Rechtsdenkmäler*, Glossar; Brunner, *D. R. G.*, II, 260 ff. With the same restricted significance we have the obsolete Danish term hof-sinde, a court official.

[14] In *Widsith* eorl is used as synonymous with theoden, chief, prince; gesith as explanatory of innweorud, house-troop (110-11). Attention has already been called to the use of these terms in *Deor's Lament*. That there were gesiths at the royal court is shown in the Gnomic Verses: 'Good gesiths shall encourage the young etheling to warfare and to ring-giving.' *Versus Gnomici*, 14-15 (Cottonian). King Higelac dwelt at home with his gesiths. *Beow.*, 1923-24. Dearly beloved gesiths accompanied Beowulf to the last great encounter (2516-18). This idea of companionship in warfare persisted as late as the time of Alfred. We read in his *Metra* (XXVI, 19-20) that 'the lord of the Greeks dearly purchased the Trojan burg with his excellent gesiths'. There were gesiths in the Jewish host that routed Holofernes' forces (*Judith*, 199 ff.) and in Abraham's company when he rescued Lot (*Genesis*, 2066-67). In the *Husband's Message* (31-34), hope is expressed that they two (husband and wife) may soon again distribute 'nailed' rings among their warriors and gesiths. The warriors who were surprised in the famous hall at Finnsburg were gesiths. *The Fight at Finnsburg*, 41-42.

with gold.[15] The general nature of the English *comitatus* seems to have been the same as of that described by Tacitus: there is the same liberality on the part of the lord, the same devotion on the part of the men.[16] That this devotion was more than a mere sense of duty appears from a passage in the Wanderer, perhaps the most artistic of all the Old English poetical productions.[17] The memories of the minstrel turn not to valor and warfare but to former joys in his lord's hall. In his dreams 'it seems to him that he is kissing and embracing his lord and laying his hands and his head on the chieftain's knee, as he formerly did in days of yore, when he enjoyed the gift-stools.'[18] That the members of the *comitatus* were as dear to their chief appears from many considerations, especially the oft-recurring phrase *swæse gesiþas*, dear gesiths. The members of the same following were no doubt also bound to each other by close ties. The runic inscription on the so-called Tunë-stone[19] seems to record the fact that the fifth century *comitatus* was a law-bound guild.[20] How this personal bond, this intimate relationship between the chief and the warrior, was formed and how long it endured cannot be answered definitely from Anglo-Saxon sources. It would seem from

[15] *C. P. B.*, I, 227: Biðjom Herjarföður i hugom sitja han geldr og gefr goll verðungo.

[16] The heroic poetry from Beowulf to Byrhtnoth (the comitatus seems to have experienced a revival after the viking incursions had begun) is a splendid commentary on these two virtues. The spirit of loyalty is also illustrated in the story of Cynewulf and Cyneheard. Even after the king was known to be slain, his men refused to listen to the assassin's promises of life and gifts; 'but they continued fighting until they all lay dead save one, a British hostage, and he was severely wounded.' *A.-S. Chron.*, 755.

[17] This poem is heathen in thought and sentiment if not in point of time. The opening and closing lines are later additions by some Christian singer. Cf. Wülker, *Grundriss*, 205.

[18] Ll. 41-45: þinced him on mode, þæt he his mondryhten
    clyppe and cysse and on cneo læge
    honda and heafod, swa he hwilum ær
    in gear-dagum gief-stolas breac.

[19] So named from its location near Tunë church in southeastern Norway. The rock is roughly hewn in the form of an obelisk and is of about the height of a man.

[20] The inscription which archeologists date about 500 reads as follows: "Ek Wivar after Woduride witada-halaiban worahto r[unor]"; in free translation, 'I, Wivar, in memory of Wodurid, my intimate companion, wrought these runes.' The word that I translate intimate companion is witada-halaiban of which the first part is probably related to Gothic witoþ, law, and the second to Gothic gahlaiba, loaf-sharer or comrade, but used by Ulfilas in the sense of soldier. *Philippians*, 2:25. The whole term probably means one belonging to a law-bound guild of warriors. Cf. Bugge, *Norges Indskrifter*, 17.

Tacitus' account that the gesith entered the *comitatus* while yet a mere youth, and certain allusions in the Anglian poetry point in the same direction.[21] But, while the institution is usually spoken of in connection with noble youths, no class of freemen seems to have been excluded from membership[22] and the relationship might apparently continue into old age.[23]

Such was the gesith as the poet saw him: a warrior devoted to a warlike lord; a hero whose joys were the battle and the banquet. The laws and the Latin sources, however, the charters, the histories and the 'lives', give us a somewhat different picture. In the Latin documents we frequently meet the term *comes*. This, in the tenth century glossaries, is translated *gesiþ*, and *comitatus* is rendered *gesiþræden*.[24] But it is not always clear that *comes* in the sense of *socius* is not meant.[25] In an eighth century vocabulary gesith is used as the Saxon equivalent of *optimas*;[26] in this case, then, the gesith is not considered as a warrior or a member of some military household, but as one of the powerful men of the realm. This is exactly in line with the use of the word in the writings of Bede, who wrote in the same century. One looks in vain through the Ecclesiastical History for any use of the term *comes* in the later sense of count or earl.[27] All we can safely say of Bede's *comites* is that they were men of power, wealth and

---

[21] Beowulf came to Hrethel's court at the age of seven. From that time on he seems to have been treated as a member of the following. The king gave him entertainment and costly gifts (2428-31). The *Wanderer* also feasted with his gold-friend in his youth (35). According to the rules of Jom no one younger than eighteen should be admitted to the brotherhood (*Jomsvikingasaga*, 24); an exception was made, however, in the case of Vagn, who became a member at the age of twelve (32). But Vagn had already killed several men and had proved himself a worthy viking (31). Cf. *Germania*, 13; Müllenhoff, *Deutsche Altertumskunde* IV, 262.

[22] Among the avengers of Byrhtnoth was an 'aged churl.' Judging from the context we should consider him a member of the ealdorman's martial following. *Battle of Maldon*, 256. Waitz believes that even serfs might become comites. D. V. G., I, 373.

[23] Old gesiths, eald-gesiðas, are mentioned in *Beowulf* (853). In the *Battle of Maldon* we read of an eald-geneat, old companion, who unquestionably was a member of Byrhtnoth's comitatus (310).

[24] *Vocab.*, 239:3, fida comes, i. fidelis, getreowa gesiða; 253:2, comes, gesið, 206:21, comitatus, consecutus vel gesiþræden.

[25] In a tenth century gloss gesith is also used to translate cliens: cliens, i. socius, þegn, gesiþa. Ibid., 205:34.

[26] *Ibid.*, 35:4.

[27] The same remark applies to dux. Of the duces we can affirm only that they were military leaders. See H. E., I. 15, 16: II. 13, 20: III, 3, 24: IV, 13, 26; V, 10. Alfred calls the dux a heretoga, host-leader, or latteow, guide.

social standing. Alfred in his translation distinguishes very carefully between *comes (socius)* meaning a mere companion and the same term as applied to an order of men. Augustine's *socii* were *geferan*;[28] the same is true of the companions *(comites)* of Edwin's queen.[29] But *comes regis* is translated gesith.[30]

The *comes* of the eighth century seems to have spent very little time, if any at all, in his lord's household. He had attained a respectable social position and kept up an establishment of his own; he even returned former favors by entertaining the king.[31] Even where the more specific title *comes regis* is employed, there is no indication that the person in question was regularly entertained at the royal vill.[32] The Anglian gesiths had, by the time when Bede wrote, become great land-owners:[33] nearly all that we read of had vills, and some even had churches on their estates.[34] How extensive these possessions were cannot be known. It is, of course, possible that the *comites* had large military followings on their estates, but the evidence for such is wholly wanting. Not even the suggestion of a gesith's *comitatus* appears in the Ecclesiastical History.

The institution of gesithship naturally gave rise to a privileged class, the *gesiþcund*.[35] To what extent we are to distinguish

---

[28] I, 25.
[29] II, 9.
[30] IV, 22.
[31] Bede tells of a king who incurred episcopal wrath by dining at the home of an excommunicated comes. *H. E.*, III, 22.
[32] King Oswin was slain at the home of Hunwald, "his gesiðes.," where he had concealed himself. *Ibid.*, III, 14; cf. IV, 22. We are told that Cuthbert once healed the servant of a "comitis Ecgfridi regis," Bede, *Opera*, II, 99. The context clearly indicates that the comes had his own home. It is interesting to note that the Frankish antrustions (some of them at least) had homes of their own. The *Salic Law* (XLII) provides that the fine for slaying a freeman "in truste" shall be three times as large as the penalty for murder in the freeman's own homo.
[33] When Colman left England he went to a Scotch island and bought a small part of it "a comite ad cujus possessionem pertinebat." Alfred's version reads: "æt sumum gesiðe þe þæt land ahte." *H. E.*, IV, 4.
[34] *Ibid.*, V, 5;....vocatus ad dedicandam ecclesiam comitis vocabulo Addi. See also *Ibid.*, V, 4.
[35] That the gesiths comparatively early became a class appears from the occurrence of such compounds as gesiðcund, gesiðman and gesiðwif. Gesiðcund as used in the earlier laws clearly indicates rank. See *Laws of Wihtræd*, 5; *Laws of Ine*, 50, 51, 63, 68. The word appears in several chapters of Ine's dooms equivalent, it seems, to the eorlcund of the Kentish laws. That a gesiðwif was a lady of rank appears from a statement in Gregory's *Dialogues* concerning 'a certain noble gesiðwif'—"sum æþele gesiðwif." *Bibl. der ang. Prosa*, V, 71. Cf. Seebohm, *Tribal Custom in Anglo-Saxon Law*, 369.

between *comites* and *'gesithcundmen'* cannot be known; but all belonging to the latter class did not enjoy the possession of great estates. We read in Ine's Law that 'if a gesithcundman who is a landowner neglect the host, he shall pay one hundred and twenty scillings and lose his land; one who is not a landowner, sixty scillings.'[36] From this we are also justified in concluding, that, before the close of the seventh century, this class, so supremely martial in its origin, had lost its passion for warfare.

How the *comes* originally came into possession of his lands can only be conjectured: but it seems reasonable to suppose that the chiefs of the Angles and Saxons, after they had risen to kingship, found distribution of conquered and confiscated lands the best way to provide for a large and growing *comitatus*.[37] Later grants were also made from time to time.[38] That it was customary to give gifts to members of the royal household is very well known. Arms, horses, rings and fragments of rings were commonly given.[39] The king of the Goths gave Widsith a ring which he in turn gave to Eadgils, his 'protecting lord, a reward to the beloved one, the lord of the Myrgings, for the lands he gave me, my ancestral possessions.'[40] Another bard, in a song almost as ancient, laments that a song-skilled rival had taken the land-right that his lord had formerly given him.[41] Beowulf gave Wiglaf 'the wealthy dwelling-place of the Wægmundings with every

---

[36] C. 51. Gif gesiōcund mon land-agende forsitte fierd, geselle CXX Scill. and þolie his landes; unland-agende LX Scill. Cf. Seebohm's interpretation of this chapter in *Tribal Custom in Anglo-Saxon Law*, 391. See also Earle, *Land Charters*, Introd., LXXX.

[37] Wholly different from this view is that of Earle, who believes the gesiths to have been "the original captains and officers of the Conquest of Wessex, men of eorlisc birth, the co-adventurers who organized and led the invasion, and who obtained a share of the conquered soil duly proportionate to their services or contributions to the successful venture." *Land Charters*, Introd., LXX. To this it may be sufficient to remark, that we do not know the plan or process of the Saxon invasions. Seebohm, the most recent writer on this subject, believes that the gesithcundman was placed over a certain number of hides, twenty, ten or fewer, "under the special obligation to provide food-rent by settling tenants upon the land." *Tribal Custom in Anglo-Saxon Law*, 422.

[38] Such was the grant of Æthilbald of Mercia to his comes Æthelric, son of the former king of the Hwiccas. K. C. D., No. 83. Another of Æthilbald's grants is made to his comes Wihtræd. *Ibid.*, No. 101. In 736 the same king gave lands (this time for church purposes, however,) to his 'honored comes Cyneberht.' *Ibid.*, No. 80.

[39] See Waitz, D. V. G., I, 376; Kemble, *Sax. in Eng.*, I, 183.

[40] Ll. 93-96.

[41] *Deor's Lament*, 39-41.

folk-right as his father possessed it.'[42] From these passages we shall have to conclude that the ancient eorl frequently rewarded his men with lands, though giving, perhaps, the usufruct only.[43] In addition, lands might be held by the title that violence gave.[44] While the evidence presented is not of such a nature as to warrant any extensive generalizing, a few things seem tolerably clear. Eorl and gesith were not originally synonymous terms: eorl referred to the old Germanic nobility, the *principes*, whose privilege it was to maintain a *comitatus*;[45] the term gesith was applied to the members of this following. It is not likely that all eorls made use of this privilege, but those that did were probably known as 'drihtens.' With the rise of kingship there seems to have come a decline in the fortunes of eorlship. The king's *comitatus*, which was, perhaps, largely recruited from the old nobility, formed the nucleus of a new privileged class. But the gesiths soon lost their militant nature and their order developed into a landed aristocracy.[46] As they had probably left the king's vil' by the time of our earliest sources, we cannot consider them a: belonging to the historic royal household.[47] Their places, howevei were not left vacant; a new order of men, the thegns, succeeds them as the king's companions. While in many essential respect: the thegn closely resembles his predecessor, the origin, the hi: tory and to some extent the character of thegnship are wholly

---

[42] *Beow.*, 2606-08.
[43] Cf. Kemble, *Sax. in Eng.*, I, 179.
[44] In one of Offa's charters we read: 'it happened in the days of Offa, king of the Mercians, that Bynna, comes regis, wrongfully appropriated this land.' *K. C. D.*, No. 164. It is by no means likely that this instance is an exceptional one.
[45] See *Riddle*, No. 95: 'I am known to the indryhten (comitatus) and to the eorls.' The terms indryhten and eorl can hardly be synonymous. *Bibl. der ang Poesie*, III, 238.
[46] The subject of the gesith as a landholder does not lie within the field of this study. The most recent work dealing with this class from the view point of manorial possessions is Seebohm's *Tribal Custom in Anglo Saxon Law* referred to above. It should be remarked, however, that his conclusions are not always likely to be correct, as, in addition to employing the comparative method to a questionable extent, he bases his conclusions almost entirely on legal evidence, thus ignoring the great bulk of Anglo-Saxon sources.
[47] The fact that the heroic poetry represents the gesiths as still abiding in the regal presence does not necessarily conflict with this conclusion. The past lives long in the realms of verse, and the "golden age" is always a favorite theme. The poems that have come down to us evidently belong to a period of transition from a time of war to an age of comparative peace, when a large military following could not very well be maintained.

different from those of gesithship and hence the subject requires separate treatment.[48]

---

[48] On the general subject of the English comitatus, the relationship existing between the eorl and his gesiths, the duties and privileges of the latter, etc., my conclusions do not differ much from those presented by Kemble and Stubbs. But Kemble sees no noteworthy difference between the gesith and the thegn (*Sax. in Eng.*, I, c. 7), and Stubbs holds that they are very closely connected, "so closely that it is scarcely possible to see the difference except in the nature of the employment. The thegn seems to be primarily the warrior gesith; in this idea Alfred uses the word as translating the miles of Bede."—*C. H.*, I, 172. As I see it, the difference between the two orders was considerable, and the gesith in my opinion was rather the warrior thegn. The gesith belongs to the earlier, more unsettled and warlike age; the thegn, to the age of national peace and organization. A general criticism that might be passed on the works of nearly all those who have written on Germanic institutions is that the elements of time and place are not sufficiently considered. In describing the comitatus historians are in the habit of using the writings of Snorre as well as Tacitus; but between these two historians lie a thousand years and more than two thousand miles, a very respectable distance in the middle ages.

CHAPTER III.

THE LATER COMITATUS IN ENGLAND: THE THEGN.

'Thegn' is an old Anglo-Saxon term, one of the oldest words in the language. Its general significance is readily determined, but its etymology has long been in doubt. Usually it is taken to be derived from an Indo-Germanic root *teq*, whence the Greek ἔτεκον begat, and τέκνού, child.[49] The term goes back into ancient Germanic times. The Old Saxon *thegan* means primarily a boy. In Old Norse *þegn* is frequently used for subject or common freeman. The Old High German form of the same word is employed to translate disciple. Nowhere does the primary significance of the term indicate high rank.[50] Furthermore, the character of a word is revealed not by its ancestry alone but also to some extent by its posterity. From *egn þ* are derived such words as *þegnian*, to serve, *þegnung*, service, and *þignen*, maidservant. And these are not late formations: *þegnian* occurs in

---

[49] Mayhew, *Old English Phonology*, 51. Others have tried to connect þegn with þeon (Gothic gaþeihan), to thrive. Leo confidently asserts that the thegn is 'he who has thriven,'—"se þe geþeah." *Rectitudines*, 168–69. Had the term first appeared at the time of the *Promotion Law*, or of the period to which it refers, this derivation from þeon might seem reasonable. But still earlier lies a long age of what does not look like much prosperity on the part of thegnhood. But slightly different is Little's explanation, "the growing one, the boy or young man." *Eng. Hist. Rev.*, IV, 724. For the Promotion Law where the expression 'he who has thriven' occurs, see Schmid, *Gesetze*, Anhang, V.

[50] The author of the *Heliand* uses thegan and kuninges thegan in such a way as to suggest the English nobleman of that same period. But this meaning is clearly a derived one and can hardly represent native usage. The poem appears to have been written during the reign of Louis the Pious, when kingship was still a rather new idea among the Continental Saxons. Perhaps Anglo-Saxon influence can be traced in the terms employed. The author knew something of Bede: he used his homilies as a source in preparing his poem. See Windisch, *Heliand und seine Quellen*, 46. If he knew any of Bede's other writings, he would find the phrase "minister regis" frequently used, a combination that he would have to translate "kuninges thegan."

Beowulf. The early history of the word thegn is one of service.[51] There is, however, no evidence known to me that would support the assumption that the original thegn belonged to an unfree class;[52] but in time the term came to be applied in Anglo-Saxon to almost every possible rank of men from serf to noble. The present discussion will be limited, as far as possible, to the thegns at the royal court.

While the institution of thegnhood may be very ancient, its importance in the king's household is of a later date. In the earliest sources there is scarcely any mention of the thegn; in the earlier Kentish dooms[53] we read of eorl and *eorlcund*, of churl and freeman, but nowhere of thegn or gesith. The first great change in terminology comes with the Laws of Withræd.[54] Gesith and thegn now appear for the first time in English legislation, but not as equivalent terms: the gesith is a member of a class, 'gesithcund,' while the thegn is a privileged individual; he is the king's thegn, while the 'gesithcundman' seems to have no master. If the king's thegn were originally a churl, he is one no longer. He can 'cleanse himself' with his own oath, while a churlish man needs three compurgators.[55] Not only has he risen above the common freeman, he has also passed the gesith.[56] If further evidence were needed to show that these two orders of men were wholly distinct, it is found in the early laws of Wessex, where the fine for breaking into the burg of a king's thegn is fixed at sixty *scillings*, and for the same offence against a landowning 'gesithcundman' at thirty-five *scillings*.[57] Nor does it seem that the gesith had declined in importance. His position with reference to the king is very nearly the same as that of the

---

[51] This fact led Kluge to look for a corresponding derivation. In an earlier edition of his *Wörterbuch* (1889) he suggested that þegn might be derived from the Germanic base• þigwa, whence Gothic þius, Old English þeon, a bondman. But he was evidently unable to overcome the phonological difficulties, for in his latest edition (1899) the suggestion is not repeated. See *Etymologisches Wörterbuch*, Degen.

[52] In the enumeration of classes in the *Lay of Rìgh* (C. P. B., I, 238), the thegns are placed among the churls or common freemen. Thegn is the son of Karl.

[53] *Laws of Æthelbirht; Laws of Hlotar and Eadric.*

[54] The "cyninges þegn" is mentioned in c. 20.

[55] C. 20, 21.

[56] The oath of a king's thegn is four times as strong as that of a churl. The fine for adultery on the part of a gesith is only twice as large as that fixed for the same crime on the part of a churl. *Laws of Wihtræd*, 5, 20, 21.

[57] *Laws of Ine*, 45.

eorl of the older Kentish laws as appears from a comparison of fines[58] and wergelds.[59] But he is soon overshadowed by the rising class of thegnhood which had placed itself between him and his king. His fortunes are clearly waning, and after the ninth century the title gesith appears no more in English law.

The terminology of the Anglian poetry is also worthy of some consideration.[60] In the Cædmonic poems the thegn is high in the royal service. The author of the Genesis, when referring to the royal household, uses the title of thegn for any member of the royal following,[61] but, more particularly for one who performs the king's commands.[62] The poet does not seem to attach any military significance to the word, though at times he does use it in the poem Judith. The guests invited to Holofernes' great banquet belonged to an inner circle of senior thegns, *yldestan*

[58] The ratio of fines for similar crimes against the king and the eorl under the old Kentish regulations was as 25:6. *Laws of Æthelbirht,* 2, 5, 6, 10, 13, 14. Under the earliest West Saxon laws the ratio of fines for breaking into the king's or the gesith's burg was as 24:7. *Laws of Ine,* 45.

[59] The earliest wergelds noted are those of Kent toward the close of the seventh century. In Hlotar and Eadric's dooms (1, 3), we read of men whose worth was three hundred scillings and others with a wergeld of only one hundred. If we double these we have the 'wers' of the six-hynde men and the twy-hynde men of the Wessex documents. But Ine (c. 70) also recognized a third class, of twelve-hynde men. It is hardly necessary to say that the wergeld of a king's thegn was twelve hundred scillings and that of a churl two hundred. Seebohm regards the six-hynde man "as probably the Wilisc man with five hides or more." *Tribal Custom in Anglo-Saxon Law,* 401. His conclusion is based mainly on two chapters of Ine's Law (24:2, 32) where the wergelds of the native Celts are fixed, and appears well founded. But most likely the six-hynde class was composed of two distinct elements. From analogous conditions in Kent we should infer that the gesithcund (which are much in evidence in Ine's legislation) were of this class. And we are distinctly told that the worth of a Celt with five hides of land was six hundred scillings. In the reign of Alfred the six-hynde man disappears. Alfred and Guthrum's peace recognizes but two classes, twelve hundred men and two hundred men. See Schmid, *Gesetze,* 100; Cf. *ibid.,* 591–95, Geldrechnung; Steenstrup, *Danelag,* 115, 171–74; Seebohm, *Tribal Custom in Anglo Saxon Law,* 352–55.

[60] On this point I shall limit myself to the investigation of what the usage was in the century of Cædmon and Cynewulf, whose productions belong to the time before 800. The ninth century, which was the period of the Norse and Danish invasions, produced nothing, it seems, in the way of literature before the art was revived at the court of Alfred.

[61] After the expulsion of Satan there was again true peace in Heaven,—'the Lord dear to all, the Ruler to His thegns' (78–81). All the dwellers of Heaven are thegns. Cf. the description of the divine courts in *Andreas* (873–76) where the angels gathering in the Lord's presence are all called thegns: "Utan ymbe æþelne englas stodon, þegnas ymb þeoden þusendmælum"

[62] Pharaoh's thegns, the princes of King James' version, who beheld the beauty of Abraham's wife, are also called ombiht-scealcas, a term of a decidedly servile origin. (1849–51; 1869–72.) When Abraham was at Gerar, Abimelech the king sent his thegns to bring Sarah to himself. (2627–28.)

þegnas.[63] When the watchmen discovered the advance of the Jewish host, they reported the matter to the eldest ruling thegns, *yldestan ealdor-þegnum*.[64] Gesith is used in reference to Holofernes' guests, not as a mark of distinction, but in the sense of companion, *wea-gesiþas*,[65] companions in woe. Farther on, the same term is applied to the warriors or leaders in the Hebrew host.[66] It will be seen that the significance of the word thegn when applied by the early Christian poets to members of the king's household is very general. Naturally it is used for freemen only. The antithetical usage of 'thegn and theow'[67] would scarcely permit us to apply the title to a serf.

There are, however, a few Old English poems of unmistakably heathen origin and of greater antiquity even than that of the Genesis.[68] These Teutonic lyrics and heroics deal largely with the life of the *comitatus* in the lord's hall—the higher life of that age. In Widsith, perhaps the most venerable of these, we meet such terms as eorl, eorlship, gesith and *duguþ*, but not thegn. Nor is there any mention of thegns in the Seafarer. The members of the *comitatus* in the Husband's Message are warriors and gesiths[69] but not thegns. In the Wanderer we find the title once in the compound *magu-þegnas*, meaning warriors.[70] While this remarkable absence of the term in the pre-Christian poetry does not prove absolutely that the thegn had not yet made his appearance among the great, it does seem to show that he had not yet thriven sufficiently to allow his own title to displace the earlier terms in the poet's vocabulary.

In Beowulf the word *þegn* has a rather general significance parallel to that which we found in the Biblical poems. On the whole, the usage implies the relationship of the *comitatus*.[71] But there were thegns at Heorot whose services must have been too

---

[63] 7-10.
[64] 241-43.
[65] 16.
[66] 201.
[67] *Phoenix*, 164-65: Æghwylc wille
    wesan þegn and þeow þeodne mærum.
[68] See chapter I.
[69] 33 : secgum and gesiþum.
[70] 62.
[71] Beowulf himself was Higelac's thegn (194, 407-8); his men are his own thegns (400, 719, 1480); the shoreward bears the same title (235). See also 123, 293, 867, 1081, 1085, 1230, 1405, 1419, 1644, 2033 et passim.

menial for noblemen. The hero himself has an *ombeht-þegn*, who takes charge of his armor when he retires.[72] There is a hall-thegn who looks after his general needs.[73] Thegns also seem to act as butlers.[74] Unfortunately, the composite character of the epic makes it an extremely unreliable source when the effort is to trace the development of any particular institution.[75] But we cannot err very much if we say that in this poem there are traces both of what the thegn once was, a trusted household servant, and of what he had recently come to be, the king's honored companion and guard.[76]

In the Latin sources king's thegn is translated *minister regis*. The title frequently occurs in Bede: all the members of the royal court seem to have been *ministri* when the Ecclesiastical History was written. The term also occurs in some of the earlier charters,[77] but perhaps in no genuine document of the seventh century.[78] The earliest land-grant to a *minister* that has come down to us, was made by Æthelbald of Mercia (716–43).[79] From this time on, there is an increasing number of charters in which *ministri* appear either as grantees or as witnesses.[80]

The results of our inquiry into the rise of thegnhood may be summed up as follows: in the laws, the charters and the poetic memorials,[81] the earliest mention of the king's thegn falls in the latter half of the seventh century or the beginning of the eighth; on the other hand, in what appears to be earlier sources, there is scarcely a single allusion to a thegn of any sort.[82] From this we

---

[72] 673.
[73] 1794.
[74] 494.
[75] For a discussion of the structure of this poem, see Müllenhoff, *Untersuchungen über das angelsächsische Epos*. Berlin, 1899.
[76] Wealhtheow's allusion to the eorls as faithful and the thegns as gentle (1228–30) is interesting, but perhaps the antithesis was not intentional.
[77] The term minister occurs in a document purporting to be issued by Wulfhere of Mercia in 664. *K. C. D.*, No. 984. But the slightest examination of the text shows it to be spurious; it is full of technical terms from Norman times.
[78] A Mercian charter of uncertain date (716?) has four ministri among the witnesses. *K. C. D.*, No. 67. A grant attributed to Wulhere and dated 624 is signed by two ministri. Birch thinks this is a genuine document, but would change the date to 674. *Cartul.*, No. 32. On close examination, however, it will be found to belong to a much later date.
[79] *K. C. D.*, No. 90.
[80] *Ibid.*, Nos. 109, 113, 117, 137, 1020, 1021 and later documents.
[81] *Laws of Wihtræd* (695–96); *K. C. D.*, No. 67 (716?); *The Genesis*.
[82] Except in Beowulf; but that epic is probably the growth of a long period of time.

shall have to conclude that the real importance of this new order of men dates from the second half of the seventh century.

In this same period the transforming power of Christianity was beginning to reshape English life and institutions. The old faith perished and with it the great *comitatus* in the heavenly halls of Woden. This fact could not fail to affect the character of the same institution on earth;[83] it soon ceased to be a martial following of warlike gesiths and became a royal guard of thegns whose lives were dedicated to the new ideal of service. Nevertheless, the royal household retained its armed character; doubtless much of the old spirit was kept alive. All men, says Eddi, trusted Wilfrid; the nobles sent their sons to him to be educated as ecclesiastics, or as servants of the king, if they should be unwilling to enter the church.[84] The phrase here used, 'that he might commend them to the king as men in arms,' has a decidedly Tacitean flavor; but a *comitatus* of the older type is not necessarily implied.[85]

As to how large the king's company of thegns was during the seventh and eighth centuries we have no information.[86] The guard of the Northumbrian king was, on one occasion at least, five or six thegns.[87] We get a vague idea of the size of King Edwin's household from Bede's account of the Princess Eanfled's baptism.[88] She was the first one of the Northumbrian people to receive that rite. Eleven others *de familia ejus* were baptized with her. Alfred understands these to be of the queen's household, þære cwene hirede. The queen was a Christian and had

---

[83] Cf. the effect of the introduction of Christianity on the Norse viking.

[84] *Hist. York*, I, 32: Principes....filios suos ad erudiendum sibi dederunt, ut aut Deo servirent, si eligerent; aut adultos, si maluissent, regi armatos commendaret.

[85] Bishop Wilfrid also kept an armed train. The jealous queen incited King Ecgfrith against him 'by eloquently recounting all the worldly glory of Saint Wilfrid the bishop, his riches, the great number of his monastic establishments, and the numberless host of his courtiers adorned with regal arms and vestments.' All this is doubtless highly exaggerated; but while we may question the regal character of the weapons, there is no reason to doubt the statement that the bishop's men bore arms. *Hist. York*, I, 34–35.

[86] There were sixty thegns in the hall at Finnsburg, but this number probably originated in the poet's imagination. *The Fight at Finnsburg*, 37–38. Cf. Waitz, *D. V. G.*, I, 357.

[87] Bede, *H. E.*, III, 26: Rex ipse....cum quinque tantum aut sex ministris veniebat [ad ecclesiam]...

[88] *Ibid.*, II, 9:...quae baptizata est...prima de gente Nordanhymbrorum cum undecim aliis de familia ejus.

brought several attendants with her from Kent, doubtless all of the new faith. If these eleven were of her men or maids, the queen's service must have been quite large for the time and place. And we should imagine the king's own to be still more numerous. But Alfred's interpretation is not the only possible one. Most likely the eleven were of Edwin's own service. Whether the author is accurate or not is immaterial. He evidently saw nothing strange in the story, and in his own day the king's household must have been quite large. In describing King Oswin's liberality, he says: 'from all sides and from nearly every province men, even of the noblest blood, rushed to his service *(ministerium)*.'[89]

The relationship between the king and his thegns seems as a rule to have been a permanent one, especially in cases where a gift of land was a consideration. But, as we have already seen, lands and honors might be lost, and with them the royal favor. However, a thegn might also be dismissed in grace. Benedict Biscop, a young nobleman, served King Oswy as *minister* and received a suitable estate from his master before he was twenty-five years old, but despising earthly possessions he left the royal service and went to Rome (ca. 653).[90] In a Kentish charter of 762 the grantor refers to himself as Æthelbirht's *minister* during the life of that king.[91] This form of statement and the fact that no title is joined to his signature lead us to infer that he had ceased to be a *minister*. A thegn, it seems, might be permitted to transfer his allegiance from one royal master to another;[92] but strangest of all, it was apparently possible for him to serve two lords at the same time, as their 'common *minister*.'[93]

The history of thegnhood after the eighth century closely resembles that of the earlier *comitatus:* the king's household became the birth-place of a new landed aristocracy. As the Anglo-Saxon

---
[89] *H. E.*, III, 14.
[90] Bede, *Opera*, II, 140.
[91] *K. C. D.*, No. 109: Ego Dunuuald minister, dum aduiuerit, inclitae memoriae regis Aethelberti....
[92] Bede tells of a thegn, a prisoner of war, who got his ransom money from the king of Kent, the son of Queen Æthelthryth's sister. The prisoner had once been the minister of Æthelthryth or of her sister; but at the time of his capture he served Ecgfrith, king of Northumbria and Æthelthryth's husband. *H. E.*, IV, 22.
[93] In 801, the Mercian king and his brother, the king of Kent, conveyed lands to "Suiðhune, nostro in commune ministro." *K. C. D.*, No. 179.

king was not in the habit of legislating for his court, the mention of his thegns in the last Kentish laws implies that they had acquired a position away from the royal presence and were no longer in constant attendance upon their master. Whether the practice of rewarding the *ministri* with lands was common during the earlier period cannot be known: all the extant charters of the seventh century are issued to ecclesiastics or to laymen for ecclesiastical purposes.[94] The same, with perhaps five exceptions,[95] is true of the eighth century grants before Offa's reign (757-96). During the second half of the century lay grantees become more numerous, and several of the transfers are to king's *ministri*. That the *ministri* were specially favored by Offa appears from two restoration charters issued by Coenwulf (798-819), under whom a clerical reaction seems to have set in.[96] Owing to warfare and unsettled conditions, the records of the ninth century are not very satisfactory; but, such as they are, they show an increasing number of grants to laymen. This tendency appears to have culminated about the middle of the tenth century. Edward's charters (901-24) are nearly all to churchmen. Under Æthelstan (925-40) there is a decided increase in the number of landed gifts to *ministri*. Of the extant

---

[94] The grant of Wulfhere (Mercia, 624 or 674) to his kinsman Berhfrith (Birch, *Cartul.*, No. 32) can hardly be considered genuine. It is signed by two bishops, Wita and Totta. Wina and Tuda are probably meant, but Tuda died ten years before the grant was made. See Stubbs, *Reg. Sacr. Anglic.*, 3.

[95] *K. C. D.*, Nos. 79, 90, 101, 117, 1001; Birch, *Cartul.*, No. 203 (apparently a duplicate of *K. C. D.*, No. 117). In No. 90 Æthelbald (Mercia, 716-43) gives land to Osred his "ministro...valde fideli qui est de stirpe non ignobili prosapia regali gentis huicciorum". This is the earliest recorded grant to a thegn. No. 117 is a grant by Uhtred (Hwiccas, 767) to "fideli meo ministro aedelmundo". No. 1001 may be a grant to a churchman. It should be added that the fact that so few charters conveying lands to laymen are extant does not necessarily lead to the conclusion that such gifts were but rarely made. The documents would not be so likely to be preserved as those of the church.

[96] The first of these relates to lands which at one time had been given by King Egbert to his thegn Aldhun; and this one, going beyond the sea, had given it to the church at Canterbury. But afterwards Offa annulled this grant and distributed the lands among his thegns, saying that it was not right for his minister to hand the estate over into the power of another: "Sed harum postmodum possessiones terrarum Offa,...immutauit suisque distribuit ministris, dicens injustum esse quod minister ejus praesumpserit terram sibi a domino distributam absque ejus testimonio in alterius postestatem dare... *K. C. D.*, No. 1020. The same year the king restored to a church at Dover certain lands "quas olim rex Offa eidem aecclesiae ablatas suis contulit ministris,..." *Ibid.*, No. 1021. In 840 Berhtulf of Mercia restored certain lands which he had taken from the church at Worcester and 'given to his own men'. *Ibid.*, No. 245.

charters dating from the reigns of Edmund (940–46), Eadred (946–55) and Eadwig (955–59), only a minor fraction record grants to the church. Edgar (959–75) was more liberal in endowing ecclesiastics, but even he distributed lands more freely among his thegns.

Occasionally the particular office of the person endowed is specified,[97] but more commonly *minister* is the only title employed. In nearly every case immunities, more or less extensive, went with the land. It seems that from the accession of Offa (757) the Old English kings made a deliberate effort to build up an aristocracy of land-owners. On the other hand, the *ministri* were eager for territorial possessions.[98] In his 'Epistle to Egbert' Bede gives us a vivid picture of official rapacity in Northumbria in the generation before Offa. The subject is monastic corruption brought about largely by the purchase of monasteries by the king's men: 'thus there are many who are called abbots and at the same time prefects or thegns or servants of the king.'[99] This condition seems to have been general all over the land,[1] and had existed, we are told, about thirty years.[2]

The thegns thus endowed with lands or local offices naturally could not be constantly present at the royal court. But their personal relationship to the king did not cease; nominally, they still belonged to his household. We read in the 'Promotion Law' that a churl might become a thegn, if he had, among other things,

---

[97] As for instance K. C. D., No. 489, a grant to "cuidam cubiculario"; *ibid.*, No. 503, lands given to "cuidam camerario", etc.

[98] The biographies of the English saints show us mere striplings hovering about the royal court, all doubtless expecting future rewards. See *Memorials of St. Dunstan*, 11; *Hist. York*, I, 4.

[99] *Opera*, II, 219: Atque ita ordine perverso innumeri sint inventi, qui se abbates pariter et praefectos sive ministros aut famulos regis appellant, qui etsi aliquid vitae monasterialis ediscere laici non experiendo... Cf. *Hist. York*, I, 410–11.

[1] There were evidently thegns in all the kingdoms. But after the establishment of the Danelaw, thegnhood seems to have flourished mainly in the south. Nearly all the royal grants of the tenth century are of lands south of the Thames; a few are located in the counties on the north bank; extremely few in the northern counties. In that region the social system was somewhat different, being based on the Norse ideas of a free yeomanry. See Steenstrup, *Danelag*, 103.

[2] The Epistola was written in 734 or 735. The movement, then, would date from about 700, or soon after the time when the thegn first appears in the sources.

a 'seat and special service in the king's hall.'[3] The term used for special service is *sunder-note*. This probably signified some particular duty, the same for all such thegns, established by custom once for all. The word seems to be thus used in Beowulf: the king had retired and a watch 'attended to the special service.'[4] Judging from the context we should take this to mean serving as a guard. In the *Rectitudines*[5] mention is made of *heafodweard*, head-ward, a service that the thegn owes to his king and the *geneat* to his lord.[6] Schmid's opinion, that this was the duty to guard the royal head when the king came into that particular region, is probably correct.[7] The term is used in a similar sense by the Anglian poets.[8] It appears from Asser's account that the thegns of Alfred's day had a similar duty to perform. 'For the *satellites* of the aforesaid king were most prudently divided into three cohorts in such a manner, that the first division remained and served at the royal court day and night for a month; when the month was ended, another division coming, the first departed for home.'[9] Here we have thegns living abroad throughout the realm, but whose duty it is to give one-third of their time to the king's service at the royal vill. Fifty years later we find the thegns making similar periodic visits to the king's court. The authority for this statement is a passage in Edmund's laws: 'And I further make known, that I will have in my household no one

[3] Schmid, *Gesetze*, Anhang V:
   And gif ceorl geþeah, þæt he hæfðe.
   fullice fif hida agenes landes,
   cirican and kycenan, bell-hus and burh-geat,
   setl and sunder-note on cynges healle,
   þonne was he þononforð þegen-rihtes weorðe.
The document is thought to date from the tenth century, but does not pretend to describe conditions as they were at the time of its authorship: it gives the law as 'it was whilom'. See Stevenson, Burh-geat-setl, in *Eng. Hist. Rev.*, XII, 489–92.

[4] Sundor-nytte beheold ymb aldor Dena (ll. 667–68).
[5] A tenth century document. See Leo, *Rectitudines*, 222 ff.; Seebohm, *English Village Community*, 129.
[6] Schmid, *Gesetze*, Anhang III, 1, 2.
[7] Cf. Old Norse höfuðvörðr, the term applied to the personal guard of the Norwegian kings. See Keyser, *Efterladte Skrifter*, II, 78.
[8] The Assyrian sentinels guarding Holofernes' camp are called heafod-weardas. *Judith*, 239. Wiglaf kept heafod-weard over the body of his dead lord. *Beow.*, 2906–10.
[9] Petrie's *Monumenta*, 495: In tribus namque cohortibus praefati regis satellites prudentissime dividebantur, ita ut prima cohors uno mense in curto regio die noctuque administrans commoraretur, menseque finito, et adveniente alia cohorte, prima domum redibat.

who has been guilty of shedding human blood, before he shall have submitted to divine penance and all that is proper, as the bishop shall instruct him in whose shire it be."[10] Evidently the members of Edmund's household dwelt in different shires.[11] Our conclusion then must be that, while there doubtless was a permanent court, there was also a body of household thegns whose presence at this court was occasional only, or at stated times, but whose duties nevertheless were definite and well understood. Analogous to this is the Norse system as described in *Speculum Regale*. The author of this work recognizes five classes among the king's servants, his classification being based on the amount and character of the service rendered. Two of these classes are made up of absentees who rarely come to the court, but who also have duties to perform, the specially important duty being to assist the king's officer in executing royal mandates in their region.[12]

That the English king would employ the thegns at his court as special agents in matters not exactly in the hands of his regular officials is almost self-evident and readily inferred from the language of the sources.[13] But that the absentee-thegn possessed any local executive functions is not so readily shown. The thegn who had thriven to the extent that he served the king and

---

[10] II, 4: Eac ic cyðe, þæt ic nelle socne habban to minum hirede þone, þe mannes blod geate, ær he hæbbe godcunde bote underfangen anc wið þa mægðe gebet on bote befangen, and to ælcum rihte gebogen, swa biscop him tæce, þe hit on his scyre sy.
The translation is disputed, the uncertain element being the word socne. Liebermann's rendering is clearly conjecture. Schmid thinks the sentence is corrupt. The translation given in the text is based on Steenstrup's interpretation (*Danelag*, 211), which appears to me to be correct, and, if accepted, makes the passage clear.

[11] This interpretation is based on the fact that the criminal seems to be subject to a shire-bishop and not to the court clergy.

[12] *Speculum Regale*, 260 ff. As will be shown later, there are good reasons for thinking that the organization of the royal court in Norway was in many respects a copy of the English hired as it was in Æthelred's day. We should therefore expect to find the English thegns of the tenth century performing to some extent the same functions as the king's men performed in Norway two centuries later.

[13] When the Lord has a special message to deliver to men, he sends his thegn or his high-thegn. See *Daniel*, 441-43; instances from the *Genesis* have been given in another connection. We read that a king once sent Saint Wulfstan, then one of his ministri, to assist a bishop in enforcing obedience. *Chronicon Monasterii de Abingdon*, II, 260. Ælfric, writing on the eve of Danish rule, speaks of thegns as ambassadors and military commanders. *Lives*, The Maccabees, 330 ff. Cf. Cook, *Biblical Quotations*, 100: Naaman a thegn.

'rode as his mounted messenger at his household'[14] evidently received his orders at court. Still, that the thegn came to be an important factor in the local administration appears from numerous passages in the laws. In Northumbria he seems to have assisted in collecting church-dues.[15] In London he evidently served as peace officer.[16] One of Æthelstan's laws provides punishment for a thegn who shall have taken a bribe.[17] The phrase, 'I and my thegns,' used in Edgar's law,[18] puts a special emphasis on this order of men and indicates that they were invested with considerable authority.

To assign a constitutional position to the holders of thegnright is, however, extremely difficult.[19] Feudal analogies will not help much to clear up matters, for all thegns did not have land.[20] It seems that the king's men were in a great measure out of the reach of the local authorities. Their land-dues were nearly all to the king.[21] Says Æthelred, 'no man shall have *soc* over a king's thegn but the king himself.'[22] Edgar magnanimously permits the townsmen to examine herds of live cattle belonging to himself and to his thegns.[23] 'In every shire and borough the king has the rights of his kingship and the thegn

---

[14] Schmid, *Gesetze*, Anhang V, 3. For a corrected translation see Steenstrup, *Danelag*, 183. Seebohm's rendering of "on his hired" as "with his household" I am not able to accept. I must also reject his translation of radstefne as "on his summons". *Tribal Custom in Anglo-Saxon Law*, 368.

[15] Schmid, *Gesetze*, Anhang II, 57.

[16] *Laws of Æthelstan*, VI, 11.

[17] V, I: 3, 4.

[18] IV, A, 6.

[19] Much of what has been written on thegnage deals with the institution mainly as it was just before the Conquest. Thus Maitland, *Domesday Book and Beyond*, 161 ff. As for the earlier thegn, Seebohm regards him as "a soldier first of all things". *English Village Community*, 135. Stubbs virtually holds the same opinion. *C. H.*, I, 172. Schmid seems to believe that the bond of service that held the thegn to the king was dissolved at some period before 900 and that subsequently thegnright was based on territorial holdings with an irresistible tendency to become hereditary. *Gesetze*, 666. An effort is sometimes made to distinguish between king's thegn and common thegn (see Pollock and Maitland, *History of English Law*, 10) but such a distinction can hardly be established before the eleventh century. While the military and territorial elements of thegnhood are important considerations, I believe they are subordinate to that of personal relationship to the king.

[20] *Laws of Æthelstan*, VI, 11: ...and þe healfum 'þam ælc minra þegna þe gelandod sy....

[21] Schmid, *Gesetze*, Anhang III, 1, *Rectitudines*.

[22] *Laws of Æthelred*, III, 11: And nan man nage nane socne ofer cynges þegen buton cyng sylf.

[23] *Laws of Edgar*, IV, B, 13.

those of his thegnship.'[24] In addition to legal privilege and social prestige the thegn apparently enjoyed great wealth.[25] Constitutional writers have generally supposed that five hides were necessary to make up a noble estate,[26] and it is quite probable that such was originally the rule.[27] If 'whilom' a churl wished to become a thegn, he had to have five hides at least;[28] but land alone was not sufficient. The development of this landed nobility extended over a period of at least three hundred years. In this evolution the rights of thegnship became hereditary[29]—soon men were thegn-born as well as churl-born[30]— and it seems unlikely that the estates could have been kept intact. On this point the charters shed no light. Æthelbald's grant to Osred, perhaps the earliest transfer of land to a *minister* of which we have the record, is of twenty *cassati*.[31] After that the charters involve land-grants of varying extent, but usually not less than five hides.[32]

But the thegn was not always merely a household servant or a local dignitary, he might also be a member of the national assembly. The privilege of membership in the king's council seems to have originated in the royal household. We have an early account of the deliberations of such a gemot in Bede's account of Edwin's conversion.[33] Prominent among the members was Cefi, the heathen *ealdorbisceop* of Alfred's version. He presided over the sanctuary in the 'town' where the council was held, and, as this was probably a royal vill, we should fancy that

[24] *Laws of Edgar*, IV, B, 2.
[25] *K. C. D.*, No. 805 (1046-60). One Toki is represented as "praepotens vir et dives minister regis". Ælfric frequently speaks of wealthy thegns. See *Lives*, I, 154; *Homilies*, II, 172; where thegns are spoken of as desiring convents to be built on their lands. The *Laws of Edgar* (II, 2) have a provision directed against such of his men as had churches on their book-lands. Wulfstan informs us that thegns frequently had serfs. *Homilies*, 162-63.
[26] Stubbs, *C. H.*, I, 173. Cf. Maitland, *Domesday Book and Beyond*, 101; Pollock and Maitland, *History of English Law*, I, 10. Little (Gesiths and Thegns, *Eng. Hist. Rev.*, IV, 723-29) combats the five-hide theory, but not with entire success.
[27] See *Eng. Hist. Rev.*, IV, 728: Little, Gesiths and Thegns.
[28] Schmid, *Gesetze*, Anhang V, 2.
[29] See *ibid.*, 666.
[30] *Ibid.*, Anhang I, 5 (Geræðnes betweox Dunsetan): ...sy he þegen-boren, sy he ceorl-boren...
[31] *K. C. D.*, No. 90 (716-43). Uhtred's grant to Æthelmund (767) conveys five tributaria. *K. C. D.*, No. 117.
[32] In many instances the lands were formerly held by the grantee's father.
[33] *H. E.*, II, 13. Cf. Freeman's view of the earlier assemblies. *N. C.*, I, 67 ff.

Cefi belonged to the royal court as king's priest. Bede is not explicit on this point: but Alfred understands the phrase *nullus tuorum* to mean *nullus tuorum ministrorum*, and accordingly translates it 'none of thy thegns;' he regards Cefi as a king's thegn.

It may be that after the establishment of Christianity the Christian bishop, who usually stood close to the king, stepped into the position of the heathen priest; when dioceses multiplied the new bishops may have been accorded the same privileges as the earlier ones. Along with the ecclesiastics and other dignitaries an indefinite number of *ministri* came to the council. These were probably designated by the king.[34] That the king controlled the membership of the assembly appears from the fact that priests were admitted to Edward's *witenagemot* but excluded by his successors.[35] Some kings admitted abbots, others did not. Nor does it seem necessary that the same ministri be in attendance from reign to reign. In one reign the attendance might be large; in the next small. The high-water mark was reached in Æthelstan's day, when more than fifty *ministri* attended a gemot.[36]

The institution of thegnship in the older sense seems to have wholly disappeared in the reign of Cnut. The name indeed remained, but apparently its application was limited to a class of men holding land by a peculiar form of tenure. And frequently the title is used so loosely in Cnut's documents as to justify the statement that to the Danes and their king thegn did not mean a member of the native nobility, but simply a subject, as it did in the North. In a royal writ from the early years of his reign, Cnut addresses all freemen as thegns *twelf-hynde and twi-hynde;*[37] and his classification of thegns into those nearest the king and 'lesser thegns'[38] suggests the elaborate system of classes that prevailed in his other kingdoms, especially Norway, where the

---

[34]Kemble seems to think that every freeman had a theoretical right to attend the witenagemot. *Sax. in Eng.*, II, 201. The same view in a more extreme form is presented by Freeman. *N. C.*, I, 68, 69, and Appendix Q. Stubbs apparently holds that the ministri who attended the council were nominated by the king. *C. H.*, I, 135, 140. Cf. Gneist, *Englische Verfassungsgeschichte*, 81–84.

[35]There can be little doubt that such documents as Nos. 337, 1082, 1084 (others could be cited) in Kemble's collection were issued at meetings of the witan.

[36]*K. C. D.*, No. 353 (931). See also No. 364 (934). Cf. Stubbs, *C. H.*, I, 140.

[37]*K. C. D.*, No. 731 (1013–20): Cnut cing gret Lyfing arcebisceop and Godwine bisceop......and ealle mine egnas twelfhynde and twihynde freondlice.

[38]*Laws of Cnut*, II, 71: 1, 2, 3.

earliest codes recognize six intervening classes between the king and the serf.[39] We are safe in affirming that the thegn was not regarded as a member of Cnut's household: as guardian of the king's person and perhaps of the royal interests throughout the realm, the house-carle had taken his place.[40] We have, however, passed the point where a discussion of thegnhood with reference to the royal court can be a fruitful one.

Before the Danish invasion, however, the *ministri* were something more than great landed proprietors with certain military obligations; they composed an aristocracy bound to the king by peculiar personal ties and forming an extension of his court into the various parts of his kingdom. From the humbler realms of household service, the order had risen, first to the plane of honor as a royal *comitatus*, and next to the plane of influence as a landed nobility. In the days of its prosperity it formed the great outer circle of the royal service. But there was also an inner circle of thegns whose duties kept them in constant attendance at the palace. These officials will be the subject of the chapters following.

---

[39] See Munch, *N. F. H.*, I, 1, 143.
[40] The house-carles will be considered in a subsequent chapter.

CHAPTER IV.

THE KING'S REEVE: *PRAEFECTUS REGIS*.[41]

At the beginning of the seventh century there seems to have been no distinction, in the Kentish kingdom, between local and central authorities. From the language used in the Laws of Æthelbirht, we should infer that the king was in direct contact with his people, that the ruler summoned the folk to the royal vill and dealt out justice in person.[42] But soon a shadowy official emerges, a sort of an intermediary between the lord and the people. The king's reeve may be as old as the English kingship, but we catch our first glimpses of him about the year 700.[43]

That the reeve was a household official in the narrower sense of the term seems to be apparent from certain allusions in the earliest sources; that he at times acted in a more public capacity seems equally clear. But in the early part of the eighth century it is difficult to draw the line between what relates to the management of the royal domicile and what may be called public administration. As the *gerefa* of later Anglo-Saxon history was a local functionary, the question naturally arises whether the early *praefectus* is not the later *praepositus, scir-gerefa* or sheriff. We shall have to consider this possibility before proceeding further.

---

[41] As the historic development of the royal reeveship differs in many important respects from that of the other household officers, I have preferred to treat the subject in a separate chapter.

[42] C. 2: Gif cyning his leode to him gehateð and heom mon þær yfel gedo, II bote and cyninge L scillinga. See also *Laws of Hlotar and Eadric*, 7. Recovered stolen property was to be brought to the king's hall, "to cynges sele," whenever possible. The same custom of royal judgment seems to have been the ruling one in Mercia. See *K. C. D.*, Nos. 210 (816) and 1026 (796–821).

[43] For the subject of the king's reeve see Kemble, *Sax. in Eng.*, II, 169–71; Stubbs, *C. H.*, I, 372; Green, *Conqu. of Eng.*, 229, 524; Schmid, *Gesetze*, 597. In none of these discussions are any satisfactory conclusions reached, mainly because the subject is usually studied from the point of view of the shire organization.

To have a shire-reeve we must have a shire, a more or less definite territorial circumscription within which the reeve exercises certain recognized authority. But to show that such an administrative area existed before the reign of Alfred is exceedingly difficult. *Scir* is an old word in Anglo-Saxon, but its territorial significance is not the most ancient. The earliest meaning that we can distinctly make out is official duties or functions.[44] In the Erfurt Glossary, which probably dates from the seventh century, *scir* is used to translate *procuratio*.[45] The word frequently appears in Alfred's version of Bede's history, but nearly always with an ecclesiastical significance. Sometimes it refers to the duties and functions of an office,[46] sometimes to the territorial limits within which these are exercised.[47] Bede's *provincia* is almost universally translated *mægþ*, a word with a tribal rather than a territorial meaning.[48] The fact that *scir* occurs almost everywhere in the Chronicle merely proves that such administrative areas existed at the time of its compilation, which can hardly have antedated Alfred's reign. More pertinent are certain chapters in the Laws of Ine. But the judge or *scirman*[49] alluded to in the first of these may be an official in the general sense, one who holds a *scir* or office. The threat that an ealdorman might lose his *scir*[50] would at first sight appear to prove the presence of a shire in Wessex as early as this reign (688?–726?). In later Saxon times the ealdorman may have been the highest official of the shire, but an examination of the use of the term in early English documents shows the impossibility of arguing from the use of this title. Any person invested with authority might be called

---

[44]The Roman term provincia has a similar history. It first signified official functions; later it was applied to the area over which an official exercised a delegated authority. See Marquardt, *Römische Staatsverwaltung*, I, 497–98.

[45]Sweet, *Oldest English Texts*, 82. For the probable date of the glossary see *ibid.*, 2, 624.

[46]Scir or bisceopscir is used to translate episcopatus (III, 21), praesulatus (V, 19), and cura episcopi (IV, 27). Cura monasterii is rendered mynsterscir (V, 19).

[47]Such as parrochia (IV, 13) and diocesis (IV, 1).

[48]The passage in which Bede narrates the conversion of the prefect of Lincoln ("praefectumque Lindocolinae civitatis.... convertit ad Dominum," II, 16) might seem to point to a shire-reeve; but Alfred disposes of the suggestion by rendering the phrase, "Lyndecylene ceastre gerefan." Ceaster is the Anglicized form of castra and signifies a city of some importance. This prefect cannot have been anything but a city-reeve, burg-reeve, or port-reeve.

[49]C. 8.

[50]C. 36:1.

an ealdorman.[51] The specific meaning that the word had in the tenth century did not appear till after the time of Alfred.[52] The legal provision referred to may mean only that a derelict official should lose his office. A stronger argument for the existence of an early shire is found in chapter 39 of the same laws, which deals with illegal moving from one shire to another. It must be remembered, however, that Ine's laws have come down to us in the form in which they were reënacted by Alfred.[53] While we cannot prove that they were changed to any extent, it seems likely that two intervening centuries would make it necessary to adapt the language to changed conditions. But even if we concede the existence of shires in Wessex before 700, we have no evidence whatever on which to base an argument for its existence in Northumbria or elsewhere. In his account of King Edwin's itineraries, Bede states that he traveled extensively *inter civitates sive villas aut provincias suas*.[54] Alfred translates this phrase thus: *betwyh his hamum oþþe be tunum.* Here would have been an excellent opportunity to use *scir;* but here as elsewhere it is wanting.

The possibility remains that the prefect may have been the chief of a more strictly local organization[55] such as the hundred. But to prove the existence of a hundred in this early period is even more difficult than to show that the shire existed. Henry Adams[56] and Emil Hildebrand[57] have suggested that the phrases *in loco* and *in regione,* frequently used in determining the location of lands, may refer to hundreds. But Steenstrup, after examining the language of the charters cited to support this view, concludes that these terms are purely geographical, not political.[58]

---
[51] In Alfred's translation of Bede's history, subregulus, primus dux, dux regis, princeps, tribunus, patricius, praepositus (of a monastery), optimas, major natu, satrap, are all called ealdormen. See I, 7, 13, 18, 34; II, 13; III, 3; IV, 12, 15, 23. The villicus who was Cædmon's master ("qui sibi praeerat") is also spoken of as an ealdorman (IV, 24); similarly the elders (majores) of a monastery (V, 19) and the chief men of a byrig (IV, 25).
[52] As shown in the above note.
[53] See Schmid, *Gesetze,* Einleitung, XXVII.
[54] *H. E.,* II, 16.
[55] He could not have been a town-reeve as that official is usually called a villicus; Bede uses that title several times.
[56] *Essays in Anglo-Saxon Law* (Boston, 1876), 1–22.
[57] *Engelska Samhällsförhållanden,* 53.
[58] Steenstrup, *Danelag,* 80–81. The author shows that the regio in but a few instances corresponds to a later hundred. He thinks these became hundreds in later times. He also shows that several of the regiones are too large areas to be hundreds, such as the regio Kent. See *K. C. D.,* No. 1019.

An examination of Alfred's Bede materially strengthens this view. *Locus* is usually translated *stow*, the common Old English word for place, *regio* is frequently rendered *land*.[59] Thus, *in regione Sudergeona* becomes 'in Surrey land.'[60] Surrey could hardly have been a hundred only. For regio in the phrases *in regione Nordanhymbrorum*[61] and *in regione quae vocatur Infeppingum*,[62] Alfred uses not land but þeodland, the land of a people or tribe. When a word is used for such large areas as Kent, Surrey and Northumbria, it seems impossible to maintain that it is the technical Latin term for the Old English hundred.

Praefectus, like its Anglo-Saxon equivalent *gerefa*, is a very general term: the reeve was merely a deputy, one whose authority is all derived from a superior. Any owner of a large estate might have and doubtless did have a reeve to whom the management was largely entrusted.[63] *Gerefa*,[64] an Anglo-Saxon text from the reign of Æthelred, is devoted to the duties of such a manorial official. There is nothing in the document that could suggest to us that the reeve under discussion might be the official of a shire; and yet he is called a shire-man, *scyrman*,[65] and 'the one who holds the shire.'[66] The king, as the greatest landowner of the realm, would be in special need of such a deputy. The author of the poem Genesis, who regards Abraham as but little less than a king, calls his steward Eliezer his *gerefa*.[67]

The earliest mention of the king's reeve in the laws is in Ine's code which dates from the same period as the Genesis. 'If the theft be a night old, let those who have seized him [the thief] atone for the guilt on the terms they may be able to arrange with the king and his reeve.'[68] In this case the reeve seems to be

---

[59] "In regione quae vocatur Loidis:" "on þam lande þe Loidis is haten" (II, 14); "in regione Gyrvlorum," "on Gyrwan lande" (IV, 6), (In a list of territorial names found in a tenth or eleventh century manuscript, the Gyrwas are represented as containing 1,200 hides. Birch, *Cartul.*, No. 297.) The island of Ely is also called a regio; in the translation we find "Elig þæt land." (IV, 19).
[60] ....on Suðrigena lande. (IV, 6.)
[61] V, 12; ..on þeodlande Norþanhymbra.
[62] III, 21: ....on þam þeodlande þe is nemned on Feppingum.
[63] A "praefectus episcopi nomine Hocca" is mentioned in Eddi's *Life of Wilfrid*, written ca. 710. *Hist. York*, I, 29.
[64] Published with a commentary by Liebermann in *Anglia*, 9:251-66.
[65] Swa sceal god scyrman his hlafordes healdan (p. 260).
[66] Hede seðe scire healde....(p. 259).
[67] Ll. 2181, 2186.
[68] C. 73: ....Swa hie geþingian mægen wið cyning and his gerefan.

acting with the king in assessing fines, a duty which naturally would fall to him as the royal steward. In the Laws of Alfred there is a significant passage relative to prisoners who are brought to the king's vill:[69] '...and let his kinsmen feed him if he himself have no meat.[70] If he have neither meat nor kinsmen, let the king's reeve feed him.'[71] It is hard to believe that there was at this time a public as well as a private treasury at the royal vill. And if there were no public funds, the reeve would have to draw on the supplies of the king's own household. The inference is that the reeve was in charge of the king's vill.[72] That such a functionary really existed is shown in a document recording a grant of land by Archbishop Æthelweard in 805. The lands in question had been given originally by 'a certain good man, Aldhelm by name, who was prefect of the royal vill in this famous state [Kent].'[73]

Thus far we have considered the reeve as an official whose functions were fiscal in the main. But he might have other duties. From the materials presented above it will be seen that the reeve assisted in certain judicial matters. In one instance a prefect was sent as ambassador across the Channel. When the Kentish king heard of the coming of Theodore of Tarsus, 'he immediately sent to him Redfrid his reeve *(praefectum suum)* to bring him across.'[74] But this same official might also be employed as a military chief. We read of prefects holding important military strongholds at Dunbar and Bromnis.[75] In 710

---

[69]This law refers only to such as have been unfaithful to vows.
[70]C. 1:2.
[71]C. 1:3: Gif he mægas næbbe oððe þone mete næbbe, fede cyninges gerefa hine.
[72]That the prefect was intimately connected with the royal court appears from a passage in the *Chronicle* for 787. We read of a gerefa who rode down to the shore to meet the Norse pirates and, not knowing who they were, tried to drive them to the king's vill: "se gerefa þær to rad and hie wolde drifan to þæs cynges tun." He is not called the king's reeve, but the context would lead us to believe that he was such an official. Æthelweard calls him exactor regis. Kemble understands this to mean that he was a burggrave. *Sax. in Eng.*, II, 171. But Æthelweard, who wrote two centuries after the fact, probably used a term which came nearest describing the functions of the reeve in his own day. A prefect in the earlier sense of the word perhaps did not exist when he composed his Chronicle.
[73]*K. C. D.*, No. 189: Hanc praenominatam terram quidam homo bonus, nomine aldhun, qui in hac regali uilla inlustris civitatis praefectus fuit....tradidit.
[74]Bede, *H. E.*, IV, I.
[75]*Hist. York.*, I, 51, 52, 54. Eddi's Life of Wilfrid. It is not sure, however, that Eddi's use of the word prefect is in line with that of Bede or the charters. It seems more likely that he has a more purely military officer in mind. Still,

Berctfrith, a prefect, led an army against the Picts.[76] As Osred ruled in Northumbria at that time, Florence calls this general *Berhtfrith regis Osredi praefectus*.[77] Wulfheard, who is spoken of as a prefect in one of Egbert's charters,[78] is mentioned twice in the Chronicle as a military leader; in 823 he invaded Kent at the head of a large army; in 837 we find him opposing the Danes.

The prefect begins to appear among those who witnessed the royal grants soon after the beginning of the eighth century. Usually only one prefect signs; so generally is this true that a document bearing several such signatures looks suspicious. Twenty-seven charters dated before the accession of Egbert (824) are signed or seem to be signed by one prefect or more. Of these, nine must be rejected as forgeries or at least considered doubtful.[79] Nearly all of these nine are signed by more than one prefect.[80] Of the remaining eighteen, thirteen are witnessed by only one such official.[81] Of the other five one most probably is signed by presbyters and not by prefects.[82] Another appears to me to be spurious.[83] A third affords no means of determining whether it be genuine or not.[84] Cynewulf's grant of 778 is too

---

the strongholds are spoken of as "urbes regis." Dunbar is located on what was then the Scottish frontier not far from Edinburgh, and was doubtless an important frontier fortress. Bromnis has not been located. Bebbanburh has been suggested and also Brunanburh. Raine (*Hist. York*, I, 51, note) suggests Broomridge.

[76] Bede, *H. E.*, V, 24: Berctfrid praefectus cum Pictis pugnavit.
[77] I, 48.
[78] *K. C. D.*, No. 1031.
[79] They are all marked with an asterisk by Kemble.
[80] Three are signed by one prefect (*K. C. D.*, Nos. 93, 145, 985); five by more than one (Nos. 73, 102, 148, 174, 178); and one by two praepositi (No. 187).
[81] *K. C. D.*, Nos. 86, 89, 108, 114, 121, 122, 127, 137, 152, 168, 1006; Birch, *Cartul.*, Nos. 208, 1334.
[82] The abbreviations p., pr. may mean presbyter, princeps, or praefectus. As the document in question (*K. C. D.*, No. 156) is an agreement between a bishop and one who lays claim to episcopal lands and is issued at a synod, I conclude that the signatures referred to are presbyterial. Excepting the king, all the witnesses are churchmen.
[83] Birch, *Cartul.*, No. 1331. This charter, dated 739, has an extensive preamble and boundaries in Saxon, which are unusual circumstances in this early period. The Saxon is the idiom of the tenth century rather than of the eighth. The copy dates from the eleventh century. However, the editors of the *Crawford Collection of Charters* (Preface, VIII) pronounce it "apparently genuine."
[84] *K. C. D.*, No. 131. The original grant of Offa to Aldred seems genuine. But immediately after this follows Aldred's grant of the same lands to a church in Worcester. The only signatures are those of Aldred and three prefects. In the text they are called principes. Two of them witnessed a charter of the following year but no titles appear. The fact that the subregulus of the Huiccas has three prefects is itself a suspicious circumstance.

mutilated to permit a final decision.[85] Aside from the great variety of titles joined to the signatures in Beorhtric's charter, there is nothing unusual about it. It is signed by two prefects.[86] The charter was issued by the king of Wessex not later than 790. A generation after, when Egbert was ruling, there were many prefects in that kingdom. Some of the grants of the great overlord are signed by four or five.[87] But the expansion of Wessex seems to have been fatal to the importance of the reeve. After Egbert's time there is not a solitary charter of genuine appearance that is witnessed by such an officer, till we reach the eleventh century; and the prefects of the Confessor's day were wholly different officials.

It is, indeed, possible that the English kings had more than one reeve before the rise of Wessex, but the charter evidence for such a statement is extremely weak. Nor can we base anything on the use of the plural in the inhibitory clause,[88] for the plural of *rex* is used as well as that of *praefectus*.[89]

As to the tenure of the prefect's office, we know nothing definite. Of the individual reigns only those of Offa and Egbert give us any information on this point. In a Mercian charter of 775 or earlier, we find the signature of Eadbald *praefectus et princeps Offae regis*.[90] In 772 we meet an Emele *praefectus*.[91] Two years later Brorda signs as prefect.[92] In 779 the title is again affixed to Eadbald's name.[93] The next year Brorda is again *praefectus*.[94] There is a grant dated 784 to Esme *comiti praefectoque meo*.[95] A charter of 788 and another of 796 are both signed by the prefect Brorda.[96] We thus know of four men

---

[85] *K. C. D.*, No. 133.
[86] *Ibid.*, No. 158.
[87] See *K. C. D.*, Nos. 1031, 1033, 1035, 1036, 1037, 1039. The last is undated; the others are from the years 824, 825 and 826.
[88] Siquis uero regum aut principum uel praefectorum....conscriptam..frangere...temptauerit. A representative formula from before 840. *K. C. D.*, No. 242.
[89] Similarly, the nullus praefectorum of Bede's Epistola (*Opera* II, 219) needs not be interpreted as meaning several contemporaneous reeves; it may mean several successive ones.
[90] *K. C. D.*, No. 127. Before this he usually appears as dux.
[91] Birch, *Cartul.*, No. 208. This is a grant of Sussex lands and Emele may have been the royal representative in that region.
[92] *K. C. D.*, No. 122. No. 121 has Brorda princeps.
[93] *Ibid.*, 137.
[94] Birch, *Cartul.*, No. 1334.
[95] *K. C. D.*, No. 147.
[96] *Ibid.*, Nos. 152, 168.

who held the office during Offa's reign.[97] This evidence necessarily leads to one of two conclusions: Offa either had more than one reeve at the same time, or for some reason limited the term of office to a few years only. I am inclined toward the former view. The extension of Offa's authority over the neighboring small states may have called forth a plurality of reeves very much as among the Merovingian Franks there finally appeared several mayors of the palace, one for each of the leading divisions of the monarchy.[98] Furthermore, a period usually comes in the history of every court, when the same official dignity is given to several men. The charters issued by Egbert, the next great overlord, present a somewhat different aspect. Offa's grants were never witnessed by more than one prefect; Egbert's usually have the signatures of several such officials, five being apparently the normal number. The notable thing is that some of these prefects later appear as *duces*.[99] What the ducal office was during the early part of the ninth century has not yet been determined; but it seems likely that the holder was a military chief.[1]

The position of king's reeve was evidently not only an important but also a lucrative one. As early as Bede's time, we find the prefects amassing great fortunes.[2] They frequently received landed gifts, such as the transfer of twenty-two hides to Wulfheard in 824.[3] Still, as a rule, the estates granted to such officials of which we have any record were not large. From the early part of the ninth century we also have the will of Abba, a Kentish reeve, which shows him to have been a man of great

[97] Eadbald, uncertain date, 757-775, 779; Emele, 772; Brorda, 774, 780, 788, 796; Esme, 784.
[98] See Waitz, *D. V. G.*, II, 2, 88.
[99] In 824 Egbert gave Wulfheard, his prefect, twenty-two hides of land. *K. C. D.*, No. 1031. The next year Wulfheard is a dux. *Ibid.*, Nos. 1035-1038. Burhard, who was a prefect in 825 (*ibid.*, Nos. 1033, 1035) is a dux in 826. *Ibid.*, Nos. 1036-1038. The prefect Alhstan also became a dux that year. *Ibid.*, Nos. 1037, 1038.
[1] There seems to be no doubt that there had been a century earlier a military official called heretoga or dux.
[2] Bede, *Opera*, II, 219. Epistola ad Ecgberctum. The author here complains of the purchase of monasteries by the prefects. See also p. 218, where the general practice is described and denounced.
[3] *K. C. D.*, No. 1031.

wealth.[4] The prefect was, it seems, frequently, perhaps always, chosen from the aristocracy.[5]

To draw any satisfactory conclusions from the materials at hand seems almost impossible. As we cannot accurately determine the scope of the terms used, we are in constant danger of admitting as evidence facts that bear no relation to the subject before us. There seems, however, to have been a court-official in the eighth century whose functions, though primarily fiscal, might be and were extended as exigencies demanded. The original reeve probably had the royal estates in his charge in the same manner as the *gerefa* of later date. Most naturally, then, matters of fines, as part of his lord's income, would come under his superintendence. From this the step is but a short one to the actual assessment of fines. The same would apply to the collection of such dues and taxes as existed at the time. The growth of these at first rather unimportant functions may explain the change of this official from chief of the royal household to royal representative in the shire.

The Old English reeveship is no doubt analogous to the office of the Merovingian *major domus*,[6] though the prefect never attained the importance of that dignitary except in one known instance. About the year 705, the Northumbrian king Eadwulf was deposed and Osred, a boy *(puer regius)* of only eight years, was raised to the kingship.[7] In the first year of his reign, a synod was held at which a communication from the Pope was heard. After the reading of this letter 'all being silent, Bertfrith, the lord next to the king in authority,' asked the archbishop to interpret it.[8] At the close of the deliberations this same

---

[4] Thorpe, *Diplomatarium*, 469–74. *K. C. D.*, No. 235.

[5] Abba gerefa's wergeld was 2000 thryms (1200 scillings), the worth of a king's thegn. The prefect of Bromnis was a comes. *Hist. York*, I, 52. Eadbald, who witnessed a number of Offa's grants, was "praefectus et princeps offae regis." *K. C. D.*, No. 127. One Ingeld was "dux et praefectus Æðelbaldi regis Merciorum." Birch, *Cartul.*, No. 203. A Kentish charter has the "Signum manus Egbaldi comitis atque praefecti." *K. C. D.*, No. 114. Esme was Offa's comes and prefect." *Ibid.*, No. 147. See also Birch, *Cartul.*, No. 448.

[6] Such is also Stubbs' opinion. See *C. H.*, I, 372. But Stubbs is in error when he identifies the earlier prefect with the later heah-gerefa.

[7] *Hist. York*, I, 89. Bede, *H. E.*, V, 18.

[8] *Hist. York*, I, 90: Post lectionem, cunctis tacentibus, **Berthfrithus**, secundus a rege princeps, ad archiepiscopum dixit: "nos qui interpretatione indigemus, quid Apostolica auctoritas dicat audire delectat."

princeps declared the will of the king and his princes.[9] He is the only one whom the narrator represents as speaking among the secular lords. His position in the synod seems on the level with that of the archbishop. Still earlier he seems to have led Osred's forces in the revolt against the wicked Eadwulf. But this same Berthfridus is doubtless the Berctfrid whom Bede calls a *praefectus* and who led the Northumbrian forces against the Picts in 710.[10]

That there were several of these prefects in some of the kingdoms toward the close of the eighth century seems evident. Apparently the importance of the office decreased as the number of holders increased. In the next century, the prefect disappears from among the charter witnesses; his title also gradually disappears from the inhibitory formulas.[11] After the accession of Alfred reeves multiply. Some are clearly at the head of shires, or towns, or boroughs; others appear to have control of royal estates.[12] The relative positions of these different classes of reeves is not so easily determined; nor does the subject lie within our field at present.

One of these, however, we cannot pass by: the high-reeve. This officer is mentioned several times in the sources, but the nature of his office is very obscure.[13] The first mention of a high-

---

[9] *Hist. York*, I, 91: Haec ea loquente, Berechtfrithus, praefatus regis princeps, respondens dixit: "Haec est voluntas regis et principum ejus ut mandatis Apostolicae sedis...obediamus."

[10] Bede, *H. E.*, V, 24.

[11] When the prefect reappears in the tenth century charters, it is as shire-reeve.

[12] After a festival at Ramsey dux Æthelwin called a local council at which Saint Oswald was received by "cunctis praefectis et militibus miro affectu." *Hist. York*, I, 465. Life of St. Oswald; an almost contemporary biography. At Edgar's coronation were present "cuncti duces, praefecti et judices." *Ibid.*, I, 436. He is praised and honored by 'pious dukes, famous thegns (militibus) and wealthy prefects.' *Ibid.*, I, 438.

[13] Kemble doubts that the office of high-reeve ever existed. He thinks the title was probably equivalent to that of the shire-reeve (*Sax. in Eng.*, II, 157, note); he also suggests that the high-reeves may have been employed as missi dominici (p. 156). Stubbs holds that the offices of prefect and high-reeve were identical: "The first of these [major] answers to the praefectus or heah-gerefa of the Anglo-Saxons." *C. H.*, I, 372. Green looks on the high-reeve as a most important and exalted official. "A second stage in the progress of kingly rule was marked by the creation, under Æthelred, of the high-reeve, the first effort of the crown to create a minister of state, a deputy of its executive and judicial power beside the hereditary ealdormen, etc. Fiercely opposed, this institution became permanent under Cnut in the "vice-royalty" of Godwine; under the Confessor in that of Harold; and from it, under the Norman kings, sprang the justiciar." *Conqu. of Eng.*, 524.

reeve is in the Chronicle for the years 778 and 779. The office, therefore, must have existed at the time of the compilation of this work, or prior to 900. Not knowing the sources of the Chronicle for this period, we can know neither the name nor the nature of the office that the Wessex historian calls *heah-gerefa*. But as the occasion was that of a revolt followed by dynastic changes, we should infer that the high-reeves who were slain at that time were military officials.

Literally translated *heah-gerefa* is high-reeve or better archreeve. From the title we should infer that the high-reeve bore the same relation to the reeves as the archbishop to the bishops. This, however, cannot be shown. But they manifestly were reeves of higher rank. In the North-people's Law, the wergeld of a high-reeve is placed at half that of an ealdorman and double that of a thegn.[14] Nowhere else is there any indication that the reeve had a wergeld of his own; in the only instance known to me where his worth is mentioned, it is the same as that of the thegn.[15] It is significant that this officer is called the king's *heah-gerefa*, while the word *cyninges* does not appear before the titles of the ealdorman or the thegn or any of the other classes mentioned in the same connection.

In one of Eadred's charters we find the signature of *Osulf heahgerefa*.[16] Three years later we find a document signed by *Osulf bebb*,[17] and another witnessed by *Osulf ad bebb. hehgr.*[18] Perhaps the meaning is that Osulf was high-reeve at Bebbanburh, a fortress of great importance in Northumbria.[19] Half a century later the Chronicle records the death of a number of Æthelred's chief men among whom were 'Æthelweard, the king's high-reeve...and Leofric from Whitechurch and Leofwine the king's high-reeve.'[20] Later in the same year we find 'Kola the

---

[14] The date of this law cannot be definitely fixed, but it cannot be much later than 900, as it supposes the existence of the 'holds' a landed aristocracy of Norse origin, which, however, soon seems to have disappeared from England. See Schmid, *Gesetze*, Anhang VII, 2:4; Einleitung, LXV.
[15] See Abba Gerefa's will, *K. C. D.*, No. 235.
[16] *Ibid.*, No. 411 (A. D. 946).
[17] *Ibid.*, No. 426.
[18] *Ibid.*, No. 424.
[19] Simeon of Durham, *Historia Regum*, II, 45: Bebba vero civitas urbs est munitissima, non admodum magna, sed quasi duorum vel trium agrorum spatium, habens unum introitum cavatum et gradibus miro modo exaltatum.
[20] 1001: And ðær wearð Æðelweard heah-gefera (!) ofslegen and Leofric æt Hwitclricean and Leofwine cinges heahgerefa.

king's high-reeve and Eadsige the king's reeve opposing them [the Danes] with the [English] host.'[21] The juxtaposition of reeve and high-reeve clearly indicates a difference in their official dignities. The following year the ealdorman Leofsige slew Æfic, the king's high-reeve.[22] In a charter dated 1012, Æthelred speaks of Æfic as his prefect and *primas inter primates meos*.[23] Thus we have several titles referring to the same person, all indicating an exalted station. With the exception of Æfic of whom we can affirm nothing, the high-reeves of Æthelred's reign seem to have been military leaders.

In the Blickling Homilies from the same period, the title is used as we at present use the word ruler in an exalted though general sense.[24] The term is applied to Biblical officers concerning whose functions the homilist could have no adequate ideas. The same is true of Ælfric's use of the word. He very frequently calls the prefect of the city of Rome a high-reeve.[25] We should be greatly in error were we to imagine from this that this office was thought similar to that of an English port-reeve. The governor of the Eternal City, the center of Christendom and the capital of the world, could not be a ruler of ordinary dignity. The homilist also speaks of high-reeves who were sent out by the emperor to govern distant regions.[26] In Ælfric's glossary the term *heah-gerefa* stands for *legatus* and *proconsul*.[27]

[21] And þær wæs Kola ðæs cyninges heah-gerefa and Eadsige þæs cyincges gerefa togeanes him mid ðære fyrde....
[22] *A.-S. Chron.*, 1002. *Flor. Wig.*, I, 155–56:..nobilem virum Eafic, summum regis praepositum occidit.
[23] *K. C. D.*, No. 719: Nam praefectum meum Æficum quem primatem inter primates meos taxaui non cunctatus in propria domo eius eo inscio perimere...
[24] See pp. 171:17, 177:14.
[25] When Gregory protested to the emperor against his election to the papacy, Germanus, the emperor's high-reeve—"ðæs caseres heah-gerefa"—destroyed the letter. *Homilies* II, 122. Germanus seems to have been praefectus urbis. In the Passion of Saint Sebastian we are told of a high-reeve Chromatius 'who ruled the city of Rome under the emperor.' *Lives*, I, 126. Cf. *ibid.*, p. 118. Sempronius, the prefect of Rome, is called heah-gerefa throughout the homily on Saint Agnes. *Ibid.*, I, 170 ff. Nero's high-reeve Agrippa advised and urged the execution of Saints Peter and Paul. *Homilies*, I, 382. The high-reeve mentioned in the homily on Saint John was also a city official. *Ibid.*, I, 72–74. See also *ibid.*, pp. 416–36.
[26] Domitian sent one Sisinnius, a high-reeve, 'a very fierce devil with many companions to the Frankish kingdom.' *Lives*, II, 182, St. Denis. Commodus sent Philippus to govern Alexandria and made him high-reeve over all Egypt. *Ibid.*, I, 24–26. Other illustrations could be produced.
[27] *Vocab.*, 114:40; 183:29.

There can be no doubt that there was, during the period of Saxon ascendency, an office that might be called a high-reeveship. The incumbent was more than a common reeve as appears from his wergeld. He is the king's high-reeve and as such was perhaps the highest appointed officer in the realm.[28] As to his functions, two significant facts are brought out: in nearly every case do we find him exercising military authority or at least connected with movements that are distinctly warlike; the high-reeves of the homilies were officials appointed directly by the emperor and sent to govern important cities and large outlying regions. Together these facts point to a dignity somewhat like that of the Carolingian *markgraf*.[29] The only English region that might require the rule of such an official would be the North-country or Danelaw. It is by no means unreasonable to suppose that the rebellious Danes were allowed less local self-rule than their fellow-subjects south of the Thames. In this connection it is also interesting to note that nearly all the definite instances of an English high-reeveship are Northumbrian.[30] It should be added, that this officer does not appear until after the prefect has disappeared. It seems most likely, therefore, that the high-reeve's office is a relic of the prefect system of the eighth century, and that as such it continued in part the functions of the earlier king's reeve. The suggestions that it might correspond to that of a *missus*, a mayor of the palace, or a modern viceroy have no support in the sources.

---

[28] Unless we regard the ealdorman as an officer receiving his appointment from the king.

[29] Cf. Waitz, *D. V. G.*, III, 369 ff. For a somewhat similar view to the one advanced above, see Ramsay, *Found. of Eng.*, I, 355. The author, however, does not discuss the general subject.

[30] *A.-S. Chron.*, 778, 779; Schmid, *Gesetze*, Anhang VII, 2, 4; *K. C. D.*, Nos. 411, 424, 426. The high-reeves mentioned in the *Chronicle* for 1001 were with the royal army and cannot be located in any particular part of the kingdom.

CHAPTER V.

THE SECULAR DIGNITARIES OF THE ROYAL HOUSEHOLD.

The members of the royal court were, as we have already seen, usually called thegns. All these, however, were not of equal rank. What marked the distinction in earlier times we do not know; but the use of such terms as 'high-thegn' and 'ruling-thegn' clearly indicates that all the king's men were not equally high in royal favor.[31] In time certain offices arose within the household, the relative importance of which formed a basis for grouping the membership. At first these offices can not have ranked very high,[32] but they gradually grew in dignity and their holders became possessed of great power, though the development in this direction did not go so far among the Anglo-Saxons as among the Franks.

At the court everything centered about the king's own person. In him all power resided, though at times he might share it with certain members of his immediate family. Of these we should first of all think of the queen. Her position, however, is not very clear: in Beowulf we find her seated beside the king,[33] and at one time a queen actually ruled in Wessex;[34] but Asser tells us that not since the days of the great Offa had a queen sat enthroned beside an English king.[35] Ælfric states, in his homily on Queen Esther, that the king ordered his men to fetch Vashti—'that she should come to him wearing her royal helmet, as such was their custom, that the queen wore a royal helmet on her

---

[31] *Satan*, 66; *Menologium*, 130; *Beow.*, 1308; *Judith*, 242.
[32] It appears from the etymology of such words as seneschal, beershal and marshal that these offices were originally held by slaves.
[33] *Beow.*, 641.
[34] Sexburh. *A.-S. Chron.*, 672.
[35] Petrie's *Monumenta*, 471.

head.'[36]. The Anglo-Saxon word for crown or its equivalent is *cynehelm*, king's helmet. The passage is significant, as it necessitates the inference that the English queen, even as late as the year 1000, was not crowned. But there are indications that the Anglo-Saxon queens had somewhat extensive households of their own.[37]

The position of the royal princes is as indefinite as that of the queen. That the king sometimes associated the heir-apparent with himself in the government is a well-known fact,[38] but such can hardly be called the rule. The princes evidently had a body of servants of their own apart from the court in general. A suggestion of this is found in Beowulf: the bereaved father looks in sorrow on his son's deserted banquet-hall.[39] Two documents from Æthelred's reign mention the seneschals of the ethelings Edmund and Æthelstan.[40] After the Conquest we find that similar privileges were enjoyed by the king's daughters.[41]

Passing from the royal family to the inner circle of court officials, we at once meet the question, whether the Old English kings had what may be called a *major domus*. This has been answered in part in the preceding chapter on the king's reeve. The prefect, at least in his public capacities, strikingly resembles the Merovingian major. Bede calls Ercenwald, the Frankish major domus a patrician;[42] but we must not infer from this that all the patricians of the English sources were such mayors. William of Malmesbury cites a letter addressed by Alcuin to *Osberto patricio Merciorum;*[43] but most likely the title was purely an honorary one. An official that might be called a *major domus* in a limited sense as head of the queen's household is alluded to in Bede: the monk Owini came 'with the queen Æthelthryth from the kingdom of the East Angles; he was the chief of her thegns

---

[36] *Bibl. der ang. Prosa*, III, 93: swa swa heora seodu wæs, þæt seo cwen werode cynehelm on heafode.

[37] The translator of Bede's history (*H. E.*, II, 9) speaks of a queen's household — "þære cwene hirede." Æthelflæd, second queen of Edmund I, in her will gives seven hides to her reeve and two hides to each of her two priests. Birch, *Cartul.*, No. 1288. Among the witnesses to one of the Confessor's charters we find a queen's butler. See *K. C. D.*, No. 813.

[38] See Plummer, *Alfred*, 89–91.

[39] *Beow.*, 2455.

[40] *K. C. D.*, Nos. 722 and 1302.

[41] *Domesday*, I, 49: Goisfridus filiae regis camerarius.

[42] *H. E.*, III, 19.

[43] *Gesta Regum*, 73.

and the governor of her household.'[44] In one of the manuscripts of Alfred's translation, he is called *oferealdorman;* in another, 'ealdorman over all her house.' This leaves us somewhat in doubt as to whether the Anglo-Saxons looked on his position as a definite office; the probabilities are that they did not. A century later, we are told that Dunstan was counted among the palatine princes—*palatinos principes*—at Edmund's court;[45] but this can mean only that he was one of the king's favorites.[46] Among those whom Harthacnut sent to exhume the body of his brother Harold, Florence of Worcester names Stir *major domus*.[47] But in a charter from the previous reign we read that the abbot of Canterbury had bribed Steorra, the king's *rædesmann*, to pay him a third of the tolls at Sandwich.[48] Stir and Steorra are probably variant forms of the same name. The person in question had evidently once been one of the king's local officials. Whether he stood in any closer relation to the court later on cannot be determined.[49]

We shall have to conclude that, so far as we know, a *major domus* in the Frankish sense of the word never existed in England. The king's reeve might have developed into a mayor, but some great constitutional change (perhaps the rise of the shire system) seems to have arrested the growth of his power and brought on a rapid decline. At other times, certain great ecclesiastics[50] or secular lords[51] appear to have wielded the power of such an official, but the office itself did not exist. English conditions were fundamentally different from those in Frankland; the limited extent of the Anglo-Saxon kingdoms made it almost

---

[44] *H. E.*, IV, 3: ....eratque primus ministrorum et princeps domus ejus.
[45] *Memorials of St. Dunstan* (London, 1874), 21.
[46] Birch prints a document (*Cartul.*, No. 1057) alluding to a "princeps domus regis" at Edgar's court; but the charter is clearly a forgery. See *Eng. Hist. Rev.*, VI, 736; Stevenson, The Old English Charters to St. Denis, 17.
[47] *Flor. Wig.*, I, 194.
[48] *K. C. D.*, No. 758 (1038, Harold Harefoot). ...and begeat....æt Steorran þe þa wæs þæs kinges rædesmann....
[49] The Abingdon chronicler speaks of a "major regiae domus Edricus" who acted as such in the early part of Æthelred's reign. But as the writer flourished in the thirteenth century no importance can be attached to his statement. See *Historia Monasterii de Abingdon*, I, 357; *Anglia Sacra*, I, 166.
[50] Such as Wilfrid and Dunstan. For the position of the latter see *Memorials of St. Dunstan*, 95.
[51] *Hist. York*, I, 428: Dux autem Æthelstanus erat pater ejus, quem semiregem appellabant proceres omnesque populi, qui tantae potestatis extitit, ut regnum et imperium cum rege tenere sua ratione dicitur.

impossible for such an official to attain any high degree of prosperity. There does seem to have been at times a head of the royal household, a ruling thegn of some importance, but his functions must have been almost wholly palatine.[52]

Among the worthies of the royal court, the first one of real prominence that we meet in the sources is the sage of the king's hall, the þyle. We find him in Beowulf, where his name is given and such prominence accorded him, that all sorts of conjectures have been made as to his duties.[53] So far as is known, the 'thyle' appears in no other Anglo-Saxon source;[54] consequently, our information regarding him is very meager. In a Latin and Anglo-Saxon glossary, of the eleventh century, *oratores* is translated *þylæs*.[55] This probably has given rise to the idea that Unferth was Hrothgar's spokesman. But that king was abundantly able to speak for himself; in oratory he might rival Ulysses, and he even tried his hand at minstrelsy.[56]

Etymologically 'thyle' is the same as the Norse þulr, the earliest record of which is probably found in the runic inscription on the Snoldelev Rock, which, according to Wimmer, dates from the earlier years of the ninth century (800–825).[57] The Eddic references are somewhat later.[58] From these it will appear that the characteristics of Norse 'thulship' were age, wisdom, extended knowledge and a seat of honor.[59] As to age we can affirm nothing in Unferth's case; but there seem to be other 'orators' mentioned

---

[52] For a somewhat different view, see Schmid, *Gesetze*, 665.

[53] The definitions of thyle given in the glossaries to the various editions of Beowulf are very general and non-committal. Grein considers Unferth a "Redner." Heyne adds to this: "der Lehnsmann am Hofe, der die Unterhaltung zu führen hat." Morris and Wyatt think him "The spokesman of Hrothgar." Earle is more definite (*Deeds of Beowulf*, 126) : "Unferth was not exactly a minstrel, but a superior in the same general line; orator, historiologer, raconteur."

[54] Unless it be in *Widsith*, 24. Cf. *Modern Language Notes*, IV, 209–12.

[55] *Vocab.*, 458 :16.

[56] *Beow.*, 2109 10.

[57] *Die Runenschrift* (Berlin, 1887), 304, 337.

[58] *C. P. B.*, I, 24. Hávamál, 1 : Mál es at þylja þularstóli á. 'It is time to speak from the thular-stool.' *Ibid.*, I, 19 : at hárum þul hlæ þu aldregi. 'Never laugh at the hoary thul.' See also *ibid.*, I, 29, 39, 62.

[59] I translate the following from Jónsson's *Litteraturhistorie*, I, 79 : 'The word thulr originally meant a sage or orator. Aged men who had lived lives rich in experience, who had studied and learned all conditions of men, who were in possession of all the knowledge of the time as to the gods and their attitude toward the world and humanity, and who, when requested, sitting in the thular-seat, imparted their knowledge—such men were the thullr.' Cf. Müllenhoff, *Deutsche Altertumskunde*, V, 288 ff. Müllenhoff rather overstates the importance of these 'orators'.

in Beowulf, one of whom, at least, was full of information and old in years.[60] Again, in the hero's account of the festivities at Heorot, we are told that 'an old Scylding, who had heard many things, told tales from afar.'[61] That Unferth 'thyle' was also possessed of information from abroad appears from his circumstantial knowledge of Beowulf's swimming-match.[62] As to his wit and abilities we have Beowulf's own testimony: 'therefore in hell shalt thou suffer damnation though thy wit is capable.'[63] He also occupied a seat of honor: he sat at the king's feet[64] where later, we are told, sat the king's minstrel after the 'sage' had passed into history. In a poem 'Concerning the Fates of Men' we read: 'one of them shall sit with the harp at his lord's feet receiving gifts.'[65]

The 'thyle'-institution was specifically Teutonic; but at the opening of the historic period it seems everywhere on the wane. Two reasons may be assigned for this: as a counselor, as one who knew the will and attitude of the higher beings, he was being superseded by the Christian priest; as a narrator of heroic events he had a dangerous rival in the *scop* or minstrel. The 'thyle', as a rule, confined himself to the past; the *scop* glorified his own age.[66] He was a singer, a poet, which the 'thyle' was probably not. Ælfric uses the word *scop* in his grammar to translate such terms as *poeta* and *vates*.[67] In Alfred's Orosius it is used for

---

[60] When peace is made between the Danes and the Heathbards, and the truce is to be confirmed by royal nuptials, a Danish warrior brings the bride to the home of the Heathbard prince. But hanging at his side the Heathman see a sword taken by the enemy from their own nation. 'Then speaks at the banquet one who sees the jewel, an old ash-warrior who remembers it all, the spear-death of men.' *Beow.*, 2029–43.
[61] *Ibid.*, 2105–6.
[62] Soon after Beowulf arrived at Heorot, the jealous Unferth 'unbound the battle-rune' and a quarrel began. He taunted the hero with having lost in the swimming-match: the result was, however, that Beowulf got the best of the 'fliting'. *Ibid.*, 499 ff.
[63] *Ibid.*, 588–89.
[64] *Ibid.*, 499–500: Unferð maþelode, Ecglafes bearn. þe æt fotum sæt frean Scyldinga.
[65] *Bi Manna Wyrdum*, 80: sum sceal mid hearpan æt his hlafordes fotum sittan, feoh þicgan.
[66] Thus it was in the North at least, where the scald, singing the exploits of his lord, seems to have overshadowed the thul, who clung more closely to the sagas. See Jónsson, *Litteraturhistorie*, 81, 321 ff.
[67] Ælfric's *Grammar* (Zupitza), 24:6, 77:2–3, 24:2, 215:8–9. The word occurs in the glossaries of the tenth and eleventh centuries with similar definitions. See *Vocab.*, 188:28.

historicus,[68] and is also applied to Terence and to the singer Tyrtaeus of Spartan fame.[69] In Alfred's *Metra* it is applied to Vergil.[70]

It is not safe to affirm that all the *scops* lived at some princely court; still, most of our knowledge of these craftsmen relates to such as struck the harp in the royal hall. The minstrel is prominent in Beowulf. He sings a great variety of things: the creation of the world and the fall of man;[71] sagas from hoary Teutonic times;[72] Beowulf's journey and perhaps his exploits of the night before.[73] His instrument was the harp, the gleewood. Where his seat was we are not told; but in the poem cited above, and which is doubtless of a later date than Beowulf, the singer is represented as sitting at his lord's feet.[74]

We are accustomed to look on the bard as a wandering singer, traveling from manor to manor and from court to court. The *scop* must have been somewhat of this character; Widsith (if that be his name) was such a wandering minstrel. The poem that bears his name is little more than a list of tribes and kings that he had visited, which list some well-meaning interpolator has padded most generously. In return for the kindness of his queenly patroness Ealhhild, he sang her praises 'through many lands.'[75] He seems to have had a companion-poet on his journeys:

'Then we two, Scilling and I, with clear voices
Before our victorious lord lifted up the song.'[76]

But not all these singers were wanderers; some seem to have been permanently employed at some princely hall. Such a one was Deor, who lost his position and tried to console himself by comparing his own ill-fortune with that of others. For 'many winters' he had a good lord and good service; he had lands for his support. Then came Heorrend, 'a song-skilled man,' and took everything, lord, lands and honors.[77]

---
[68] Sweet's Edition, 32 :28.
[69] *Orosius*, 56 :29.
[70] *Metra*, 30 :4. *Bibl. der ang. Poesie*, III, 338.
[71] *Beow.*, 90 ff.
[72] *Ibid.*, 874 ff.; 1068 ff.
[73] *Ibid.*, 871–74.
[74] *Bi Manna Wyrdum*, 80.
[75] *Widsith*, 97–99.
[76] *Ibid.*, 103–04.
[77] *Deor's Lament*, 38–41.

From the evidence at hand we may conlcude that the *scop* was a singer of the old heroic lays[78] and a poet who told the notable events of his own day in verse. Though the bard and the 'thyle' differed essentially in both aims and themes, there is no reason why the same person might not sometimes act in either capacity: to draw the lines firmly between the two seems impossible. In the heroic period the minstrel was a personage of some consequence; but when the English people came into the full light of history, the sage and the singer were both on the decline, though the latter may have lingered somewhat longer than the former. Most likely the minstrel remained an interesting member of the princely household, but he is soon overshadowed by other dignitaries.[79]

A Mercian charter dated 811 has the signature of one Æthelheah *pedes sessor*.[80] This title at once suggests the 'thyle,' Unferth, who sat at the feet of the Danish king;[81] but the association is no doubt a fancied one. In a document of the following year Æthelheah appears as *pedisecus*.[82] Cuthred *pessesor* (!) witnessed a grant of the same year,[83] but in another charter of uncertain date he, too, is *pedisecus*.[84] The title occurs in three other Mercian documents dated 824,[85] 825[86] and 831[87] respectively. Eastmund *pedisecus,* who signed a Kentish charter in 856,[88] seems to have been the last of his class to witness a grant of which we

---

[78] Deor's repertoire is to some extent given in his 'Lament'.
[79] I find no reference to court poets in English sources later than 800. They are alluded to in the poems *Bi Manna Cræftum* and *Bi Manna Wyrdum* which some poems have ascribed to Cynewulf. His authorship is by no means certain, but the poems seem at least to fall within the Anglian period of Old English literature which can hardly extend much beyond the eighth century. For the various views on this subject see Wülker, *Grundriss*, 196–200.
The court minstrel reappeared in England with the Danish conquest. Some of the songs sung at Cnut's court have been preserved. See *O. P. B.*, II, 155 ff.
In the Welsh laws of Howell the Good, we find an elaborate company of entertainers provided for under the leadership of the *bardus familiae*. See *Ancient Laws of Wales*, 771.
[80] *K. C. D.*, No. 196.
[81] *Beow.*, 500. Cf. Kemble, *Sax. in Eng.*, II, 117.
[82] *K. C. D.*, No. 199: Sign[um] man[us] Aeðelheah ped[e]sec[i].
[83] Birch, *Cartul.*, No. 340: Signum manus Cuðredi pessessoris.
[84] *K. C. D.*, No. 1028: .... Cudred pedise[cus].
[85] Birch, *Cartul.*, No. 378: Ego Bola pedisecus.
[86] *K. C. D.*, No. 220: Ego bola pedisecus.
[87] *Ibid.*, No. 227: Ego aelfred pedisecus.
[88] *Ibid.*, No. 281: Ego eastmund pedesecus.

have any record.[89] Turning to the glossaries we find *pedisequus* and *sequipedas*, the one used as the equivalent of thegn, the other of *ministri*.[90] The masculine form of the word is, however, of rare occurrence except in the charters. More common is the feminine *pedissequa*, which an eighth century gloss renders 'thignen,'[91] maid-servant. This significance the word retained till the close of the Saxon period.[92]

It will be observed that the use of the title *pedisecus* is practically limited to Mercian documents of the first half of the ninth century. In this same period the title *minister* also begins to appear in the charters. But this title, so common in the next century, is not used by any one subscribing to a grant signed by a *pedisecus*. And I do not believe that the word *minister* occurs in any of the documents referred to except the last, which records a grant to a king's *minister*.[93] It is my opinion that *pedisecus* is a localism and simply a pedantic translation of thegn. That there ever was an official at court bearing such a title is extremely improbable.[94]

Of the four traditional chiefs of the Teutonic king's household, the seneschal, the marshal, the chamberlain and the butler, we hear but little before the tenth century.[95] The butler and the

---

[89] The title occurs in three tenth century charters, twice in the text and once in a group of titles following the episcopal signatures: (a) A grant by Eadred (946) to "Wulfric pedissequus". *K. C. D.*, No. 411. The language and style are very inflated. The word minister is nowhere used. (b) A grant to "pedissequus Uhtred Child". The style of this charter is unusual, as it seems to be "alliterative and poetic", but otherwise the document seems normal. Birch, *Cartul.*, No. 911. (c)....et ceteri duces disciferi, pedissequi et ministri. *Ibid.*, No. 1211. This may be the statement of some later copyist. Cf. No. 911.
[90] *Vocab.*, 507:32, 494:2.
[91] *Ibid.*, 38:15,
[92] *Ibid.*, 262:30, 294:23, 466:38, 467:1; *Flor. Wig.*, I, 207 (Queen Edith's maid); Liebermann, *Gesetze*, I, 172, Quadripartitus (in opposition to domina).
[93] *K. C. D.*, No. 281.
[94] Kemble considers the pedisequus a court official, but cannot determine his functions. *Sax. in Eng.*, II, 117. Von Maurer believes that pedissequi was the general term for the inferior servants at court. *Hofverfassung*, 196.
[95] On the subject of the higher palace officials writers on English history give us nothing beyond a few general statements. Says Kemble (*Sax. in Eng.*, II, 105–06): "The four great officers of the Court and Household in the oldest Germanic kingdoms are the Chamberlain, the Marshal, the Steward and the Butler". The error here lies in the use of the word "oldest". Stubbs (*C. H.*, I, 372–73) speaks of "the praefectus or heahgerefa", disc-thegn, cup-bearer and horse-thegn. But, as has already been shown, to equate the praefectus and the Frankish major domus, as Stubbs seems to do, is rather misleading. Freeman (*N. C.*, V, 287) agrees with Stubbs except in that he uses the term staller

chamberlain appear to be mentioned in Beowulf, but the poet says nothing of a marshal or a seneschal. In his will Alfred remembers his household thegns in the following words: 'And the men who serve me, to whom I recently at Eastertide gave wages *(feoh:* property), two hundred pounds let there be given to them; and let it be divided among them, to each one as would be due him after the manner in which I recently divided [wealth] among them.'[96] This implies that the royal servants were not of equal rank and dignity, but of the classification we are told nothing. But from about the middle of the tenth century, we have a most important document, the will of King Eadred, which gives us most valuable information on this point. The order of bequests is as follows: To the state; to the archbishop; to the bishops and ealdormen; to the seneschals, chamberlains and butlers; to the king's priests; to his stewards; to other servants (and kinsmen?).[97] The grouping of the palace officials together with the amount of each bequest shows conclusively that three, the seneschal, the butler and the chamberlain, were the high court-officials in Eadred's time.[98] There is no mention of a constable or a marshal.

Of these three dignitaries, the butler is the first to appear in the sources. The Anglo-Saxon word for cup-bearer is *byrel* or *byrele,* one who bears. Possibly this word also includes the seneschal idea, but that can hardly be the case with *beor-scealc,* which is also used. It seems that the cup-bearers of the earliest

---

for horse-thegn; the history of stallership will be given in a succeeding chapter. Ramsay considers the horse-thegn and the staller two different officials; he speaks of 'the Burthegn, the Discthegn, the Horsthegn and the Stallere or Constable'. *Found. of Eng.,* I, 525. Green has a different grouping: "The hordere, the staller, the dishthegn and the cupthegn". *Conqu. of Eng.,* 523. I propose to show in the course of this chapter and of chapter VII that the staller was not known in England in Alfred's day as has been claimed, that the hoarder was never a court official in Saxon England, that the Confessor's chamberlain also acted as treasurer, and that the marshal was not a very important functionary before the Norman Conquest.

[96] *K. C. D.,* No. 314 (880-885): ....and ðam mannum ðe me folgiað, ðe ic nu on eastertidum feoh sealde, twa hund punda agyfe man him; and dæle man him betweoh, ælcum swa him to gebyrian wille, æfter ðære wisan ðe ic him nu dælde....

[97] *Liber de Hyda* (London, 1866), 153-55; Birch, *Cartul.,* No. 912.

[98] The bishops and ealdormen are given 120 mancuses each; the three high court officials 80; the mass-priests 50; the stewards 30, etc.
....and ælcan gesettan discðegne and gesettan hræglðene, and gesettan biriele, hund eahtatig mancusa goldis. *Liber de Hyda,* 153-55; Birch, *Cartul.,* No. 912.

sources were women;[99] but when we come to the age of the Beowulf poem, we find that men were also employed in the service.[1] The Danish chieftain necessarily had several, perhaps many, butlers;[2] and in the later narrative sources the word cup-bearer, as a rule, also appears in the plural form. When Æthelflæd entertained King Æthelstan, the butlers filled cups and beakers of all sizes and bore to the feasters till the day was ended.[3] The royal thirst must have been intense, for it required a miracle to slake it. Folcard tells us of a banquet given by Archbishop John to King Osred and his nobles; the cup-bearers found the supply of mulse, wine and beer inexhaustible.[4] Ælfric in his homily on Esther also uses the plural form.[5]

It seems probable that over all these cup-bearers there was a chief butler. Perhaps Æschere held such a position at Hrothgar's court; for a common butler he has too many titles.[6] At Archbishop John's banquet referred to above, the king called the butler Brihtred to him and praised him for his excellent service.[7] In the supplement to Ælfric's vocabulary, *magister calicum* is translated *yldest byrla*.[8] Asser tells us that Alfred's mother was a 'daughter of Oslac, Æthelwulf's famous butler.'[9] It seems reasonable to assume that the cup-bearers whose signatures ap-

---

[99] In the Laws of *Æthelbirht* (14, 16) fines are decreed for violating the honor of an eorl's or churl's bierele. Nothing is said about the maid who bore the king's cup, though a parallel law relates to a similar crime against the king's maid (10). It is more than likely, however, that some of those who served in the king's hall were women. It seems that the feminine head of the household had some important duties in this connection. Hrothgar's queen passes the cup to the doughty ones in Heorot. *Beow.*, 615, 1169, 2016 ff. The queen of the Geats performed a similar service in Hygelac's hall (1981–82). Hrothgar's daughter also bore the ale-stoop (2020–21). The wife of a comes who was miraculously healed by John of Beverly (A. D. 686) immediately arose and offered the cup to the bishop and his men. Bede, *H. E.*, V. 4. The same custom prevailed in the North. See *O. P. B.*, I, 50, 333.

[1] *Beow.*, 495: þegn(....se þe....scencte scir wered.
[2] *Ibid.*, 1161: Byrelas sealdon win of wunder-fatum.
[3] *Memorials of St. Dunstan*, 18: ....pincernis, ut assolet in regalibus conviviis, cornibus, sciphis, aliisque indiscretae quantitatis vasibus totum diem propinantibus.
[4] *Hist. York*, I, 254–5. But Folcard wrote after the Conquest.
[5] *Bibl. der ang. Prosa*, III, 93.
[6] He is called beorscealc, æðeling, aldor-þegn, runwita, rædbora, the king's eaxl-gestella, and is said to be of gesiðes had.
[7] *Hist. York*, I, 255.
[8] *Vocab.*, 189:29. Cf. Book of *Genesis*, 40:9.
[9] Petrie's *Monumenta*, 469.

pear in charters were chief butlers.[10] In Eadred's will, however, no distinction is made between chief and subordinate. Eighty mancuses are given 'to each legally appointed butler,'[11] thus implying equality as well as plurality.

The functions of butlership were such as we should naturally associate with the office. The cup-bearers performed their duties at the banquets in the royal hall. The first cup was offered to the king. Ælfric tells us in his life of Saint Martin that at Maximus' banquet they bore to Caesar,

'As it customary was, wine on a dish;
But he ordered the butler to offer it first to Martin.'[12]

The principal beverages served were mead and beer, though ale, wine and mulse were also counted necessary to successful feasting.[13] We should infer that the chief butler was also charged with the duty of keeping the king's cellar well supplied with tuns and casks.[14] We do not know that he had any other duties. The butler's office was no doubt an honorable one;[15] but it never

---

[10] *K. C. D.*, No. 86. A Kentish charter dated 740 and signed by the butler Dunwalh. Kemble believes it genuine but admits that the year and the indiction disagree. I should say that the use of the title pincerna at such an early date is a very suspicious circumstance. *Ibid.*, Nos. 148, 265, 320; rejected as forgeries by Kemble. Birch, *Cartul.*, No. 328. Given by Ceonulf of Mercia and Kent, 809. This is the only charter dated before 958 and bearing a butler's signature that can seriously claim to be genuine. *K. C. D.*, No. 1214 (958). Signed by "Ælfwig regis pincerna". Eadwig gives two cassaturas to Keneric his propincernarius. What this title signifies is not clear. Du Cange does not have the word. *Ibid.*, No. 1224 (959). Signed by Æthelsige pincerna. *Ibid.*, No. 1294. Æthelred (1000) gives lands to Abingdon monastery "sicut Wulfgarus meus uidelicet pincerna obtinuit". *Cf. ibid.*, No. 1280. *Ibid.*, No. 813. Edward, 1062: "Ego Wigodus regis pincerna. Ego Herdingus reginae pincerna". This is perhaps the only queen's butler in Anglo-Saxon times of whom we have any record.

[11] Birch, *Cartul.*, No. 912.

[12] Ælfric's *Lives*, II, 258. It would seem that the use of the word byrel in this passage and in Eadred's will proves definitely that it was the Anglo-Saxon equivalent of the Latin pincerna. Kemble suggests that it may have been, adding, however, "but I am not aware of its occurrence". *Sax. in Eng.*, II, 111.

[13] See *Vocab.*, 128, for a list of Anglo-Saxon drinks.

[14] The importance of having a supply of beverages on hand is well expressed in *Beowulf* (769) where the terror of the Danes when they awoke to find the hero grappling with the monster is likened to the 'terror of ale-dearth' (ealuscerwen).

[15] *Hist. York*, I, 449 (assassination of Edward): Circumstabant eum undique armati viri, cum quibus et pincerna humili officio astabat ministrando. This would indicate that not all cup-bearers enjoyed a high rank; at the same time we must not infer that the position of all was a humble one. The king was on a journey and this particular pincerna may not have been a regular butler.

attained the dignity among the Anglo-Saxons that it enjoyed across the Channel.

Grouped with the butler and the seneschal in Eadred's will, we find the *hrægel-weard,* or keeper of the wardrobe.[16] This term is an unusual one for a high official, and, furthermore, we should expect some title that would suggest the chamberlain. Still, it seems that the keeper of the royal chambers also had charge of the wardrobe.[17] The usual Old English word for chamberlain is 'bur-thegn,' though 'bed-thegn' is also used.[18] In his homily on Esther Ælfric calls Ahasuerus' seven chamberlains his seven 'bur-thegns;[19] but the two who conspired against the king's life are merely *bur-cnihtas.*[20] Ælfric evidently considered them of a lower order of servants. 'Bur-thegn' is again used in the homily on Judith.[21] The servants performing the corresponding duties in the poem Judith are *ambyhtscealcas.*[22] In the Latin sources the terms used are *camerarius* and *cubicularius.* There can be no doubt that all these terms—'bur-thegn,' 'bed-thegn,' 'rail-thegn,' *camerarius, cubicularius, custos cubile*—refer to the same official, the keeper of the king's chamber.[23] It is possible that the *camerarius* was subordinate to the *cubicularius,*[24] but I am in-

[16] In *Beowulf* there is a mention of a hall-thegn (sele-þegn, 1794) who seems to have looked after the nightly comforts of the guests; but we are not told whether his duties also extended to the king's bed-chamber. In an anonymous document addressed to Edward the Elder, there is an allusion to a 'rail-thegn'. *K. C. D.,* No. 328: ælfric wæs ða hrælðen. As he had been appointed by Alfred to assist in settling a dispute regarding certain lands, he may have belonged to his court. The Benedictine Rule provides for a hrægelhus, where the robes are kept in charge of a 'rail-thegn'. *Bibl. der ang. Prosa,* II, 55. A gloss from the tenth or eleventh century translates vestiarius with hrægl-weard, *Vocab.,* 279:19.

[17] Thus it was among the Merovingian Franks. See Waltz, *D. V. G.,* II, 2, 72-73.

[18] That the bur-thegn had charge of the royal chamber appears from the use of the word bur. Though not always limited to chamber, this term usually contains the idea of privacy. Wealhtneow's apartments to which Hrothgar retired for the night, were 'bowers'. *Beow.,* 921. The tun where Cynewulf visited his mistress also had a bower. *A.-S. Chron.,* 755. If the chamberlain were in charge of the entire hall, he might be called a 'sele-thegn' or a 'heal-thegn'. Such a one seems to be mentioned in one of the charters: Heal-ðegen Scearpa. *K. C. D.,* No. 742. But it is more than likely that the term in this case has become a proper name.

[19] *Bibl. der ang. Prosa,* III, 93. Be Hester, 33-36.

[20] *Ibid.,* ll. 212-14, 278.

[21] *Ibid.,* III, 111, 113.

[22] *Judith,* 37-38.

[23] *Vocab.,* 198:6, camerarius, burþen; 216:21, Cubicularius, custos cubili, bed-þegn; 124:17, 18, Cubicularius, burþen, Camerarius, bed-þen These definitions are all from the tenth century.

[24] Cf. Brunner, *D. R. G.,* II, 101: Der merowingische Kämmerer heisst thesaurarius oder cubicularius..... Er hat Unterbeamten camerarii genannt. Im

clined to consider the titles absolutely identical. It is true, however, that the latter is the term most commonly met with.[25] In 963 Edgar gave lands 'to his very faithful *camerarius* called by the noble name Winstan.'[26] In 972 there is another transfer of lands to Winstan now *cubicularius*.[27] If there had been any advance in his case, the office of *cubicularius* must have been the superior one.

It appears that there were several chamberlains serving the Anglo-Saxon king at the same time. Edgar's grants are to three different persons: Æthelsie, Titstan and Winstan.[28] Eadred's will also implies plurality: 'and to each legally appointed railthegn eighty mancuses of gold.'[29] According to William of Malmesbury, Edmund Ironside was slain by two of his *cubicularii*.[30] Three chamberlains are mentioned in Domesday as belonging to the Confessor's court: Aluric,[31] Hugo,[32] and Wenesi.[33] But what the usual number was, we do not know; nor can we affirm that there was a chief chamberlain before the reign of Edward the Confessor, during which period Hugelinus (Hugo) apparently held such a position, as will be shown presently.

The functions of the Anglo-Saxon bower-thegn were doubtless analogous to those of the Continental *camerarius*. He had charge of the king's private apartments including his bed and his wardrobe; he stood close to the royal person: audience had to be sought through him.[34] And, in addition to guarding the king's

---

karolingischen Sprachgebrauch ist umgekehrt der camerarius der oberste Schatzbeamte, während cubicularii, saccelarii und dispensatores seine Unterbeamten sind.

[25] I find no reference to a camerarius in any apparently genuine document later than 963. In Domesday, however, camerarius is the title commonly used. Three of the Confessor's camerarii are mentioned in the survey. One of them is Hugo, evidently the Hugelinus of one of Edward's charters, in which he is spoken of as cubicularius and bur-thegn. K. C. D., No. 904.

[26] Ibid., No. 503.

[27] Ibid., No. 572.

[28] Ibid., Nos. 489, 503, 572, 1247. The grant to Titstan is dated 962; Winstan and Æthelsie received lands in 963; Winstan received an additional grant in 972.

[29] Birch, Cartul., No. 912.

[30] Gesta Regum, 217.

[31] Domesday, I, 151: Hoc manerium tenuit Aluric camerarius R. E.

[32] Ibid., 208: ....et ipsi vendiderunt Hugoni camerario Regis Edwardi.

[33] Ibid., 151: Hoc manerium tenuit Wenesi camerarius R. E.

[34] William of Malmesbury. Gesta Regum, 274: [A blind man is healed by King Edward.] Postremo, ad regis curiam veniens, vestibulum camerae, adversantibus cubiculariis, frustra diu trivit; sed perstitit.... But the historian's narrative may have been colored somewhat by the customs of his own time.

camera, he seems to have had the keeping of his master's treasures.[35]

Our earliest sources represent the king as possessing much hoarded wealth. The nature of this early hoard is revealed in the allusions to gifts that were given. These included everything necessary for military equipment or masculine adornment, especially swords, rings and horses.[36] But there were also articles of a more strictly commercial value used in payment, such as small rings and fragments of rings;[37] hence the common appellations ring-giver *(beah-gyfa)* and ring-distributor *(beaga-brytta)* that we find applied to the king in Old English verse.[38] But while the existence of a treasure can be shown to be an ancient fact, it is not so easy to find a treasurer. The old poets describe the king as acting in this capacity: he was the hoard-guardian. Nor can we always point to a localized treasury. King Eadred deposited his 'land charters and even old treasures from preceding kings' in various monasteries, especially in the one with which Dunstan was connected.[39] But it seems that at least as early as

---

[35] On this point writers on English history are not wholly in agreement as the following citations show:

Lappenberg, *Hist. of Eng.*, II, 380: The chamberlain....was also the royal treasurer. The garments of the king were under the care of a keeper (hrægl-thegn).

Kemble, *Sax. in Eng.*, II, 106: The names by which the chamberlain was designated are Hrægelþegn....Cubicularius, Camerarius, Búrþgen, perhaps sometimes Dispensator, and Thesaurarius or Hordere.

Green, *Conqu. of Eng.*, 523: In the time of Ælfred, the great officers of the court were....the hordere, the staller, the dishthegn and the cupthegn.

Freeman, *N. C.*, V, 291: The King's "Hoarder" was as old as the King's "hoard".... The Old English Kings had their *hoard*, and the hoard under its Hoarder must always have been a special department of administration.

Ramsay, *Found. of Eng.*, I, 524: But the Anglo-Saxon kings had a Treasurer, the *Hordere* or Keeper of the king's Hoard, who received the moneys due to him from the sheriffs and other reeves....

Lappenberg and Kemble hold with varying degrees of confidence that the chamberlain had charge of the treasury. Green follows Kemble. Freeman and Ramsay appear to consider the treasury a distinct department.

[36] *Beow.*, 1046–48: Swa manlice, mære þeoden,
　　　　　　hordweard hæleþa, heaþo-ræsas geald
　　　　　　mearum ond madmum.

[37] Müller, *Vor Oldtid*, 539–40: [Describing archeological discoveries in Schleswig from the period of the migrations.] 'Among other things brought to light were nineteen bars and fragments of large rings and five small rings, all of gold and evidently intended for use as currency'. (Author's translation.)

[38] It is interesting to note that the Old Norse baugr, A.-S. beag, a ring, is used in the earliest Norwegian laws as a unit in computing fines, wergelds, etc. See *Norges gamle Love*, V, 92. Cf. *Laws of Æthelbirht*, 6.

[39] *Memorials of St. Dunstan*, 29: ....quamplures scilicet rurales cartulas,

the reign of Cnut, the royal hoard had been definitely located at Winchester. One of Harold Harefoot's first acts was to seize the royal valuables there in the queen's possession in that city.[40] The treasury remained at Winchester till the Conquest and was continued there by the Conqueror.[41]

The old word hoard seems to have persisted as a designation of a large accumulation of valuables,[42] though toward the close of the Old English period we also find the word *haligdom* used.[43] It would seem natural that the person in charge of all this would be called a *hordere,* and certain writers on Anglo-Saxon subjects tell us that such was the case.[44] I have, however, yet to find the first bit of contemporaneous evidence for such a statement. The Laws of Æthelstan contain two significant passages relative to the hoarder: 'Concerning barter. And let no man dispose of cattle by barter except in the presence of the reeve, or the mass-priest, or the landlord, or the hoarder, or some other reliable man.'[45] And again concerning theft: 'Likewise, if it be that any one of the king's hoarders or of our reeves was in collusion with the thieves who had done the stealing, be it the same to him.'[46] The hoarders

---

etiam veteres praecedentium regum thesauros, necnon et diversas propriae adeptionis suae gazas sub munimine monasterii sui fideliter custodiendum.

Ramsay (*Found. of Eng.*, I, 304) infers from this that Dunstan was the king's treasurer. "He made Dunstan act as his treasurer, placing all his valuables, including the title-deeds of his private estates (rurales cartulas) under his charge at Glastonbury". But this is clearly incorrect as we are expressly told that Dunstan was only one of many with whom such documents were deposited. On page 31 of the *Memorials* we read: ....misit circumquaque ad congregandas facultates suas....per hoc enim vir Dei Dunstanus, velut alii regalium gazarum custodes ibat; ut quas causa custodiendi secum habuerat regi reportaret.

[40] *Flor. Wig.*, I, 190: Is [Harold]....misit Wintoniam suos constipatores celerrime, et gazarum opumque, quas rex Canutus Alfgivae reliquerat reginae, majorem melioremque partem ademit illi tyrannice.....

[41] *Domesday*, III, 65: ....qui debebant geldum portare ad thesaurum regis Wintoniae....

[42] A translation of II *Kings.* 20;13, reads as follows: 'Then he took the envoys from abroad into his treasure-house and showed them his gold-hoard'—"geiewde his goldhord". See Cook, *Biblical Quotations*, 13:2.

[43] Haligdom may, perhaps, mean the place where the treasures were kept; but the context usually indicates that the valuables themselves are meant.

[44] See Green, Freeman, and Ramsay, cited above.

[45] *Laws of Æthelstan*, II, 10: Be hwearfe. And nan man ne hwyrfe nanes yrfes butan þæs gerefan gewitnesse, oððe þæs mæssepreostes, oððe þæs landhlafordes, oððe þæs horderes, oððe oðres ungelygenes mannes. Liebermann (*Gesetze*, I, 156) translates *hordere* with Schatzmeister. This is misleading, if not absolutely incorrect.

[46] *Ibid.*, II, 3, 1: ....eac swilce cynges hordera oððe ure gerefena, swylc þæra þeofa gewita wære, þe staledon, beo he be þam ilcan. Liebermann's translation, Königskämmerer, is clearly incorrect.

alluded to in these laws were manifestly local officials merely. They are grouped with local functionaries, and, furthermore, it would be unreasonable to suppose that the higher dignitaries of the court could be expected to witness petty commercial transactions all over the country.

We get a clue to the real meaning of hoarder in the monastic literature of the time. In a tenth century vocabulary, *hordere* is given as the equivalent of *cellerarius* or keeper of provisions.[47] Ælfric uses the word similarly in his homilies: Saint Benedict, he tells us, ordered his hoarder to give a needy subdeacon a glass of oil,[48] "because they eat oil in that country with their food as we do butter."[49] The monastic hoarder is mentioned in the Chronicle along with the churchwarden and the rail-thegn.[50] The word can have but one translation: steward. The hoarder of the first law quoted was probably the landlord's steward, who might represent his master when cattle were to be exchanged. The official of the second law clearly had charge of a royal estate, as the context shows that he was in charge of serfs;[51] he is also spoken of as 'our' hoarder. We are safe in concluding that there never was at any time in English history prior to 1066 a court-official whose duties were primarily fiscal and whose functions gave him a name. The *thesaurarius* came with the Normans.[52]

As has already been suggested, however, it seems that Edward's chamberlain acted as his treasurer.[53] With the establishment of a fixed treasury came a new formula into the English chancery. Thus in one of Cnut's charters: 'And of these writings there are three, one at Christ Church, another at Saint Augustine's and the third in the king's treasury (or sanctuary).'[54] Similar terms are used in two other documents: *in thesaurum regis;*[55] *mid þise*

---
[47] *Vocab.*, 330 :18.
[48] *Homilies*, II, 178.
[49] Thorpe's translation.
[50] *A.-S. Chron.*, 1131: circeweard and hordere and reilþein.
[51] The guilty one shall lose his serfs. Schmid (*Gesetze*, 613) believes that this particular law refers to a "Schatzmeister, welcher aber, gleich dem Gerefa, als Verwalter der königlichen Güter erscheint....".
[52] See *Domesday*, I, 49: Terra Henrici Thesaurarii.
[53] The evidence that follows has, I believe, been neglected by writers on English history. They have, it appears, based their conclusions mainly on the etymology of the word hordere and on Frankish analogies. See Kemble, *Sax. in Eng.*, II, 106. For the Continental practice see Waitz, *D. V. G.*, II, 2, 73; III, 502; Brunner, *D. R. G.*, II, 101; von Maurer, *Hofverfassung*, 192.
[54] *K. C. D.*, No. 1327: And ðissera gewrita synd þreo,.... and ðe þridde is inne mid ðæs kynges halidome.

kinges halidome.[56] There is therefore nothing strange in the statement made by the historian of Ramsey that the charters of that monastery which were received during the Confessor's reign were deposited in the royal treasury *(gazophylacium)* and kept by Hugelinus the chamberlain.[57] Four facts speak in favor of the correctness of this information: it was the practice in the first half of the eleventh century to deposit documents in the royal treasury;[58] in the reign of Henry II[59] such valuables would probably go to the royal exchequer and not to the king's camera, so that the chronicler could not have been influenced by the custom of his own time; we gather from an Old English vocabulary that the bower-thegn was the keeper of documents;[60] the name of the chamberlain is correct.[61] While more evidence might be desired, whatever there is points toward the conclusion that, at least during the closing years of the Saxon monarchy, the chamberlain guarded the royal hoard.[62]

The third great court-official was the seneschal or *disc-þegn* as he is called in Anglo-Saxon.[63] So far as I know, there is no

---

[55] *K. C. D.*, No. 932: Haec scripta tripliciter consignantur,....aliud in thesaurum regis,....

[56] *Ibid.*, No. 931: Nu sinden ðise write þre, on is mid ðise kinges haligdome ....

[57] *Chronicon Ramesiensis*, 170-71: ....decrevit rex omnia, ordine quo gesta sunt vel relata, literis Anglicis ad monimentum futurorum declarari, ejusdemque ccripti medietatem in gazophilacio, ubi quaecunque habebat praecipua et pretiosa erant reposita, ab Hugelino cubiculario suo diligenter conservari.

[58] See charters cited above.

[59] The chronicle was probably composed in that reign. See *Chronicon Ramesiensis*, Preface, XXII.

[60] *Vocab.*, 19:19: Cancellarius uel scriniarius, burþen. The scriniarius was the official of the scrinium, the depository of the king's valuable documents. See *Du Cange*.

[61] *K. C. D.*, No. 904: Hugelino cubiculario.

[62] Green classifies the duties of the chamberlain as follows: "Of all the officers of the court, he was far the most important, (1) as head of the whole royal service; (2) as exercising control over the royal palace or household, wherever it might be, and charged with care "de honestate palatii seu specialiter ornamento regali": (3) as receiver of royal dues for the crown lands, and head of the royal gerefan....; (4) as dispensator of the crown; and (5) through this and in his charge "de donis annuis militum" as head of the household troops; and (6) of the budding diplomatic service." *Conqu. of Eng.*, 523-24. It is hardly necessary to say that for all this there is no authority in the English sources. It is merely an effort to apply Hincmar's system to the Saxon court.

[63] The word stiweard seems also to have been used with much the same meaning. *Vocab.*, 223:7: Discoforus, discifer uel stiweard. But most probably this term was applied to the seneschals of lesser lords only. The king's steward in the tenth century, as Eadred's will shows us, was an official wholly different from the dish-thegn and of much less importance. In the Latin sources the

mention of such a functionary before the accession of Æthelstan.[64] A charter from the beginning of his reign (926) is witnessed by Wulfhelm *discifer regis*.[65] We next hear of the seneschal in connection with the death of King Edmund (946) : Florence of Worcester reports that he fell while trying to shield his *dapifer* who had gotten into serious difficulties in trying to remove an uninvited guest from the banquet.[66] We find that Eadred in his will (before 955) bequeathes 'to each legally appointed dish-thegn' the same amount of gold as to each butler or chamberlain.[67] Four *disciferi* witnessed charters in the reign of Eadwig (955–59) : Ælfheah,[68] two by the name of Ælfsige,[68] and Ealdred.[69] The last named signs a document dated 958. The next year Wulfgar *discifer* signs a charter given by King Edgar.[70] This is the last mention of a king's seneschal before the time of the Confessor.[71]

The master of the royal tables, like his colleague of the cellar, does not seem to have been a specially important personage at Edward's court. At any rate we hear little of him. The statement in the Book of the Hyde, that Edward made Harold his seneschal,[72] must be discredited, as it has no support in contem-

---

seneschal is called discifer, discoforus and sometimes dapifer. *Vocab.*, 126:38 : Discifer uel discoforus, discþen. (Ælfric, ca. 1000.)

[64] We should expect to find such an official in Bede's account of King Oswald and his dining with Aidan the bishop; but we are told only that the viands were served on a silver dish. *H. E.*, III, 6. In *Exodus* (131) there is an allusion to a 'meat-thegn' but he was not a royal official. The title occurs in a forged charter attributed to Offa (785). *K. C. D.*, No. 149; cf. Kemble, *Sax. in Eng.*, II, 109, where this document is apparently accepted as genuine.

[65] *K. C. D.*, No. 1099. A document from the same year has the following peculiar close: "Ego Cyneferð episcopus subscripsi, et ceteri Duces, ministri, disciferi, testes". Birch, *Cartul.*, No. 658. This looks like the work of a forger, who has been unable to secure a list of dignitaries that he dared make use of.

[66] *Flor. Wig.*, I, 134. No earlier source mentions a seneschal in this connection. William of Malmesbury calls the official in question a dux. The fact that he was the one who challenged the guest does, however, give some support to the opinion that he was the master of the feast. Ramsay accepts Florence's statement without question. *Found. of Eng.*, I, 297.

[67] Birch, *Cartul.*, No. 912.

[68] *K. C. D.*, Nos. 1191, 1196, 1197. The last two are copies of the same document. Ælfsige was a common name at that time.

[69] *Ibid.*, No. 1214.

[70] *Ibid.*, No. 1224.

[71] Florence alludes to a dispensator in Harthacnut's reign (I, 194), but while dispensator and dishthegn may have meant the same to him, they did not to the Anglo-Saxons generally. To Ælfric dispensator meant reeve. See *Genesis*, 43:16, 23 ; 43:19; 44:1. Cf. *Pastoral Care*, 63 (brytnere). Kemble and Green identify the dispensator with the chamberlain. *Sax. in Eng.*, II, 106; *Conqu. of Eng.*, 523.

[72] *Liber de Hyda*, 288, 290.

porary sources. Such an office might have been commensurate with such an ambition as Harold's at the time when the statement was written, but not at the time indicated. The charters give us little help. A document dated 1060 has the *signum Raulfi regis dapiferi* and the *signum Asgæri regis dapiferi*.[73] But as we shall find that Edward had two stallers bearing such names, I am inclined to consider this the work of a forger or of a later copyist who did not know what staller meant.[74] A charter of two years later has the signatures of *Adzurus regis dapifer* and *Yfingus regis dapifer*.[75] It is possible that we again have the names of stallers, that Adzurus is Asgarus and Yfing, [L]ifing. It will not do to assume, however, that staller and *dapifer* are equivalent terms: historically the two offices are wholly distinct, and they also seem to differ in functions and in relative importance.[76] It is in Domesday that we find the most reliable references to Edward's stewards, and these are by no means satisfactory. Ednod *dapifer* held five manors in Edward's day,[77] and of nine hides belonging to that king in Huntingdon Alanus his *dapifer* held two.[78]

In addition to the seneschals who served the king directly, there were other officials with similar duties serving the various members of the royal family. Among those present at Wynflæd's suit (in Æthelred's reign) was 'Æfic the dish-thegn of the ethelings.'[79] Some time in the same reign Æthelstan Etheling willed eight hides to 'Ælmere his seneschal.'[80] About the year 1006 the etheling Edmund purchased certain lands, his dish-thegn Leofwine witnessing the transfer.[81]

On the duties of the dish-thegn the sources are not very explicit. "His especial business was to superintend all that apper-

---

[73] *K. C. D.*, No. 808.
[74] The difficulties that the Normans experienced in their efforts to comprehend Saxon terms is well illustrated in a passage from Michel's *Chroniques Anglo-Normandes*, 234 (quoted by Ellis in introduction to *Domesday*, XXIX, note) : Esegarius regie procurator aule, qui Anglice dicitur stallere, i. e., regni vexillifer.
[75] *K. C. D.*, No. 813.
[76] See Chapter VII for a discussion of the stallership.
[77] I, 69 : Haec V maneria tenuit Ednod dapifer T. R. E. He seems also to have been staller. See *Eng. Hist. Rev.*, XIX, 92.
[78] I, 206b : De eadem terra habuit Alanus dapifer ejus II hidas.
[79] *K. C. D.*, No. 693: æfic þara æþelinga discten...
[80] *Ibid.*, No. 722 : ...Ælmere minen discðene...
[81] *Ibid.*, No. 1302 : ....Lofwine æðelinges discðen...

tained to the service of the royal table, under which we must probably include the arrangements for the general support of the household, both at the ordinary and temporary residences of the king."[82] With this general statement the subject will have to be dismissed.[83]

· Of the fourth great official of the Germanic courts, the master of the horse, I shall have something to say in a subsequent chapter. We have no reason to think that he was an important official at the English court before the Danish dynasty. In the tenth century, the glorious period of Anglo-Saxon kingship, the inner circle of the royal household service counted but three dignitaries: the butler, the chamberlain and the seneschal.[84]

---

[82] Kemble, *Sax. in Eng.*, II, 109.

[83] On this matter Continental analogies throw but little light. See Waitz, *D. V. G.*, III, 499; VI, 329; Brunner, *D. R. G.*, II, 101.

[84] Since the above was written J. H. Round has published a paper on "The Household of Edward the Confessor" in *Eng. Hist. Rev.*, XIX, 90-92. In this he appears to include the marshal, the constable and the treasurer among the high officials of that king. I have elsewhere in this chapter given my reasons for identifying the treasurer with the chamberlain; the Henricus Thesaurarius that Round refers to evidently held the office of treasurer at the time when the survey was made (see *Domesday*, I, 49); but there is no evidence that he served Edward in that capacity. He was one of the tenants-in-chief in William's day. There is a reference to a constabularius who held such an office in Edward's day (*ibid.*, I, 151); but elsewhere the same person is spoken of as staller (*ibid.*, I, 146b, 148b, 218b). I conclude, therefore, that Edward had no constable at his court. It is, of course, possible that the duties of such an official may have been exercised by the staller. Edward evidently had a marshal, but he does not seem to have been classed with the more important officials.

CHAPTER VI.

THE KING'S PRIEST. THE CHANCERY.

The royal household in the middle ages had its ecclesiastical as well as its secular side.[85] The king's priest did not rank with the high officials of the palace in dignity, yet, his influence in affairs of state was far-reaching and profound. It is true, the importance of the chaplainship would depend largely on the character of the chaplain. When Wilfrid was growing into maturity, the Northumbrian king, wishing to make him his 'inseparable companion,' asked that he be ordained to the priesthood.[86] It is readily seen that with such an aggressive, almost gigantic spirit as the king's religious guide, the policies of government would to a large extent be determined in the royal chapel. However, the bishop decided that Wilfrid was better fitted for episcopal duties, and he never became royal chaplain.

The first priest connected with an English court of whom we hear anything was the one who accompanied the princess Bertha when she left Gaul to become queen of Kent.[87] But this man of God, Liudhard by name, does not seem to have made his presence felt among the Kentish people to any appreciable extent. Of a different type was Paulinus, the spiritual adviser of Edwin's queen, through whose persistent efforts the conversion of Northumbria was begun.[88] Bede mentions several other royal chaplains serving at Northumbrian courts,[89] but after his time we hear little of

---
[85] The subject of the royal chapel is discussed by Kemble in *Sax. in Eng.*, II, 113–17; also by Green in *Conqu. of Eng.*, 524–28. Green's discussion contains a great deal of information, but his use of sources has been uncritical and his conclusions are often incorrect.
[86] *Hist. York*, I, 13.
[87] Bede, *H. E.*, I, 25.
[88] *Ibid.*, II, 9. *Hist. York*, I, 353.
[89] About the middle of the seventh century a priest Utta, "multae gravitatis ac veritatis vir," brought Eanfled from Kent to become queen of Northumbria. Bede, *H. E.*, III, 15. He may have been a royal chaplain. Eanfled brought her own confessor with her, a Kentish priest named Romanus. *Ibid.*, III, 25. In 660 the Northumbrian king had a confessor whose name was Caelin. *Ibid.*, III, 23. In 665 one Eadhed was chaplain at the same court. *Ibid.*, III, 28.

the king's priest before the reign of Alfred.[90] Asser speaks of the chaplains—*capellanos suos*[91]—serving at Alfred's court, and names two, "Ethelstan and Werewulf...Mercians by birth and erudite."[92] The king himself names two more, Grimbald and John.[93] But he speaks of these as his teachers rather than as his confessors. Ecclesiastics were numerous at Alfred's court, but the king called them not so much because they were holy men as because they were learned.[94]

During the reign of Alfred's successor, the king's presbyter seems to have been especially honored: he was admitted to the circle of the wise. At least we shall have to suppose that the presbyters who witnessed Edward's charters were, some of them if not all, the king's own priests. The documents bearing such signatures are comparatively numerous in this reign.[95] When

[90] According to Alfred's laws (38, 2) fighting in the presences of the king's priest was punished by a heavy fine. But the fact that the priest in this case is coupled with the ealdorman's deputy leads me to think that the law does not refer to the court chaplain, but to the parish priest acting in an official capacity at the folk-moot.
[91] Petrie's *Monumenta*, 496.
[92] Asser (Giles' translation): *Six Old Eng. Chron.*, 70.
[93] In the Preface to Gregory's *Pastoral Care*. On the subject of Alfred's chaplains see Plummer, *Alfred*, I, 136 ff.
[94] Preface to *Pastoral Care*: 'Even as I learned from Plegmund my archbishop, and from Asser my bishop, and from John my mass-priest.' It is not probable that all these were continuously at the royal court; but some time or other they had been in the king's personal service. It will be remembered that Asser was asked to divide his time, giving certain months to the king. Plummer thinks that Alfred "established, probably after the example of Charles the Great, a Court school, for the education specially of the sons of the upper classes, in which books of both languages, Latin and Saxon, were read." See *Alfred*, 135.
[95] List of presbyters whose signatures occur in Edward's charters:

Year	900.	903.	903.	904.	904.	904.	901-9.	901-9.	909.	909.	909.	909 (?).	910 (?).	910 (?).	909.
Tata	+			+	+	+	+								
Werulf	+	+			+	+	+	+	+	+	+	+	+	+	+
Beornstan	+	+			+	+	+	+	+	+	+	+	+	+	+
Æthelstan	+			+	+	+	+	+	+	+	+	+	+	+	+
Walda	+														
Johan					+	+	+								
Searu					+	+	+								
Thoneulf					+	+	+								
Thald					+										
Brichtulf															
Ælfstan							+								
Ealhstan								+	+	+	+	+	+	+	+
Wulfric								+							
Æthelbyrht								+							
Yoelbeard								+							
No. in *K. C. D.*	1077	1080	335	337	1084	1085	1087	1088	1090	1091	1092	1093	1094	1095	1096
No. in Birch, *Cartul.*															620

This does not include *K. C. D.*, Nos. 331 and 342, which are apparently spurious. Kemble questions them. Nos. 597 and 598 in Birch are also excluded for the same reason.

we consider the number of bishops and *duces* who were also present as witnesses, it seems clear that most of these charters must have been issued when the national council was in session. The normal number of presbyterial signatures is four, though the earlier documents frequently have more. The names of Werulf,[96] Beornstan and Æthelstan are found with great regularity as the appended table shows. The same is true of Tata and Ealhstan; the latter apparently succeeded the former, as the last document bearing Tata's name is the first in which Ealhstan's signature occurs.[97]

After the death of Edward the power of the presbyter seems to have declined. Æthelstan thoroughly reorganized the *witan*,[98] and the priest disappeared.[99] In the succeeding reigns up to the accession of Cnut, the sources have little to say about the king's chaplains except as partakers of the royal bounty.[1] Cnut seems to have revived the custom of calling in his priests to witness land transfers. There are, however, only eight documents given during his reign that have presbyterial signatures, the earliest dating from 1024.[2] Six of these bear Eadwold's name; four have Stigand's signature; Ælfwine has signed three; eight other priests have witnessed one document each. In the charters of Edward the Confessor such signatures are met with quite frequently.[3]

The position of confessor at the royal court was no doubt both an honorable and a profitable one. In Eadred's will the king's

---

[96] *K. C. D.*, No. 1094, has Werulf dux which may be a scribal error for Werulf presbyter.

[97] The list of presbyters would be materially reduced if we omit No. 1088 in Kemble. This charter relates wholly to ecclesiastical affairs, and the priests whose names appear in this document only may have belonged to the episcopal and not to the royal household.

[98] See Stubbs, *C. H.*, I. 140.

[99] Two charters of 931 have the signatures of "Godescealc sacerdos minister". *K. C. D.*, Nos. 1104, 1106. But it is not clear that this priest was a royal chaplain. Cf. No. 1135, where there is an allusion to "Godescallus abbas abbunduniae". The charter is an evident forgery, but the scribe may have been correctly informed as to the name of the abbot at this period.

[1] Birch, *Cartul.*, No. 803. Edmund, 945. A grant to "cuidam presbytero meo, cui nomen Æthelnodus". *K. C. D.*, No. 1165. Eadred, 948. Signed among others by Heremod presbyter who apparently was a court priest. Birch, *Cartul.*, No. 1288. Æthelflæd second queen of Edmund wills two hides to each of her two priests, Alfwold and Æthelmær. *K. C. D.*, No. 1200. Eadwig (956) endows his "fideli Byrthelmo presbytero" with lands at Cenigton. Soon afterwards the grantee disposes of these lands and in this transaction he appears as bishop. *Ibid.*, No. 1201.

[2] *K. C. D.*, Nos. 741, 743, 745, 746, 751, 1318, 1322, 1324.

[3] See *ibid.*, Nos. 787, 791, 792, 793, 796, 800, 813.

chaplains rank next to the great palatine officials, the seneschal, the butler and the chamberlain: 'and to each of my mass-priests that I have appointed to attend on my relics, fifty mancuses of gold and five pounds in pennies, and to every one of the other priests, five pounds.'[4] We shall have to conclude from this that the number of ecclesiastics at court must have been comparatively large.[5] It seems likely that each of the principal members of the royal family had his own confessor or chaplain.[6] Some of them must have had several.[7] I have been able to find the names of more than twenty persons who were royal presbyters in the days of Edward the Confessor.[8] The greater number of these appear in sources that cannot be questioned, such as the Chronicle and Domesday.

The chaplain's reward was land,[9] or an abbacy, or a bishopric, as soon as a vacancy should appear. I have already suggested that the king's confessor, if a man of strength and spirit, would be a powerful factor in shaping governmental policies, and might thus give the church undue influence in the state. But the institution was two-edged; more often it helped the king to maintain his position as lord of the Anglican church. The chaplain might become strongly attached to his lord and thoroughly subservient to the king. His chaplainship might also become a stepping-stone to higher honors. In the Northumbrian kingdom episcopal appointments seem generally to have come after service in the king's chapel.[10] There is, however, little evidence that the Eng-

---

[4] Birch, *Cartul.*, No. 912. (The translation is from *Liber de Hyda*, 349.)

[5] Chaplains were also numerous at the Carolingian court. See Waitz, *D. V. G.*, III, 525.

[6] Cf., *ibid.*, III, 525: Die Gemahlin des Königs oder Kaisers hatte einen eignen Capellan.

Attention has already been called to the queen's chaplains mentioned by Bede and to the priests endowed by queen Æthelflæd in her will. Æthelstan Etheling also remembered his mass-priest in his will. *K. C. D.*, No. 722. The queen's priest Walter was given a bishopric in 1060. *Flor. Wig.*, I, 218.

[7] See Birch, *Cartul.*, 1288. Æthelflæd's will.

[8] Cf. Green, *Conqu. of Eng.*, 526–27.

[9] The royal grants to presbyters in the ninth century have been referred to. *Domesday* mentions several of Edward's priests as landholders. "Wlmarus presbyter regis" held two small areas in Buckingham and Bedford. I, 151, 210b. "Esmellt capellanus regis Edwardi" had a little plot of ground in Kent. I, 1b. Edward is also said to have given certain lands in Huntingdon to "Vitali et Bernardo presbyteris suis". I, 208.

[10] Caelin did not get such a position for himself, but he may have been influential in securing it for his brother. Bede, *H. E.*, III, 23. Eadhed, after serving some time as royal capellanus, became bishop of Lindsey. *Flor. Wig.*, I, 243.

lish kings tried to control the church through the episcopal patronage before the Danish period.[11] Three of Cnut's chaplains are known to have been rewarded with bishoprics: Ælfwine in 1032,[12] Duduc the next year[13] and Eadsie in 1038.[14] Stigand, another of Cnut's presbyters, received similar honors in Edward's reign. Cnut's policy in church appointments was continued and further developed by Edward the Confessor. Apparently the king had but little worldly goods to spare for his friends,[15] but with offices he was more liberal. Giso,[16] Heca,[17] Hereman,[18] Stigand,[19] Ulf,[20] and William,[21] all of the king's own chapel, were given episcopal sees in this reign. Kynsige whom Edward made archbishop of York was probably one of Cnut's chaplains.[22] Walter, the queen's priest, was also rewarded with a bishopric.[23] Leofric, chancellor and doubtless king's presbyter, was placed in charge of two western sees.[24] Godric, the son of one of the royal chaplains, received an abbacy.[25] Regenbaldus was elevated to the chancellorship.[26] It is not strange that this persistent policy of

[11] Examples are Alfred's appointment of Plegmund to the see of Canterbury (Plummer, *Alfred*, 139), and the advancement of Byrhtelm in 956. See *K. C. D.*, Nos. 1200, 1201.
[12] *A. S. Chron.*, 1032: [Vacancy in the see of Winchester.] And Ælfwine þæs cynges preost feng þærto.
[13] Stubbs, *Reg. Sacr. Angnc.*, 19. Cf. *K. C. D.*, No. 1318.
[14] *Flor. Wig.*, I, 193: ..regis capellanus Eadsius in archiepiscopatum successit. But he seems to have received episcopal honors in 1035. See Stubbs, *Reg. Sacr. Anglic.*, 19.
[15] On the landed estates held by Edward's priests see the references to *Domesday* cited above.
[16] *K. C. D.*, No. 835: [Wells, 1061.] Sciatis nos dedisse Gisoni presbytero nostro episcopatum hunc apud vos.
[17] *A.-S. Chron.*, 1046; also 1045, 1047, 1048: [Sussex, 1047.] Heca cinges preost feng ðarto.
[18] *Ibid.*, 1043: [Ramsbury.] Hereman þes cynges preost feng to þam biscoprice.
[19] *Ibid.*, 1042: [East Anglia, 1043.] Stigand preost wæs gebletsod to bisocpe to Eastenglum. Cf. *K. C. D.*, Nos. 751, 1318, 1322, 1324.
[20] *Ibid.*, 1049: [Dorchester, 1050.] Eadwerd cing geaf Ulfe his preoste þæt bisceoprice.
[21] *Ibid.*, 1048: [London, 1050.] ...and wes Willelm þæs cynges preost gehadod þærto.
[22] *Ibid.*, 1053. Stubbs (*Reg. Sacr. Anglic.*, 20) gives the year as 1051. Kynsige signed one of Cnut's charters as presbyter in 1026, *K. C. D.*, No. 743.
[23] *Flor. Wig.*, I, 218: (1060.) Et Herefordensis praesulatus...capellano Edgithae reginae Waltero Lotharingo est datus.
[24] *Ibid.*, 199: [Exeter and Crediton.]...regis cancellario Leofrico...datus est praesulatus.
[25] *Ibid.*, 211: [Winchcombe, 1053.] Godricum, regis capellani Godmanni filium abbatem constitueret.
[26] Regenbaldus will be discussed later in this chapter. The corrections and additions in brackets are mainly from Stubbs. *Reg. Sacr. Anglic.*, 19-21.

selecting the spiritual lords of the realm from the king's own immediate household should have produced dissatisfaction and even opposition.[27] The practice, however, did not originate in England; it is at least as old as the Carolingian monarchy. Charlemagne not only exercised complete control over episcopal appointments,[28] but also selected the prospective candidates and had them trained at his own court.

The royal chapel at the Frankish court was directly in charge of a chief presbyter to whom all the other chaplains were subordinate. He was usually known as the *summus capellanus* or *archicapellanus*,[29] and his office carried with it great influence in ecclesiastical affairs not only at the local court but in the empire at large. It seems likely that such a dignitary existed at the Anglo-Saxon court also; but on this point our sources maintain an absolute silence.

In addition to their priestly functions[30] the clerks of the royal chapel may have had certain notarial duties.[31] Documents were regularly issued on the king's authority, and it is difficult to see who but some ecclesiastic could have produced them; for the knowledge and skill necessary in drawing up such documents in those days were not inconsiderable.[32] As a rule, the early English charters do not state by whom they were written; there are a few exceptions, but many of these are spurious or at least doubtful.[33] An examination of these will reveal the fact that nearly all, the doubtful and the probably genuine,[34] claim to have been drawn up

---

[27] See Kemble. *Sax. in Eng.*, II. 115.
[28] Waitz, *D. V. G.*, III, 420.
[29] *Ibid.*, 517 ff.
[30] For the duties of the chaplains at the Carolingian court, see *ibid.*, 522.
[31] Cf. *ibid.*, 523 ff.; Brunner, *D. R. G.*, II, 114.
[32] For the state of learning in early England, see Plummer, *Alfred*, 81–82.
[33] In two of Ine's charters (*K. C. D.*, Nos. 45, 48) dated respectively 699 and 701, Winberht is represented as being the scribe. The first of these is clearly a forgery; the second. a wholly different document, may be genuine. More than doubtful are two documents dated 605 (*ibid.*, Nos. 3. 4) and approved by "Angemundus referendarius." The referendarius was a Merovingian official; his title seems never to have been born by any English functionary. A charter dated 682 (Birch, *Cartul.*, No. 62) contains this statement: "Ego Aldhelm hanc scedulam scripi et subscripsi." He may have been the Aldhelm who was abbot of Malmesbury six years later. See *ibid.*, No. 71. A rather suspicious charter from 793 was ostensibly drawn up by Tilhere the king's priest. *Ibid.*, No. 268. See also *K. C. D.*, No. 555 (a very questionable document): Ego Aldred abbas ...hanc libertatis singrapham scripsi.
[34] *K. C. D.*, No. 1191 (Nos. 1196 and 1197 are copies of this): Ego Daniel, iubente rege, hanc syngrapham dictaui. Daniel was bishop of Rochester at this

by some ecclesiastic; also that the scribe usually did not reside at court.[35] The series of such documents extends well past the middle of the tenth century.[36]

This leads directly to the question, was there a royal chancery in Anglo-Saxon times? The evidence just presented, though by no means conclusive, declares against the existence of such an institution at least before the reign of Æthelred. It is true, these charters may be exceptional; but in that case the existence of a chancery would be a matter of common knowledge. In a Supplement to Ælfric's Vocabulary, which cannot be earlier than Æthelred's reign, we find *cancellarius* defined as *scriniarius* or 'burthegn.'[37] It is certainly possible that the keeper of the king's strongbox might also act as royal notary; but the probabilities are that the glossarist was trying to explain a term that he did not clearly understand.

Earlier students of Anglo-Saxon history looked on the English chancery as a most ancient institution. Lappenberg traced it back to the reign of Æthelbirht of Kent.[38] Spelman found it in the days of Edward the Elder.[39] "From Edgar," according to Palgrave, "the office may be traced more distinctly."[40] But recent writers agree with Kemble that not "till the reign of Eadweard the Confessor is there the slightest historical evidence in favor of

---

time, 956. See Stubbs, *Reg. Sacr. Anglic.*, 15. *K. C. D.*, 1166: Ego Dunstanus abbas indignus cartulam, inde imperante domino meo rege Eadredo, composui, et propriis digitis meis perscripsi. Dunstan was abbot of Glastonbury. The charter is brief and business-like, in every way worthy of the great prelate. (949.) *Ibid.*, No. 534: Ego Wulfsie episcopus hanc chartulam....perscribere iussi. (967.)

[35] A document from the middle of the eighth century closes with this sentence: 'Alda, the king's gefera, he wrote it.' *K. C. D.*, No. 95. It is possible that gerefa was intended instead of gefera; the latter, however, is a good Saxon word meaning companion. Alda may have been a man of learning occupying a position at court like that of Asser in Alfred's time.

[36] An apparently genuine charter from 1065 seems to have been composed by "Brihtricus abbas". *K. C. D.*, No. 817.

[37] *Vocab.*, 190:19.

[38] *Hist. of Eng.*, II, 381: "As early as in charters of Æthelbirht of Kent we meet with a Referendarius, probably the same dignity as that bearing from the time of Eadward the Elder the name of Chancellor." Cf. Kemble, *Sax. in Eng.*, II, 114, note. In *K. C. D.*, Nos. 3, 4, an Angemundus referendarius is mentioned, but these two charters are glaring forgeries.

[39] Palgrave, *English Commonwealth*, II, 345.

[40] *Ibid.* The author was evidently deceived by the many forgeries purporting to emanate from Edgar's councils and of which No. 555 in the *Codex* may serve as an example: "Lam decreuimus roborare et de sigillo nostro iussimus sig illare."

such an office."[41] That a chancery existed just before the Conquest cannot be doubted. Much of the evidence for such an institution in Edward's day is, indeed, questionable; but we shall not be able to reject all. Florence of Worcester tells us of a Leofric chancellor who was given episcopal honors in 1046.[42] There is a grant of lands to Harold dated 1062 which is witnessed by *Regenbaldus regis cancellarius*.[43] Several evident forgeries also bear the signatures of this same priest or chancellor. His name and title also occur in a document drawn up in the Saxon idiom and apparently above suspicion, a donation to the Old Minster at Winchester, witnessed by 'Edith the lady, Stigand the archbishop, Harold earl and Rengebold chancellor.'[44] "He occurs repeatedly in Domesday, where he is distinguished as 'Canceler,' 'Presbyter' and 'de Cirencestre.' "[45] He seems to have been one of the few officials of Edward's court who were taken into the service of the Conqueror.[46]

The chancellor was the chief scribe of the royal court. All the king's secretarial forces were subject to his orders. His principal duty was to prepare the royal documents or to have them properly drawn up by his notaries.[47] He was also the customary keeper of the royal seal,[48] and so closely is this symbol associated with the chancellor's office that when we find the one we should expect to find the other. There is little evidence for the use of a seal before the Confessor's time.[49] The historian of Ramsey, writing in the twelfth century, tells us that none of the charters belonging

---

[41] *Sax. in Eng.*, II, 114. See also Stubbs, *C. H.*, I, 381; Green, *Conqu. of Eng.*, 526.
[42] *Flor. Wig.*, I, 199. I see no reason for doubting the statement. It is true, the author wrote after the Conquest and his authority is unsupported, but Florence seems to have had exceptional advantages for getting information relative to his own time and region. Leofric was given sees not far from Worcester.
[43] *K. C. D.*, No. 813.
[44] *Ibid.*, No. 891: Rengebold cancheler. Cf. *Eng. Hist. Rev.*, XI, 732, note.
[45] Round, *Feudal England*, 421.
[46] In one of his charters (quoted by Round in *Feudal England*, 422) William speaks of Regenbald as his priest, "minan preoste."
[47] Cf. Waitz, *D. V. G.*, III, 513–515; Freeman, *N. C.*, V, 290.
[48] Cf. Stubbs, *C. H.*, I, 381.
[49] Offa's seal, found attached to a document in a French monastery, may be left out of account as the charter cannot be genuine. For the document see Birch, *Cartul.*, No. 259. Cf. Stevenson's discussion in *Eng. Hist. Rev.*, VI. 736–42: The Old English Charters to St. Denis. The words sigillabant and sigillare occur occasionally in the charters, but I do not believe they will be found in any genuine document.

to that establishment and dating from Edgar's day had seals.[50] He also tells us that the charters from Edward's reign were provided with such authentications.[51] The Confessor's seal is, furthermore, mentioned in the most reliable sources of the period, the Chronicle[52] and Domesday.[53] But it is probably not true, as certain writers assert, that Edward was the first English king who had a seal.[54] In a document entitled Wynflæd's Suit, apparently an account of a shire-moot held some time in Æthelred's reign, this sentence occurs: 'Then sent the king his seal by Ælfhere the abbot to the gemot at Cwicelmeshlæwe.'[55] If this document is genuine, and it seems to be, we shall have to say that the royal seal was used in England at least as early as the tenth century.

The evidence before us seems to show that there was a chancery during Edward's reign; that his two chancellors were churchmen; that the office of chancellor, at least while Regenbald held it, was one of great power and profit.[56] There seems to have been a royal seal and hence, perhaps, a chancery in Æthelred's day;[57] but for the earlier period all the evidence is negative. It should be said, however, that the final word on this subject cannot be spoken before a thorough study of originals has been made and the documents issued in each particular reign carefully examined and compared.[58]

---

[50] *Historia Ramesiensis*, 65: Notandum vero quod nullis eaedem scedulae sigillorum impressionibus sunt munitae....

[51] *Ibid.*, 161, 167.

[52] 1048: ða com Sparhafoc abbod to him mid þæs cynges gewrite and insegle.

[53] I, 78b: ...in ipsa aecclesia inventus est brevis cum sigillo R. E. See also pp. 208, 374 et passim. Much of the Domesday evidence on this point has been collected by Freeman. *N. C.*, V, 526, note. A few of the impressions of the Confessor's seal seem to have been preserved; Birch describes three of them. See *Catalog of Seals in the Department of MSS. in the British Museum*, I, 2–3.

[54] Stubbs, *C. H.*, I, 381: "Edward the Confessor, the first of our sovereigns who had a seal, is also the first who had a chancellor." For a similar view see Green, *Conqu. of Eng.*, 526.

[55] *K. C. D.*, No. 693: þa sende se cyning be æluere abbude his insegel to þam gemote æt cwicelmes-hlæwe....

[56] Regenbald held land in five counties and controlled the revenues of sixteen churches. See Round, *Feudal England*, 426.

[57] The introduction of the chancery into England will be discussed in the concluding chapter of this study.

[58] The subject will doubtless be exhaustively treated in Stevenson's forthcoming work, *The Anglo-Saxon Chancery*. Stevenson's view of the general question is presented briefly in *Eng. Hist. Rev.*, XI, 731–44. See also Round, *Feudal England*, 421–30: Regenbald.

CHAPTER VII.

THE INNOVATIONS OF CNUT AND THE DANES.

That the Danish conquest of England should have produced certain changes in the institutional life of the conquered nation seems inevitable. The new king was a Dane; his councillors and trusted men were aliens like himself. His court seems to have been largely Scandinavian not only in personnel (as appears from the signatures to Cnut's charters) but in speech and spirit. The praise-lays that the Danish conqueror heard at his regal banquets were not such as would delight a Saxon ear.[59] The influence of an alien court on the constitutional development of a people is a matter of great importance.[60] With the general question of Scandinavian influence the present study is not concerned. This chapter will be limited to the consideration of two institutions that appeared in England with the Danish dynasty: the stallership and the royal guard or corps of house-carles.

With regard to the staller the view commonly held is that this office was equivalent to that of the earlier horse-thegn[61] and that it may have been borrowed from the Frankish court,[62] as the

---

[59] See *C. P. B.*, II, 155-56. Only a few fragments of the poetry sung in praise of Cnut have come down to us.

[60] As a rule writers on English history conclude with Green (*History of the English People*, I, 100) and Stubbs (*C. H.*, I, 219-20) that the influence of the Northmen in the shaping of Anglo-Saxon institutions is a negligible quantity, as the invaders, having essentially the same speech and customs as their brethren in Britain, could have but little to contribute. On the other hand, Steenstrup, the Danish historian of the viking age, finds the legal and political systems of Old England permeated with Norse terms and institutions. While few would accept all of Steenstrup's conclusions, no one who has examined his work will deny, that he has shown, that the earlier English opinions on this subject are untenable and that for an adequate understanding of the institutions of England in the eleventh century a considerable attention must be given to Norse sources. See *Normannerne*, especially Vol. IV, *Danelag*.

[61] See chapter VIII.

[62] Lappenberg, *Hist. of Eng.*, II, 381: In the instance of the Marshal even the usual Anglo-Saxon denomination of stallere (comes stabuli) indicates its

Anglo-Saxon title staller (supposedly derived from Latin *stabularius* or *comes stabuli*[63]) seems to indicate. Till recently it was thought that the Norse *stallari* was this same Old English official introduced into Norway, perhaps some time in the tenth century.[64] It is my purpose to show that the converse is more probably true: that the stallership is Norse in name and origin, and that it came into England with the Danish host.[65]

The earliest appearance of the Norse staller is in the sagas dealing with the times of Olaf Trygvesson about the year 1000.[66] He appears in the reign of Saint Olaf as a most important state official;[67] there can be no doubt that Björn, the staller of that reign, is an historic person. But even if we reject the accounts in the sagas of the two great Olafs, we still have in the court-poetry of the time sufficient evidence for the existence of such an official among the Northmen in the early part of the eleventh century. Sighvat the Poet, the roving scald who sang the exploits of Cnut 'the Mighty' at the English court, alludes to the Norwegian staller in his poems.[68] In the English sources this official appears for the first time in one of Cnut's charters;[69] the document is undated but was probably given in the year 1032.[70] During the Confessor's reign the title occurs frequently, but nearly always in legal documents only.[71]

If the staller's office is of Norse origin, the institution must be studied in the light of the Norse sources rather than of the Frankish. It may be urged, however, that, even if it did come into England with the Danes, the etymology of the term shows an unmistakably Frankish-Roman origin. But it does not seem necessary to derive *stallari* from *stabulator* or any other Latin

---

Roman origin; for he is seldom designated 'cyninges hors-thegn.' Cf. Kemble, *Sax. in Eng.*, II, 108; Green, *Conqu. of Eng.*, 523.

[63] Stubbs, *C. H.*, I, 383, note: The name is derived from the *comoo stabuli* of the Byzantine court.

[64] See S. R. D., III, 156; Keyser, *Efterladte Skrifter*, II, 81, note.

[65] Cf. Steenstrup, *Danelag*, 125, where the subject of origin is briefly treated. Steenstrup was the first to suggest that the Norse term stallari is probably older than the Anglo-Saxon stallere.

[66] See *Fornmannasaga*, II, 331. Cf. Keyser, *Efterladte Skrifter*, II, 80.

[67] Snorre. *St. Olaf's Saga*, 55.

[68] *C. P. B.*, II, 129, 134.

[69] *K. C. D.*, No. 1327: þored steallare. The name is Danish.

[70] It bears the signatures of bishops Ælfsige and Ælgelric (Æthelric). The former died in 1032, the same year in which the latter received his appointment. See Stubbs, *Reg. Sacr. Anglic.*, 18, 19.

[71] It occurs once in the *Chronicle* (1047): man utlagode Osgod stallere.

term of like import; it seems much more natural to connect it with *stallr*, an Old Norse word meaning much the same as modern English *stall*.[72] This word has a Germanic origin and is only a distant relative of the Latin *stabulum*.[73]

The stallership was of great importance in the North during the eleventh and twelfth centuries. Langebek believes there was such an official in Denmark as early as Cnut's reign;[74] the probabilities favor this view; still, no historic example can be produced before 1085.[75] Several are known to have born the title in the next century; but after 1200 the dignity declined and was overshadowed by that of the marshal.[76] The position of the staller in Saint Olaf's household may best be illustrated with a citation from Snorre's history: 'King Olaf located his court at Nidaros [Throndhjem]. There was built a large kings-hall with doors in both gables. The king's high-seat was in the middle of the room;[77] on the inner side sat Grimkell his court-bishop, and next him his other priests; on the outer side sat his councillors. In the other high-seat opposite the king sat his staller, Björn the Stout, and next him the guests.'[78] Thus the staller was next to the king in dignity; by the time the *Hirdskraa*[79] received its final form, he ranked second among the court officials, the chancellor holding first place.

That the English staller occupied a correspondingly high position, the sources clearly indicate. In a twelfth century account of the miracles of Saint Edmund, Osgod Clapa, at one time staller, is spoken of as of so great power, 'that, as standing next to the king, he was not to be feared less than the king himself.'[80] This, of course, is gross exaggeration, still, it testifies to Osgod's great fame. In Hermannus' work on the same subject, he is

---

[72] It is used in this sense in the Eddic poems of the early tenth century. See C. P. B., I, 227, 309. Keyser suggested this etymology in his work on the mediaeval constitution of Norway. *Efterladte Skrifter*, II. 81.
[73] See Kluge, *Etymologisches Wörterbuch*.
[74] S. R. D., III, 156, note.
[75] *Ibid.*: An. 1085, Petrum stabellarium invenimus.
[76] *Ibid.*: Sub Waldemaro II et postea stabularii titulus et dignitas vilescere et exolere coepisse, inque ejus locum Marescalci nomen et officium inolscere videtur.
[77] Near the north wall.
[78] *Saint Olaf's Saga*, 55.
[79] A law governing the royal household in Norway, amended and promulgated by Magnus Lawmender (1263-80).
[80] *Memorials of St. Edmund's Abbey*, I, 135: ....ut secundus a rege non minus quam rex ipse cunctis formidandus haberetur.

called *major domus*.[81] The importance of the office is also apparent from the language used in contemporary charters. In the king's writs, usually composed in Old English and peculiar to the half century just preceding the Conquest, the staller is frequently addresed along with the earl and the bishop.[82] From this juxtaposition of earl, bishop and staller we should infer that the last named had some authority in the shire. But I cannot find that any particular territory comes under the exclusive authority of any particular staller.[83] The great prominence of this official also appears when we consider him as a land-owner. 'Æsgarus a certain staller' is spoken of in the *Historia Eliensis* as having forcibly seized on lands belonging to the monastery of Ely.[84] The 'land-hunger' must have been strong in him; an examination of Domesday will show that Æsgar staller was one of the greatest landholders in England at the time of Edward the Confessor; he had estates almost everywhere.[85] Almost the same can be said of Radulfus staller.[86] There can be no doubt that the stallership was the highest dignity at the Old English court when the Anglo-Saxon period came to a close.

As to the functions of this official the English sources give us very little information, and the Norse court-laws are of too late a date to be relied on for conditions in the eleventh century. The Norwegian staller in the thirteenth century had duties along three principal lines: he served as the king's spokesman on public occasions; he acted as chief and judge of the henchmen and presented their requests to the king; he provided horses or other means of transportation for his master's journeys.[87] But it seems, from

---

[81] *Memorials of St. Edmund's Abbey*, I, 54: Inter quos quidam major domus Osgodclap cognomine vocitatus.

[82] *K. C. D.*, No. 855: Eadward king gret Wiliem biscop, and Harold eorlle, and Eogar stallere, and alle mine þegnas and mine holde frend on Middelsexum frendlice. See also Nos. 828, 843, 845, 859, 864.

[83] Æsgar is addressed on matters in Middlesex (*K. C. D.*, No. 855), Kent (No. 828) and Hertford (No. 864); Eadnoth on an affair in Southampton (No. 845); Robert on an Essex matter (No. 859); on a matter of business in Kent Edward addresses the archbishop, the bishop of Rochester, earl Leofwine and two stallers, Æsgar and Robert the son of Wymarch (No. 828).

[84] *Historia Eliensis*, I, 216: Æsgarus quidam stallere...

[85] *Domesday*, passim. The name appears as Asgar, Asgarus, Ansgerus, Angerus, Esgarus, etc.

[86] *Ibid.*, passim.

[87] *Norges gamle Love*, II, 411. Munch, *N. F. H.*, IV, 1, 601. Keyser, *Efterladte Skrifter*, II, 81. For the duties of the constable elsewhere on the Continent and in England at this period, see Stubbs, *C. H.*, I, 483–84. The Norwegian stallere differed from the constable in being primarily one who spoke to

the allusions to this same official in the Eddas, that his duties were much the same in the days of Saint Olaf and Cnut, except that in those days he was also a leader of the host.[88] Which of these duties devolved on the English staller we do not know. The fact that Eadnoth, a former staller, commanded an army in 1067,[89] suggests that the office may have been of a somewhat military character. Eadnoth must, it seems, have had some experience as a leader in war. He may have had charge of the royal stables, but the sources do not show it. There seems to have been a lower official, a king's marshal, who looked after the royal steeds. Florence of Worcester, writing soon after the Conquest, speaks of Ecgulf, Alfred's horse-thegn as *Ecgulfus strator regius*.[90] Again, in his account of the expulsion of the Normans in 1052, he mentions *Ælfredum regis stratorem* among those who were permitted to remain in the land.[91] This is, doubtless, the *Alueredus marescal* who is mentioned in Domesday as holding lands in Edward's day.[92] There was also one Roger who held the marshalship before the Conquest.[93] In the following reign the marshal was a far more important official. William had no staller.

The kings of Norway evidently had several stallers at the same time,[94] though one of them may have enjoyed a headship.

---

the populace on behalf of the king, and not one who commanded his armies. The 'court-law' says nothing of military duties.

[88] The poets do not speak of the staller as a spokesman, but as such he is frequently alluded to in the sagas. See Snorre, *St. Olaf's Saga*, 68, 80. As an intermediary between the king and his henchmen we find Björn staller alluded to (Björn fell in battle, 1030). The poet praises him as a counselor and for having won favor for him with the King. *C. P. B.*, II, 129. Björn staller was a leader at Stiklestad where Saint Olaf fell (1030). At the battle of the River Niz (1052) Ulf staller, "he the king's friend, bade us lay his ship in the forefront of the battle by the side of the king's...." *Ibid.*, II, 224. (Vigfusson's translation.)

[89] *A.-S. Chron.*, 1067: Eadnoð stallere heom wið gefeaht. *Flor. Wig.*, II, 3: Eadnothus, qui fuit Haroldi regis stallarius....

[90] *A.-S. Chron.*, 897. *Flor. Wig.*, I, 115.

[91] *Flor. Wig.*, I, 210.

[92] III, 216: Comes habet unam mansionem quae vocatur Stratona quam tenuerunt Alueredus marescalcus et Osbernus episcopus die qua rex E. fuit vivus et mortuus. See Round, The Officers of Edward the Confessor: *Eng. Hist. Rev.*, XIX, 90.

[93] *Domesday*, II, 59. .... videntibus duobus hominibus scilicet Rogero marescalco et quodam Anglico.... The occasion was a transfer of land by Harold's house-carle Scalpinus to his wife. The transaction seems to have taken place while Edward was still king. From his name and the fact that the other witness has his nationality so distinctly stated, we should judge that Roger was a Norman.

[94] The Norse court-poets in speaking of the stallers frequently use the plural. See *C. P. B.*, II, 129, 134, 141.

It is possible that Cnut also had more than one such official at his court, but one only is mentioned in the records.[95] There were in all, so far as we know, eight stallers in Edward's reign: Bondig, Eadnoth, Ælfstan, Æsgar, Leofing, Osgod, Rodbertus and Roulf or Radulfus. Several of them, usually three, served at the same time. One of the earliest, and perhaps the most famous of them all, was Osgod Clapa. He was a Northman and probably served in the same capacity under the Danish kings.[96] His term of service ceased in 1047.[97] Ælfstan, whose name and title appear in a document from 1044,[98] seems to have been associated with him in the office. Æsgar first comes to our notice in 1052;[99] he seems to have continued staller till the close of the reign.[1] His colleagues in the years 1052 and 1053[2] were Leofing and Roulf. After the last named date we hear no more of Leofing. A document that Kemble places between 1060 and 1066 has the signatures of three stallers: Esegar, Roulf and Bondig.[3] Bondus, Boding or Bondi staller is mentioned in Domesday, but not very frequently;[4] in one entry he is called *Boding constabularius.*[5] Eadnoth is the only one of Edward's stallers whom we know to have continued as such under Harold.[6] He is mentioned but once or twice in the great survey.[7] *Rodbertus regalis palatii stabilitor,* who, as we are told by the Con-

---

[95] *K. C. D.*, No. 1327: þored steallare. He was evidently a Dane. It is possible that one Tovi served as staller under Cnut, but the fact is not mentioned in any contemporary document. For a statement of the case see Freeman, *N. C.*, I, 521 ff.

[96] He was apparently connected with Cnut's household, as his signature is affixed to several charters given by that king. See *K. C. D.*, Nos. 1319, 1324, 1327. It was at his house at Clapham that Harthacnut died.

[97] *A.-S. Chron.*, 1047: Man utlagode Osgod stallere. After he was outlawed he turned viking and harried the English coasts (1049). He died in 1054.

[98] An agreement between Ægelric and bishop Eadsige signed by "Ælfstan stealloere." *K. C. D.*, No. 773.

[99] *Ibid.*, No. 956: ..and on Esgeres stealres [gewitnesse] and on Raulfes steallres and on Lifinges steallres...

[1] *Ibid.*, No. 828 (1066): Eadward king gret....Esgar stallere..

[2] *Ibid.*, No. 1337. Ælfgifu's bequest.

[3] *Ibid.*, No. 822. Birch (*Cartul.*, No. 929) places it between 1052 and 1070. The same names occur in *K. C. D.*, No. 813, with these titles: Esgarus regiae procurator aulae; Radulphus regis aulicus; Bundinus regis palatinus.

[4] I, 146b, 148b, 218b.

[5] I, 151.

[6] *Flor. Wig.*, II, 3: Eadnothus qui fuit Haroldi regis stallarius....Cf. *A.-S. Chron.*, 1067; *K. C. D.*, No. 845.

[7] I, 58b: Ednod stalre tenuit T. R. E.... There is also a reference to one Alnodus stalro (III, 415) who held lands in Edward's day. I take Alnodus to be a scribal error for Eadnodus or Adnodus.

fessor's biographer, was present at the king's death-bed,[8] was doubtless the *Roberd Wymarche sune stallere* to whom greetings were sent in a royal mandate of 1066.[9] *Rodbertus filius Wimarchi* became a great landowner after the Conquest. His name occurs almost everywhere in Domesday, though perhaps not as Edward's staller.

Of the nine or ten stallers whose names have come down to us, the earlier three, Thored, Osgod and Tofig (if he ever held the office) were Danes. Bondig's name has also a decidedly Norse appearance. Of the later ones, two, Radulfus and Rodbertus, were probably Normans. The remaining three were presumably Saxons.

In 1033, the year after the first mention of the staller,[10] we note the earliest appearance of another Danish institution, the king's guard, usually known as the house-carles.[11] Writers on English history have paid considerable attention to this 'military household' and generally agree in ascribing its organization to Cnut; but on the origin and composition of the guard, its nature, its purpose and its final fate, the most diverse opinions are expressed.[12] The difficulty seems to be that no one has made a critical study of all the available sources. Of these there are three groups: the English documents from the eleventh century; the Norse poems from the same period and, for some purposes, the sagas and the laws; and the Danish histories of the twelfth century, the writings of Sveno and Saxo. Of these the second group is ignored or misunderstood by English writers,[13] while

---

[8] *Lives of Edward the Confessor* (London, 1858), 431.
[9] *K. C. D.*, No. 828.
[10] *Ibid.*, No. 1327.
[11] *Ibid.*, No. 1318. The grantee is called a minister in the document itself, but in an Anglo-Saxon rubric his title is translated huscarl.
[12] These will be noted in their proper places.
[13] Lappenberg (*Hist. of Eng.*, II, 247–48) seems to have been the first writer on this subject who also used the Danish sources. His statements are gathered largely from Sveno and Saxo. Kemble follows Lappenberg in almost every detail. *Sax. in Eng.*, II, 118–24. He makes some use of the English charters, but, after all, adds but little to our knowledge of the subject. Freeman (*N. C.*, I, 297–98, 497–500) attempts a critical study of the Danish sources and in most respects his conclusions are correct, though stated with many misgivings and much doubt. His treatment of the subject is by no means satisfactory; still, it is, perhaps, the best available in English. Freeman wholly ignores the Norse sources. Ramsay (*Found. of Eng.*, I, 413–16) gives considerable attention to Cnut's guard, especially to its probable numerical strength. The subject is also treated, though very briefly, in Traill's *Social England*. The contributors, Oman (I, 184) and Powell (I, 135), apparently accept the conclu-

Scandinavian historians[14] pay too little attention to the first. It should be added that Sveno's work has not, to my knowledge, been read in the light of other and earlier sources, as it should be to yield definite information.

English writers since the time of Kemble have looked on the royal guard of Cnut and his successors as "only a revival of the comitatus"[15] and therefore essentially English. On the other hand Munch[16] and Steenstrup[17] trace the institution back to the famous viking fraternity of Jomburg in the tenth century. It seems probable that neither of these views is wholly correct. Taking up the English view first, we shall find that there was a profound difference between the old Anglian 'hearth-guard' and the mercenary bands that Cnut distributed in 'camps and castles.' Neither the name nor the institution can be found in the English sources before the Danish period. *Huscarl* is a Norse word,[18] and one of the oldest in the language. In the Eddas it is used sometimes for servant[19] and sometimes for henchman.[20] But when we come to the court-poetry of the first half of the eleventh century we find the latter significance the dominant one.[21] House-carle, then, is the general term for member of a royal household; but when the early writers speak of the English house-carles,

---

sions of Freeman and, in part, those of the Norwegian historian, P. A. Munch. Green's statements relative to the house-carles (*History of the English People*, I, 100, *Conqu. of Eng.*, 414-1o) are extremely unreliable.

[14]These are particularly Munch (*N. F. H.*, I, 2, 473) and Steenstrup (*Danelag*, 127-54). Steenstrup's discussion of this subject is by far the most thorough thus far produced either in England or in the North.

[15]Kemble, *Sax. in Eng.*, II, 124. Freeeman (*N. C.*, I, 297-98) and Powell (*Social England*, I, 135) accept this view.

[16]*N. F. H.*, I, 2, 473. Munch holds that the remnants of the Jomburg guild entered into Æthelred's service, thus forming the corps afterward called the house-carles.

[17]*Danelag*, 147. Steenstrup believes that Cnut's household law, the Lex Castrensis of Sveno, was modeled on the Jomburg laws.

[18]It does not appear in the Anglo-Saxon Chronicle before 1036.

[19]The house-carles of the Atla Lay (placed by Vigfusson among the oldest epics of the Edda) must have been servants at court. They could not have been among the feasters for they helped Gudrun to burn the hall. *C. P. B.*, I, 51.

[20]*Ibid.*, 336.

[21]Sighvat, one of Cnut's scalds, complains of efforts made to bribe St. Olaf's house-carles. *C. P. B.*, II, 124. He says in praise of King Olaf: "We have both made a good bargain: thou hast got a good house-carle and I have got a good liege-lord." *Ibid.*, 149. Thiodolf describes a battle and says: "We lessened the number of the earl's house-carles." *Ibid.*, 201. (The translations are Vigfusson's.)

they use the more specific term þingamenn[22] the whole guard being known as the þingamannalíþ[23] The origin of this word is a matter of dispute: most probable seems the explanation of those who derive it from Anglo-Saxon þegnung, þenung or þening, meaning service.[24] The form 'thenigmen' occurs in Alfred's will and evidently means trusted servant.[25] The genitive form appears in 'theningmannagemot,' a word that occurs in a document from Edgar's day.[26] The Norse 'thingamanna' could easily be formed from 'theningmanna.'

When we come to consider the corps of 'thingamen' as an organized guild, it will become clearly apparent that the institution as well as the name was unknown in England before the last great Danish invasion. But before proceeding with such an examination, it will be necessary to consider the argument of those who connect the corps of house-carles with the mighty *comitatus* of Jom. During the period of the viking-raids the Danes established themselves among the Slavic Wends in the region of present Pomerania. To guard their interests there they built the famous stronghold of Jomburg,[27] near the town of the same name.[28] This was the retreat of the Jomvikings, a brotherhood of pirates, bound by laws and regulations which the sagas give quite circumstantially. Membership was limited to warriors between the ages of eighteen and fifty. Every viking was sworn to revenge his fellows. Women were excluded from the stronghold. No member was permitted to absent himself for more than three days at a time. All news was first to be reported to the commanding chief. The leader also was to act as judge. Law-

---

[22] I believe this word or any form of it occurs but once in the English sources and then in a Norman-English document, the *Leges Henrici Primi*, 15: "Denagildum quod aliquando þingemannis dabatur."

[23] See Steenstrup's *Danelag*, 130 ff., for a discussion of the various forms in which these words appear in the Norse sources.

[24] Such is Steenstrup's view (*Danelag*, 133). It seems rather strange, however, that the guard should be known by a Norse name in England and by an Old English name in the North. Other writers have tried to connect it with thegn.

[25] *K. C. D.*, No. 314. The thenigmen are to assist the ealdormen in distributing the wealth bequeathed.

[26] *Ibid.*, No. 1258.

[27] Its establishment seems to date from the reign of Harold Bluetooth, Sweyn's father. The subject is discussed in the opening pages of Steenstrup's monograph, *Venderne og de Danske.* Cf. *Saxo,* 325; *Knytlingasaga,* 1.

[28] *Saxo,* 325: Apud Iulinum. Adamus calls the place "nobilissima civitas Iumne." II, 19. The sagas speak of Jomsborg and Jomsviking. Jom was situated on the island of Wollin at the mouth of the Oder.

breakers were banished.[29] The only truly historic chief of the Jomvikings was the shrewd and treacherous earl Sigvaldi. With his leadership came a growing disregard for the laws of the guild,[30] and its power rapidly declined. The last great exploit of the Jomvikings was the attack on Norway which the crafty King Sweyn had induced them to make. At Hiorunga Bay Sigvaldi's fleet met that of Earl Hakon and was completely crushed.[31] Sigvaldi saved himself by flight.

Of the subsequent history of Jom almost nothing is known. Many of the vikings seem to have enlisted in Sweyn's service when he invaded England, or, what is more likely, they may have made independent raids on the English shores. Sigvaldi may have died in England in the great massacre of 1002, for in 1009 we find his brother Thorkil the Tall coming to England to revenge a slain brother.[32] Later in the year came another fleet under the leadership of Heming, Thorkil's brother, and Eilif.[33] The saga tells us that, when the corps of 'thingamen' were established in London and Slesswick, Eilif and Heming were in command.[34] There probably were such bands, but most likely they were in Æthelred's service;[35] for in 1011 that king purchased peace and Thorkil became his man.[36] It is reasonable to suppose that Heming, the chief at Slesswick, followed his brother's example. The saga tells us that after Sweyn's death the English plotted a massacre of the two garrisons, which in great part

---

[29] *Jomsvikingasaga*, 24. There were several other interesting regulations, but the ones given are the most significant. Whether these vikings originated them may well be doubted. I am inclined to believe that we have in them a statement of the rules governing the ideal comitatus. As the pirates at Jom composed perhaps the greatest comitatus ever organized in the North, it is reasonable to suppose that these laws were in force there; and that later tradition should also ascribe their authorship to the Jomburg chiefs is not strange.

[30] Women were admitted to the fortress 'two nights or three, and the men were also at times absent longer than the law permitted.' *Jomsvikingasaga*, 34.

[31] According to Munch (*N. F. H.*, I, 2, 104) this battle was fought in 985–86. Storm in his edition of Snorre's history (*Olaf Tryggvesson's Saga*, 35) dates it 994.

[32] *Gesta Regis Cnutonis*, I, 2: ...ut fratrem suum inibi interfectum ulcisceretur. Cf. the Jomburg laws.

[33] *Flor. Wig.*, I, 160–61 (1009): ....exinde, mense Augusto, alia classis Danorum innumerabilis, cui praeerant duces Hemingus et Eglafus....

[34] *Jomsvikingasaga*, 50. Slesswick has not been definitely located.

[35] The term 'Thingamen' (serving-men?) may have arisen at this time and from this service.

[36] *A.-S. Chron.*, 1012 (1011?): ða bugon to þam cyninge of þam here XLV scipa.... Thorkil is found acting with Æthelred the next year. *Ibid.*, 1013.

succeeded.[37] Heming was killed, but Eilif escaped. Thorkil deserted Æthelred about this time,[38] perhaps because he now had another brother to revenge.[39] The vikings in England gathered about young King Cnut.

In the account of the massacre the saga relates that Thord,[40] a member of the Danish garrison at London, went out one day 'to the house of the woman who followed him.'[41] Her home was outside the fortress—*utan borgar*—; she was evidently an English woman, at any rate she knew the plans of the English. Anxious to save her lover, she endeavored to induce him to remain with her till morning; failing in this, she revealed to him what her countrymen were plotting. From this it would seem that the London corps was governed by Jomburg laws.[42]

But while admitting the presence of Jomvikings in Cnut's forces and higher councils when he finally got control of all England, I cannot subscribe to Munch's opinion that the corps of house-carles was simply the Jomburg remnant somewhat transformed.[43] If the sagas are correct there could not have been much of a remnant after the great massacre of 1015. And what of that splendid army that Cnut and Thorkil led to England that same year? 'In that host there was neither slave nor freedman, nor any one weak with old age; all were nobles, all vigorous with the strength of complete manhood, fit for all manner of battle, and so speedy that they despised the fleetness of cavalry.[44]

---

[37] *Jomsvikingasaga*, 51. This must have occurred about 1015. The English sources are silent on this point, still, the story seems to have some foundation. Heming disappears from English history about this time, while Eilif (Eglaf) is found witnessing charters a decade later. See K. C. D., No. 728. The massacre, if it occurred, serves to explain not only Thorkil's defection but also the great efforts put forth by the Danes to conquer England once for all. For a fuller form of this argument see Napier and Stevenson, *Crawford Collection of Charters*, 139–42.

[38] *Gesta Cnutonis*, I, 2. He came to Denmark with nine ships.

[39] Cf. Jomburg laws.

[40] The editors of the *Crawford Collection of Charters* (148) suggest the possibility that this person may have been the one who later signed a charter as staller. (149.)

[41] *Jomsvikingasaga*, 51: 7da dag jola gekk Þorðr utan borgar til husa konu þeirrar er honum fylgði.... The Icelandic idiom implies a mistress, not a wife.

[42] It will be remembered that these laws required that all news be reported first to the chief; that members of the corps should not be absent for more than a definite period; that women should be kept outside the fortress.

[43] N. F. H., I, 2, 473.

[44] *Gesta Cnutonis*, II, 4.

The author of this *Encomium*[45] also describes the splendor of the ships and the armament. He is, indeed, not to be taken too seriously; but Cnut no doubt led a valiant, well-equipped host. It is no doubt true that Danes and Jomvikings formed the larger part of Cnut's guard, as finally organized,[46] but by no means the whole. According to Saxo the warriors differed much in race, language and character.[47] The sagas bear similar testimony.[48] That the idea of forming such an organization should have been borrowed from Jom is also very improbable: more likely it was derived from the early court of Norway where a similar guard seems to have existed at least a century before the pirate-guild on the Oder was formed. The corps of house-carles was apparently not only a royal guard but also a standing army to occupy and defend the realm,[49] and keep the new subjects in awe and obedience. Such a force existed at the Norwegian court perhaps as early as the ninth century. In Hornklofi's Ravensong the valkyrie asks: "How does the generous prince deal with the men of feats of renown *that guard his land?*" The raven replies: "They are well cared for, the warriors that cast dice in *Harold's court*. They are endowed with wealth and with fair swords, with the ore of the Huns, and with maids from the east."[50] Hornklofi was Harold Fairhair's minstrel. That king was also a conqueror: his realm had been consolidated only after ten years of struggle.[51] The royal guard *par excellence* was the king's 'bear-sarks,' or 'wolf-coats' as the poet calls them. These were the king's select champions,[52] warriors in whom the *furor athleticus*[53] was exceptionally strong.

---

[45] The *Gesta Cnutonis* is also known as the *Encomium Emmae*.
[46] Traill, *Social England*, I, 135: The enlistment of a number of the banished sea-rovers of Jom under Thurcytel the Tall was the nucleus of the force of housecarles. (F. Y. Powell.)
[47] P. 352. Saxo also tells of a Slavic prince who joined Cnut's household. Cf. Kemble, *Sax. in Eng.*, II, 120; Freeman, *N. C.*, I, 497.
[48] But the sagas add that the majority were Northmen: "oc mest af danscri tungo." *Morkinskinna*, 111.
[49] Freeman, *N. C.*, I, 498: They were a standing army in days when a standing army was a new thing. See also Kemble, *Sax. in Eng.*, II, 118-119; Green, *Conqu. of Eng.*, 414-15; Ramsay, *Found. of Eng.*, I, 414.
[50] *C. P. B.*, I, 256-57. (Vigfusson's translation. The italics are mine.)
[51] The dates usually given are 860-70.
[52] *C. P. B.*, I, 257: Wolfcoats they call them, that bear bloody targets in battle, that redden their spear-heads when they come into fight, when they are at work together. (Vigfusson's translation.)
[53] See Cleasby and Vigfusson, *Icelandic Dictionary*, Berserkr.

They guarded the forecastle of the king's ship, standing just behind the keepers of the royal standard.[54] Some of the sagas give twelve as the number of these wolf-coats, Egil's saga being the most explicit on this point.[55] Christianity did not look with favor on the bear-sark, and for that reason, perhaps, we find no trace of such select warriors among the house-carles. But otherwise the guard of 'thingamen' recalls Harold's Norwegian 'hird.' The wolf-coats and their associates were carefully selected;[56] they guarded the realm as well as the king's person; they were in a sense mercenaries.

As to the time when the royal guard was established in England the sources do not agree. Several of the sagas assume its existence before the death of Sweyn (1014).[57] The *Knytlingasaga* states that it was formed immediately after his death by the Danish chiefs then in England.[58] But the chronology of the sagas is not to be trusted. It seems probable, however, that the term 'thingamen' came into use during the wars with Æthelred, for we find that in Thorrod's praise of Earl Erik the men who followed the earl against Ulfcytel are alluded to as 'thingamen.'[59] Sveno and Saxo hold that Cnut selected the men, organized the corps and promulgated the guild-law. This is the view generally accepted.

According to Sveno, Cnut's army contained men of all degrees of bravery, nobility and wealth. The king proclaimed that only those would be admitted to his chosen guard who bore two-edged swords with hilts inlaid with gold.[60] He tells us that the wealthy warriors made such haste to procure properly ornamented swords, that the sound of the sword-smith's hammer was heard all through the land.[61] Thus the guard was made up wholly of

---

[54] Snorre, *Harold Fairhair's Saga*, 9.
[55] C. 9: En berserker kouungs xij voro i soxum.
[56] *C. P. B.*, I, 257: The wise king, I trow, will only enrol men of high renown among them that smite on the shield. (Vigfusson's translation.) This is said particularly of the bear-sarks, but the regular guardsmen are also spoken of as "men of feats of renown." (256.)
[57] *Jomsvikingasaga*, 50: Sveinn konungr setti þingamamannalið i tveim stö- .... The *Saga of Saint Olaf* (9) assumes the existence of the thingamannalith before 1009, perhaps as early as 1002.
[58] C. 7.
[59] *C. P. B.*, II, 105. Erik assisted Cnut in his invasion of England. He was made earl of Northumberland in 1016. See *Crawford Collection of Charters*, 144-48.
[60] Sveno, *Lex Castrensis*, 2. (S. R. D., III, 144.)
[61] *Ibid.*

such as could add splendor to the royal retinue.[62] It has been thought that this selection was made in 1018.[63] It could hardly have been later, as in that year Cnut sent his fleet back to Denmark, retaining only forty ships.[64] The guard existed in 1023; Osbern reports that a great multitude of house-carles were present at the translation of Saint Elphege's remains in that year.[65] An exact date cannot be fixed; it is also possible that the corps was to some extent a growth.

The laws governing Cnut's military household may be summarized as follows from Sveno's *Lex Castrensis:* The house-carles should be seated at the king's tables according to their eminence in warfare, priority of service or nobility of birth.[66] To be removed to a lower place was counted a disgrace.[67] In addition to daily fare and entertainment the warriors received wages;[68] according to Saxo these were paid each month.[69] The bond of service was not permanent but could be dissolved on New Year's Day only.[70] All quarrels were to be decided on the oaths of two house-carles in the gemot of the corps, the *Huskarlesteffne,* where the king was also to be present.[71] Members guilty of minor offences, such as not caring properly for the horse of a fellow-guardsman, were given lower places at the king's tables.[72] If any one should have been thrice convicted of such misdeeds, he was to be given the last and lowest place at the tables, where no one was to communicate with him in any way; the feasters might, however, throw bones at him with impunity.[73] In controversies

---

[62] Saxo (351) appears to think that personal bravery more particularly characterized the house-carles: "Jamque frequens ad Kanutum miles defluxerat, animis quam impensis onerosior. Plerisque enim amplior uirium quam morum grauitas inerat...."

[63] Such is the view of Steenstrup (*Danelag,* 138) and Freeman (*N. C.,* I, 297). Ramsay (*Found. of Eng.,* I, 414) holds that "the institution is carried back to the time when Thurkill's fleet was taken permanently into Æthelred's pay in 1014."

[64] *A.-S. Chron.,* 1018.

[65] Wharton's *Anglia Sacra,* II, 146: Divisus ergo a Rege Archiepiscopus cum ingenti Huscarlium turba praecedentes subsequitur. On the credibility of Osbern's account see Hardy, *Catalogue of British History,* I, 622.

[66] Sveno, *Lex Castrensis,* 5.

[67] *Ibid.*

[68] *Ibid.,* 6.

[69] *Saxo,* 351.

[70] Sveno, *Lex Castrensis,* 7.

[71] *Ibid.,* 8: ...in colloquio quod dicitur Huskarlesteffne...

[72] *Ibid.,* 5.

[73] *Ibid.*

160   BULLETIN OF THE UNIVERSITY OF WISCONSIN.

over lands and plunder the oaths of six house-carles were required, the six to be selected by lot from the division to which the accused belonged; but the power to decide still lay with the gemot.[74] Whoever should slay a comrade should lose his head or be driven into exile;[75] the Danish text says, 'he shall be driven off the king's estates with nithing's word, and shall be exiled from every land under Cnut's rule.'[76] *Crimen majestatis,* or treason, was to be punished by death and the confiscation of all the criminal's property.[77]

These regulations were put into their present form four or five generations after their presumptive origin. We cannot, therefore, accept them as evidence without further investigation as to what extent they are to be credited, if they are to be credited at all.[78] It should be observed first of all that the house-carles in Sveno's law are the house-carles of the king of Denmark. In the twelfth century there seems to have existed at the Danish court a military guild whose traditions went back to the elder Cnut.[79] Scandinavian investigators apparently agree that by the end of the twelfth century, when the *Lex Castrensis* was put into writing, the corps had ceased to exist as a guard.[80] But Sveno tells us that, in the days of King Nicholas (1103-34), Christiernus, his own paternal grandfather, belonged to the guild and was tried for the murder of a fellow house-carle.[81] There seems to

---

[74] Sveno, *Lex Castrensis,* 9.
[75] *Ibid.,* 10.
[76] *S. R. D.,* III, 162: ...tha skal han wrakas aff konungs garthe meth nithings orth, oc fly al land, ther Knut war konung lwer. Cf. *Lex Castrensis,* 10: ...cum proboso nuncupationis vocabulo, id est nithingsorth, ejectus abscederet.
[77] Sveno, *Lex Castrensis,* 14.
[78] The attitude of historians toward this work has been various. Danish investigators usually accept it without question, as do also Lappenberg (*Hist. of Eng.,* II, 247-48), Kemble (*Sax. in Eng.,* II, 119 ff.) and Ramsay (*Found. of Eng.,* I, 413). Freeman, on the other hand, has his doubts: "That Cnut did organize strict laws for the government of the force there is no reason to doubt; but I confess that in the Leges Castrenses, as we have them, there is much that has a mythical sound." *N. C.,* I, 497.
[79] Absalom's authority was the king himself. It is Absalom's work that Sveno claims to have translated.
[80] It is generally thought that the guard had developed into a new nobility, that the members no longer resided at court, and that a desire to know the obligations of these new aristocrats to their lord was responsible for Absalom's compilation.
[81] Sveno, *Lex Castrensis,* 11. This grandfather was a man of prominence; two of his brothers were bishops and two others were "proceres."

be no reason to doubt this statement, as on this matter the author ought to be well informed. We may safely conclude that the guard existed in Nicholas' day and that its origin belongs to some earlier date. The four preceding reigns were brief and turbulent;[82] it is not likely that such an institution as the one we are considering could have arisen in that period. The Danish sources assume that the guard existed in the earliest of these reigns, that of Harold (1076–80) and certain changes in its laws are attributed to him.[83] Sweyn Ulfsson, the father of these five kings and a nephew of the great Cnut, was an able and vigorous monarch. His reign was comparatively long (1047–76), and, if the corps described by Sveno in the *Lex Castrensis* is a purely Danish institution, it probably originated while he was king. He may have found the guild already organized in Denmark, or he may have formed it along English lines with warriors who had served in Cnut's guard as a nucleus.[84] It seems reasonable to suppose that the organization of house-carles in Denmark was, in a sense, a continuation of the great English corps.

It will not do to insist that Sveno and Saxo are correct in every detail as to the laws proclaimed by Cnut; during the intervening period certain changes had been made, several of which Sveno indicates.[85] But, if the *Lex Castrensis* is read in the light of the earlier sources, I believe it will be found that on the more important points, the origin of the corps, its membership and its corporate nature especially as revealed in its judicial authority and organization, Sveno's account may be accepted as fairly reliable. It may also be found that the 'law' is not wholly new,

---

[82] Harold, 1076–80; Saint Cnut, 1080–86; Olaf, 1086–95; Erik, 1095–1103.

[83] See Holberg, *Dansk Rigslovgivning*, 4 ff. But the evidence for Harold's emendations are by no means conclusive.

[84] The restoration of the old royal line in England doubtless caused many Northmen to return to Denmark. Cf. *A.-S. Chron.*, 1047. Sweyn himself probably served in England under Harthacnut. His brother Osbern was in England till he was expelled. See *Adamus*, III, 13. Sveno (11) speaks of an old warrior, Bo Hethinsson, at one time a house-carle at Cnut's court, who was called on in the days of King Nicholas to declare the ancient customs of the guild in the case of murder. The story is improbable. If Bo served in Cnut's guard he would be extremely aged at the time indicated. Cf. Freeman, *N. C.*, I, 498.

[85] Such as substituting fines for capital punishment. *Lex Castrensis*, 12. Cf. *Saxo*, 356. For the probable later additions to Cnut's guild-law see Holberg, *Dansk Rigslovgivning*, 37.

but is to a great extent a statement of old household customs common to the North and older than the power of Cnut.[86]

The manner in which Cnut selected his men must have been to some extent an innovation. It seems to have been customary for the Scandinavian king to give a sword to the one who entered his service.[87] If the henchman was to be signally honored, the pledge would be a splendid blade with a gold-mounted hilt.[88] It will readily be seen that if the English guard was as large as has been represented to us,—three thousand men or more—the king would be put to great expense. But if each house-carle furnished his own sword, not only would the royal treasury be spared, but Cnut would also secure a guard drawn largely from the nobler and wealthier classes. The statement that a house-carle might leave his lord's service needs no comment. From numerous passages in the Norse laws and sagas it is evident that the relationship need not be permanent.[89] The further statement that Cnut released his men on New Year's eve only must be considered in connection with the fact that on this, the seventh day of the Christmas festival, it was customary for the Norse king to pay his house-carles their lawful wages,[90] to honor the more worthy ones with gifts and perhaps to make certain changes in the personnel of the guard.[91] The custom seems to be at least

---

[86] Ramsay (*Found. of Eng.*, I, 413) also looks on the Lex Castrensis as an ancient code, but apparently for a priori reasons only.

[87] When Sighvat the Poet entered Saint Olaf's guard (ca. 1016) he composed a poem of which the following fragment has come down to us: "I willingly received the sword from thee, king, nor shall I ever repent it. We have both made a good bargain; thou hast got a good house-carle and I have got a good liege-lord." *C. P. B.*, II, 149. (Vigfusson's translation.)

[88] The sword that Sighvat received seems to have been of such a character. He says in speaking of his pilgrimage: "War-weary I left the gold-wound battle-rod, which the king gave me.... I laid down the silver-hilted weapons and took up the consecrated staff. *Ibid.*, 143. (Vigfusson's translation.) Cf. *Ibid.*, 246.

[89] In Norway the duties of the house-carles ceased with the king's death. Violations of the court law were punished by expulsion. *Norges gamle Love*, II, 399, 435 ff.

[90] Keyser, *Efterladte-Skrifter*, II, 87.

[91] As the court was a law-bound guild of which the king was only a member, though a powerful one, no one could obtain membership except by consent of the house-carles. It was practically impossible to consult the whole guard at any other time than at the great festivals. It was, however, not always necessary to consult all. The 'Court law' of the thirteenth century speaks of this as an old custom: 'they shall ask admission to membership according to old custom:' "sem forn er siðr til." *Norges gamle Love*, II, 439. Cf. *ibid.*, 422.

as old as the time of Saint Olaf.[92] We are told that the king provided entertainment for his men, but we need not take this to mean that the house-carles always dined in the king's presence. It was customary for the Norse king to eat and drink with his assembled guard at certain great festivals only.[93] The house-carles were then seated according to rank[94] and to be moved to a lower place was doubtless counted great dishonor. In earlier days the henchmen seem to have enjoyed great freedom at these banquets.[95]

That the Norse house-carles received regular wages in the twelfth century is clear;[96] but what the custom was in the days of Olaf and Cnut, we do not know. Still, Sveno's statement that the English house-carles were mercenaries is doubtless correct. The saga calls them *málamenn,* men receiving wages.[97] Florence of Worcester speaks of them as *solidarii*[98] and William of Malmesbury calls them *stipendiarii.*[99] In addition to wages the chiefs evidently received landed estates. Of charters granting such favors to house-carles but few are extant;[1] most of our evidence on this point comes from Domesday. Thirty-three house-carles are mentioned in William's survey as holding lands prior to the

---

[92] Snorre tells us of a gift given to Sighvat on a New Year's eve. *St. Olaf's Saga,* 172: 'He had, as he was accustomed to do, collected his valuables to distribute them as gifts of friendship on the eighth eve of Christmas.' Then quoth Sighvat (*C. P. B.,* II, 150): 'Swords gold-mounted are standing there; I would gladly take it, if thou wouldst give me any one of them; I have served thee long.'

[93] The 'guests' dined with the king at Christmas and Easter only. *Speculum Regale,* 259.

[94] *Norges gamle Love,* II, 143.

[95] *C. P. B.,* II, 149. Sighvat, when the court was crowded: "Ye are thronging about the good young king, and elbow each other so that I cannot get a word from Olaf." (Vigfusson's translation.) It should be added that the rude table-manners described by Sveno had evidently disappeared almost entirely by the time the Lex Castrensis was written. See *Speculum Regale,* 241 ff.

[96] *Ibid.,* 257 ff.

[97] *Knytlingasaga,* 7.

[98] I, 204.

[99] *Gesta Regum,* I, 282. In speaking of the English at Hastings.

[1] *K. C. D.,* No. 1318. Cnut grants "VII terrae mansas...meo fideli ministro ....Boui." To this is added a rubric in Anglo-Saxon in which Bovi is called house-carle.

Ibid., No. 843. Edward confirms a grant to Westminster "swa full and swa forð swa ðurstan min huskarll hit furmest of me heold."

Ibid., No. 871. Edward confirms the right of Urk his house-carle to what wreckage might strand on his shore.

Conquest.[2] Usually it is stated that the holder was King Edward's house-carle.[3] In only one instance does a house-carle holding land in Edward's reign hold the same estate in William's day.[4] Nearly all the lands are located in the southern shires, more than half being in the counties of Middlesex, Buckingham and Hertford. No house-carle seems to have acquired lands in the old Danelaw.[5] It has been observed by Steenstrup that the estates held by house-carles are of rather moderate sizes,[6] ranging from half a hide to fifteen hides,[7] the average being about four. But this writer overlooks the fact that great landed wealth in those days consisted less in large manors than in a number of estates sometimes contiguous, but freqently not.[8] However, it is by no means likely that all the house-carles received lands or that those who were thus rewarded were given large estates.

---

[2] Summary by counties.
Buckingham, 7. I, 146b, 147, 149, 152, 152b.
Hertford, 5 (including one of Leofwine's). I, 136b, 138, 138b, 140, 140b.
Middlesex, 5 (including one of Harold's). I, 129, 130, 130b.
Gloucester, 3. I, 164, 167.
Suffolk, 3 (not king's house-carles). II, 441b, 442.
Bedford, 2 (including one of Algar's). I, 213, 216, 217.
Cambridge, 2 (including one of Wallef's). I, 195, 202.
Somerset, 2. I, 95, 99.
Surrey, 2. I, 36.
Essex, 1. II, 59 (Harold's house-carle).
Sussex, 1. I, 17.
Berks. Rex Edwardus habuit XV acras in quibus manebant huscarles. I, 56.
Dorset. In Dorecestre T. R. E. erant CLXXII domus. Hae pro omni servitio regis se defendabant et geldabant pro X hidis, Scilicet ad opus Huscarlium unam markam argenti..I, 75. (Similar payments were due from Brideport, Shaftesbury and Warham.
See also Steenstrup, *Danelag*, 151-53, where a somewhat similar table is found. The figures given above are, however, somewhat fuller than those of Steenstrup, who seems to have overlooked several entries.

[3] Several of those referred to in the table above were earls' house-carles and it is possible that a few of the remaining ones may have borne the title as a proper name. But in all such cases it is likely that the bearer at one time had belonged to the guard.

[4] I, 99: Huscarle tenet unam virgam terrae quam ipsemet tenebat T. R. E.

[5] It is true that we have been able to locate but a small number of such estates, but it is also true that titles are often omitted in the survey, especially in the case of Edward's tenants. Some of the house-carles may have been classed with the thegns. Thus we have Burcardus Huscarle (I, 146b) and Burcardus teignus (I, 147). See also I, 152b, 217, 130b, 138, Alli and Achi.

[6] *Danelag*, 153.

[7] *Domesday*, I, 130: [Stanwelle, 15 hides.] Hoc manerium tenuit Azor Huscarle R. E....

[8] Azor Huscarl had a manor of 15 hides in Middlesex (*ibid.*, I, 130); but other lands in the same county belonged to an Azor whose title is not given. As this name is not a common one, it is possible that the same person is meant in all cases. An Azor Huscarl also held lands in Buckingham. *Ibid.*, I, 152b.

According to the *Lex Castrensis* Cnut's guard was an organized guild with a code of laws defining the rights and duties of the members and a house-carle-gemot—*huskarlesteffne*—by which these laws were applied. On this point also the Norse parallel is both interesting and instructive. In the household of the Norwegian king as early as the twelfth century and perhaps earlier, the *hirþstefna*, or assembly of the henchmen, was the ruling authority in all matters affecting the membership. It passed on the admission of new members, tried offences and expelled or otherwise punished the guilty. In theory at least, its power exceeded that of the king who was merely a member of the guild.[9]

Returning to the subject of Cnut's guard, we shall find that Sveno's statement as to its corporate nature is supported by the best contemporary source, the Anglo-Saxon Chronicle. Certain events recorded in that document receive an added significance when studied in the light of the *Lex Castrensis*. During the reign of Edward the Confessor, Swegen, the son of Godwin, became implicated in a revolt. He fled, but later returned and slew Beorn, a nephew of Cnut and a brother of Sweyn, then king of Denmark. 'And the king and all the *here* declared Swegen a nithing,' says the Chronicler.[10] When we consider the crime, the court and the verdict, it becomes clear that we have here a formal act of the house-carle-gemot.[11] *Here*, in Anglo-Saxon, is usually, perhaps always, applied to an alien, generally a Danish host,[12] the native levy being known as *fierd* or *fyrd*. It will be remembered that, according to Sveno's statement of the 'court-law,' any one who was accused of slaying a fellow-housecarle should be tried by the house-carle-gemot and if guilty should be exiled and given the 'nithing-name.' Beorn must have been one of the chiefs of the royal guard, else we should look for

---

[9] For the organization of the Norwegian hirð see Keyser, *Efterladte Skrifter*, II, 77 ff.

[10] *A.-S. Chron.*, 1049 : And se cing þa and eall here cwædon Swegen for niðing.

[11] Freeman (*N. C.*, II, 67–68) sees in this the action of "a military gemot." The *here* he thinks "consisted of the king's *Comitatus* of both kinds, of the thegns bound to him by the older and more honorable tie, and also of the standing force of the House-carles, or at any rate of their officers." But the historian of the Conquest can find no other instance of such a "military gemot" in English history and has to content himself with references to Tacitus' Germania and to his own study of Greek federations (67, note).

[12] Bosworth–Toller, *Anglo-Saxon Dictionary*, *Here*: It is the word which in the Chronicle is always used for the Danish force in England, while the English troops are always the *fyrd*.

action on the part of the *witan* and not of the 'host.' *Morkinskinna*, a collection of Norse sagas, declares that such was the case: 'and this was the beginning of the conversation between Asmund and Sweyn the king, that Sweyn Godwin's son had slain Beorn his father in the thingamannalith.'[13] The term nithing is Norse both in origin and content. The group of crimes known to the Northmen as nithing-deeds was not so regarded by the Anglo-Saxons.[14]

Further evidence for the existence of such a gemot is found in the entries of the Chronicle recording the banishment of Godwin and his family (1051). In refusing to punish the citizens of Dover as the king had ordered, the great earl practically assumed the attitude of a rebel. Forces were gathered on both sides; in speaking of these the Chronicle uses the term *fierd*.[15] In the hope, however, of reaching a peaceful settlement of the whole matter, the king called the *witan* to meet in gemot at London, at the same time also ordering out the *here*.[16] Manuscript D calls this meeting a *stefna*,[17] a term which recalls the *Huskarlesteffne* of the *Lex Castrensis* and the *Hirþstefna* of the Norse laws. The two phrases, *bannan ut here* and *setton stefna ut to Lundene,* probably mean that the house-carles were called to meet in formal gemot. At this meeting Swegen was outlawed a second time.[18] Godwin's case came next. 'But it was not agreeable to him [Godwin] to heed the summons of the king and the *here* that was with him; so he left during the night. And the king had a *witenagemot* the next morning and declared him an outlaw, and all the *here* [outlawed] him [Godwin] and all his sons.'[19]

---

[13] 86: ... at Sveln Guþina son hafþl vegit Biornu favþur hans i þingamanna liþi vestr a Englandl.

[14] In this I follow Steenstrup (*Danelag,* 27). This author further contends that the word did not appear in England before Danish times.

[15] MS. D., 1052.

[16] MS. E., 1048: ða geræbde se cyning and his witan þæt man sceolde oðre syðan habban ealra gewitena gemot on Lundene to hærfestes emnlhte and het se cyning bannan ut here.....

[17] MS. D., 1052: ...and setton stefna ut to Lundene. Steenstrup (*Danelag,* 182-83) places stefna among the Norse terms that crept into the Old English vocabulary during this period. Cf. Bosworth-Toller, *Anglo-Saxon Dictionary,* stefnian.

[18] Swegen had been restored to his rights in 1050 according to *Chron.* C.

[19] *A.-S. Chron.,* 1052, Ms. D.: And man utlagode ða Swægn eorl his oðerne sunu. Þa ne onhagode him to cumenne to wiðermale ongean þone cyng and agean þone here þe him mid wæs: for ða on niht awæg. And se cyng hæfde þæs on morgen witenagemot anu cwæð hine utlage and eall here hine and ealle his suna.

We are distinctly told that before the trial Godwin was summoned to make his defense before the king and the *here*, and that the latter body also acted when he was finally exiled. Everything considered, it is hard to escape the conclusion that the *here* was the corps of house-carles[20] and that this body was an organization with extensive jurisdiction over its own membership—a guild such as Sveno and Saxo describe.

But while the general constitution of the guild was unquestionably Norse in character, the judicial process of the housecarle-gemot seems to have been derived from non-Germanic sources, more particularly from canon law, either directly or indirectly through Anglo-Saxon legislation.[21] Of the legal principles that seem to have had an Old English origin, the most noteworthy is the employment of the 'fore-oath:' the accuser was required to swear that in presenting his charges he was innocent of all guile and was not moved by hatred or evil intent.[22]

Of the guild as a military organization we know very little. According to Sveno the corps was limited to three thousand men;[23] Saxo gives six thousand as the number.[24] While neither of these writers can be relied on in matters of detail like this, it is likely that Sveno's statement is very near the truth.[25] The

---

[20] If this explanation of the events of 1049 and 1051 has been proposed before, it has escaped my notice. Cf. Freeman, *N. C.*, II, 406: "I was puzzled fifteen years back at finding what appeared in one account as an Assembly of the Witan, described in the other as a gathering of armies. I did not then so well understand as I do now that in those days an army and a Witenagemot were very nearly the same thing." See also Kemble (*Sax. in Eng.*, II, 231) who also holds that Godwin was exiled by the witan.

[21] On this point I accept Holberg's conclusions in his comparative study of the Lex Castrensis and other legal systems of the same age, and from which I translate the following: 'We find in this process the same mixture of Roman and Germanic law that is again found in canon law; and there is not a single point that does not find its prototype in the process which in those days was employed by state and church in England and in France. In other words: there is in the process of the Lex Castrensis no trace of any application of Norse or Danish legal principles.' *Dansk Rigslovgivning*, 79-80. Holberg uses Saxo's account as the more specific on this point.

[22] *Saxo*, 354. Cf. Schmid, *Gesetze*, 578, where the fore-oath (for-að) is discussed and references given to the laws of Æthelstan and Cnut. See also Holberg, *Dansk Rigslovgivning*, 48.

[23] *Lex Castrensis*, 2: Cujus summa tria millia militum selectorum explevit.

[24] P. 351: Ceterum Kanutus, tria prememorata regna circuiens, clientelam suam, sex millum numerum explentem, sexaginta nauigiis...distinxit.

[25] Saxo tells us they were distributed among sixty ships. But one hundred to an eleventh century ship seems a rather high average. Harold Hardrada's great Dragon, perhaps the one in which he sailed to England in 1066, had seventy oars. This ship was, however, exceptionally large. See *C. P. B.*, II, 209.

Lex Castrensis implies that all were gathered about the king, but such could hardly have been the case. Saxo expressly denies it: in the summer they were abroad guarding the realm; in the winter they were quartered throughout the kingdom.[26] Saxo also tells us that a house-carle might have a home of his own.[27] There would be nothing strange about such an arrangement, but we cannot know to what extent the author is reading later Danish conditions back into English history. It appears from Sveno's 'law' that the corps was divided into four divisions and that these were again divided into smaller troops;[28] but on this question the contemporary sources are silent.[29]

As to the final fate of the guild, three different views have been advanced. Ramsay holds that the last house-carle was dismissed in 1051.[30] Munch reaches the same conclusion, but believes the guild was revived by Harold.[31] Nearly all others who have written on the subject believe that it existed without interruption till 1066.[32] This diversity of opinion arises from the use of the term *litsmen* in the Anglo-Saxon Chronicle. If the word is Old English, it should mean sailor[33] and no difficulties will arise. If the term is of Norse origin it may mean warrior[34] and it would be possible to conclude that the entry recording the dismissal of 'all the *litsmen*'[35] refers to the house-carles. But the Chronicle also

---

The sagas speak of ships of all sizes, from such as hold twenty to others holding more than two hundred men. I should say that sixty would be a fair average. At that rate, if we connect the corps of house-carles with the forty ships that Cnut retained in 1018, it would number about 2,400 men, while Saxo's sixty ships would bring it up to 3,600. There is a fairly satisfactory discussion of this question in Ramsay, *Found. of Eng.*, I, 415–16.

[26] P. 351: Eandem, estate pro tuendo imperio excubantem, hyeme contuberniis discretam alere consueuit.

[27] If a house-carle was summoned to appear at the gemot, notice was served once at his home and twice at his place at the king's tables; if he had no home, thrice at the king's tables. See *Saxo*, 354.

[28] *Lex Castrensis*, 9. Cf. Steenstrup, *Danelag*, 141–46.

[29] Kemble suggests (*Sax. in Eng.*, II, 122) that the stallers may have commanded the house-carles. As we found that there were several of these officials at the same time, three perhaps, it seems reasonable to assume that the corps was divided in England as it was in Denmark, one staller commanding each division. But this is mere conjecture and must be treated as such.

[30] *Found. of Eng.*, I, 450–51.

[31] *N. F. H.*, II, 169, 320.

[32] Such is the opinion of Freeman (*N. C.*, III, 499), York Powell (*Social England*, I, 135) and Steenstrup (*Danelag*, 140).

[33] Bosworth-Toller, *Anglo-Saxon Dictionary*, Lidmann.

[34] It is thus used by one of the scalds in speaking of the Norse forces at Stamford Bridge. *Morkinskinna*, 119. *C. P. B.*, II, 193.

[35] *A.-S. Chron.*, 1050. MS. C.: .... þæs ylcan geares he sette ealle þa litsmen of male.

tells of nine ships of *litsmen* that were dismissed the year before: 'and they left the country with ships and with everything.'[36] The language here used would point to a naval force rather than to a land force such as we should expect the royal guard to be. Furthermore, it seems impossible that the Chronicler could have had the house-carles in mind, for we find these mentioned at a later period. The king's house-carles are referred to in connection with Earl Siward's invasion of Scotland in 1054.[37] Florence of Worcester, in his account of the Northumbrian rebellion of 1064, gives the names of two Danish house-carles.[38] That the corps existed in 1066 is hard to deny. William of Malmesbury tells us that Harold had scarcely any troops at Hastings but mercenaries: *stipendiarios et mercenarios milites.*[39] Snorre speaks of the 'thingamen' as fighting at Stamford Bridge.[40] Morkinskinna recounts the discussion among the Northmen when Harold's plan to aid Tostig became known: 'and there is also that troop called thingamen, which has been selected from various lands.... and they are the most valiant warriors, mighty and courageous, so that the prowess of one thingaman is considered equal to that of two of the best Northmen.'[41] This disgusted Ulf staller and he replied in extemporized verse: 'It is no use for the king's marshals to turn into the fore-castle, if two of us, lady, are to fly before one Thingman. I did not learn this in my youth.'[42] Evidently great apprehension did exist among the Northmen.[43] That the corps of house-carles was truly a valiant band was proved not only in the victory of Stamford Bridge but also in the defeat at Senlac.[44]

[36] 1049, MS. C.: ....on þyson ylcan geare Eadwerd cing scylode IX scypa of male; and hi .oron mid scypon mid eallon anweg...

[37] *A.-S. Chron.*, 1054: Ac his sunu Osbarn and his sweostor sunu Sihward and of hio huscarlum and eac þæs cynges wurdon þær ofslægene

[38] I, 223: Danicos huscarlas Amundum et Reavensvartum...

[39] *Gesta Regum*, I, 282: ....nam praeter stipendiarios et mercenarios milites, paucos admodum ex provincialibus habuit.

[40] *Harold Hardrada's Saga*, 94: Riddarar 20 riðu fram or þingamannaliði....

[41] P. 111.

[42] *C. P. B.*, II, 2.2. (Vigfusson's translation.)

[43] The king of Norway began preparations early in the spring before his English namesake (who was consecrated in January) could have proceeded very far with organizing a new force of house-carles. And had the corps been dissolved by Edward,' the fact would have been known at the Norwegian court, especially as Tostig was with the Norse king.

[44] No doubt there were individual house-carles who survived Senlac: but the organization evidently perished in that battle. House-carles are mentioned in

Before dismissing the subject it may be well to review briefly the history of the institution as it appears from the author's point of view. The guard of house-carles did not originate in England, nor was it first organized by King Cnut, it was a rather highly developed form of the Norse *comitatus* transplanted to English soil. In Norway we find such a corps as early as the ninth century; in England in the first quarter of the tenth; and in Denmark it had a vigorous existence a hundred years later. The traditions of the Danish court, however, refer the organization of the guild to the time of King Cnut, and the probabilities are that the corps in Denmark was at least as old as the English guild. Cnut's father, Sweyn, as overlord of Norway, certainly knew the customs of the Norwegian court, and he, too, may have had some sort of a military household. At least we know that there were warriors at all the courts in Scandinavia in that period, and that they were often, perhaps generally, called house-carles. It is therefore possible that the Danish conqueror brought such a corps with him when he invaded England, but if he did the guard was later enlarged by the admission of kindred elements: Jomvikings, Norse vassals and English warriors. This reorganization apparently occurred about the year 1018, and it seems likely that a guild-law governing the household was promulgated very soon afterwards. This was no doubt mainly a collection of older customs with such additions as circumstances demanded. That a *comitatus* of Scandinavian origin should have such a body of rules is not at all strange: the sagas of the next century have much to say of the laws that governed the conduct of the vikings. A runic inscription from about the year 500 also seems to indicate that the *comitatus* was a law-bound guild even at that early date. Furthermore we have the laws of the Norse court of the thirteenth century and these make specific reference to an older court-law. The house-carles were mercenaries in England as in Norway and in addition to wages, or what passed as wages, they appear to have enjoyed the privilege of dining in the royal presence, though perhaps only on certain festive occasions. The corps as an organized guild exercised its authority in the gemot of house-carles where the king was present, not as a master but as an influential member. Most likely the house-carles had to be

---

the Chronicle in connection with the uprising of 1070, but it will be observed that they were Danes and were found among the rebels.

consulted whenever the king proposed to admit new members to the guild; such at least was the case in Norway. The character of the household was mainly military, though not exclusively so: the Norwegian king could employ his house-carles in various administrative capacities, and we know that English house-carles were at one time employed in collecting royal revenues.[45] The membership was comparatively large, about three thousand in England, it seems, but if we consider Cnut's exceptional position this number is not unreasonably great. The Norwegian kings in the generation following Cnut's death had two hundred and forty house-carles of various grades at their court and many more elsewhere in the kingdom. Edward the Confessor continued the guard, but apparently reduced it materially. It appeared for the last time in organized force on the field of Senlac, where it perished fighting for Saxon kingship. In the North, however, the corresponding corps lived on for two or three centuries. In Denmark the guild developed into a new nobility; but in Norway we find the king's house-carles as late as the close of the thirteenth century still organized as a martial brotherhood and serving their royal master within the hall and without according to the laws of the guild.

---

[45] *Flor. Wig.*, I, 195: Hoc anno [1041]....Heardecanutus suos huscarlas misit per omnes regni sui provincias ad exigendum...tributum.

CHAPTER VIII.

THE LESSER OFFICIALS AND SERVANTS OF THE COURT.

The four high officers of the Germanic courts represented the various departments of the household service. The great officials were the chiefs in charge. Each of these divisions no doubt had its full quota of lesser officials and inferior servants, the number varying with the importance of the department and the splendor of the court. As to the titles, numbers and duties of these, the English sources are not very explicit, but information is not wholly wanting.

In Eadred's will there is mention of an official who seems to have been connected with the service of the seneschal, namely the king's steward. That the latter was considered much inferior to the former appears from the fact, that while the seneschal was given eighty mancuses, the steward received only thirty.[46] The title does not occur very often; the mention in Eadred's will is the earliest known. We read of an earl's steward at Bamborough in 1093,[47] and of William of Eu's steward who was hanged in 1096;[48] the latter is called *dapifer* by Florence.[49] And in the entry for 1120 the Chronicler makes this very significant statement: 'on that journey were drowned the two royal sons...and very many of the king's household, stewards and chamberlains and butlers....'[50] The fact that no seneschal is mentioned in the account naturally leads to the inference that steward was the Saxon word for *dapifer* in the twelfth century. Even in the

---

[46] Birch, *Cartul.*, No. 912: And ælcan gesettan stigweard þritig mancusa goldes.

[47] *A.-S. Chron.*, 1093: Hine sloh Moræl of Bæbbaburh, se wæs þæ eorles stiward and Melcolmes cinges godsib.

[48] *Ibid.*, 1096: And his stiward Willelm hatte...het se cyng on rode ahon.

[49] *Flor. Wig.*, II, 39.

[50] ...and swyðe manega of þæs cynges hired, stiwardas and burþenas and byrlas....

tenth the words must have meant very much the same, as a gloss of that period has *discoforus, discifer vel stiweard*.[51] But in this case there must have been some difference between popular usage and usage at court.[52] In the half century just before the Conquest the office seems to have become general all over the country, but its functions are in every case such as we should assign to the seneschal.[53] It seems evident that in monastic establishments and in the house-holds of the king's vassals the two titles were used without much discrimination, and that after the Conquest the steward took the seneschal's place at the royal court also, in much the same way as the marshal superseded the constable.[54] But such a development could hardly have been possible if the stewards did not have some connection with the service of the king's tables in the earlier period.

The word *stigweard* is a compound of *stig* (Mod. Eng. sty), an enclosure, or if need be a building, and *weard* (Mod. Eng. ward), a guardian. The steward was originally the guardian of the enclosure; so much is clear from the etymology. A service of this sort has an interesting parallel at the Norse court. The king of Norway in the twelfth century[55] had a group of household servants called 'guests,' **gestic**.[56] These were the outer guards of the royal establishment (the *hirþmenn* kept the inner guard), but they also served as spies in times of war and rode royal

[51] *Vocab.*, 223:7.
[52] See Eadred's will.
[53] In Leofgifu's will (*K. C. D.*, No. 931, undated but placed by Kemble late in the Saxon period) lands are given to three stewards, all servants of the testatrix. They cannot have been reeves, for a reeve is also remembered in the will. The stewards are placed well at the head among the different groups making up the household. In a body of guild rules from the same period (*ibid.*, No. 942) a steward occurs, plainly as one who has general over-sight over the hall and other property of the guild. His permission must be obtained before a member can bring in more than a certain number of men. He also appears as the legal representative of the guild. The duty of distributing the bequests in Bishop Ælfric's will (*ibid.*, No. 759, placed late in the Danish period by Kemble) seems to be assigned to the stewards who are supposed to know which of the servants are to be remembered: "and sela man mina cnihtas þa mina stiwardas witan XXXX punda."
In Ælfric's vocabulary stiweard is translated economus. *Vocab.*, 129:13. This title occurs in two charters (*K. C. D.*, Nos. 1006, 622); but it cannot be affirmed that a king's official is meant in either case. According to Du Cange, oeconomus was sometimes used in the feudal period for dapifer or seneschal.
[54] Stubbs, *C. H.*, I, 373-74; Luchaire, *Hist. des Inst. Mon.*, I, 172.
[55] The sagas place this institution as early as the beginning of the eleventh century.
[56] See Cleasby and Vigfusson, *Icelandic Dictionary*, Gestr.

errands generally. The number of guests was always exactly half that of *hirþmenn* and their wages were also half as great. Still earlier we find a similar institution in Wales. On the subject of the king's retinue, the Latin translation of the old laws reads in part as follows: *Licitum regis est habere XXX^a sex homines equitantes in commitatu suo, id est, XX^{ti}IIII^{or} officiales suos, et duodecim hospites preter familiam, et optimates, et pueros, et iocculatores, et pauperes.*[57] As in the Norse household, the number of the lower officials is just half that of the higher. Furthermore, *hospes* in its general significance, is equivalent to guest. The Welsh word is *gwestai* which the English translator derives from *gwesdva*, entertainment dues: "a term used for the provision or money-payment in lieu of it, due to the lord from the *uchelwyr* or free-holders."[58] The translator of the Welsh laws thinks the *gwestai* were "the persons who brought the *gwestva* or entertainment-dues from each *maenol* or manor to the lord."[59]

It is extremely probable that there were officials in Old England whose duties resembled those of the Welsh *gwestai*. The Anglo-Saxon king had a right to demand a certain amount of provisions from at least some of his subjects, the *feorm* or *firma unius noctis*.[60] These dues may have been collected by the stewards and in that case we can readily understand how the later importance and significance of stewardship might be attained. The Norse guests and the English stewards resemble each other, it seems, in being primarily guards, and in their rank in the household. The stewards and the *gwestai* both appear to have duties connected with the king's tables. The guests and the *gwestai* are alike in their titles, which in both cases are rendered *hospites* in Latin.[61] There is also the fact that in both house-

---

[57] *Ancient Laws of Wales*, 772. Cf. Seebohm,*Tribal System in Wales*, 163.
[58] *Ancient Laws of Wales*, Glossary.
[59] *Ibid.*, 4, note. On the subject of the probable relationship between the gwestai and the gestir, see also Steenstrup, *Danelag*, 124.
[60] In a Mercian charter from the close of the eighth century the grantee is released from all secular obligations to king or 'prince' "except in the matter of these dues, namely, for tue rent at Westbury two tuns full of clear ale, and a coomb full of mild ale, and a coomb full of Welsh ale, and VII oxen, and six wethers, and XL cheeses and VI 'lang þero' and thirty ambers of rye corn, four ambers of meal, contributions to the royal vill." K. C. D., No. 166. Thorpe, *Diplomatarium*, 39–40. Thorpe's translation. Cf. Seebohm, *Tribal Custom in Anglo-Saxon Law*, 431.
[61] The Norse may have originated in a misunderstanding of the Welsh.

holds these officials are exactly half as numerous as the higher officials. The parallels, however, though interesting and worthy of some consideration, are by no means complete: the results reached after the most careful comparison still belong to the field of conjecture. But, if all these institutions have a common origin, the probabilities are that it was English. The Saxon court was the oldest of the three and doubtless exerted a powerful influence over the other two.

The Old English king seems to have been a great lover of the chase and was well provided with fowlers and falconers. These servants we know mainly from the charters[62] and Domesday. All the *venatores regis* were, however, not connected with the chase: Ælfric in his Colloquy introduces us to a class of huntsmen whose occupation would scarcely be classed among the sports; their duties seem rather to have been to supply the king's tables with meats. Their methods were hardly noble, the net being a favorite instrument in the pursuit of their calling.[63] All the fruits of their labor belonged to the royal master.[64]

The king's *venator* seems to have paid no attention to birds; they belonged to the province of the falconer or *accipitrarius*.[65] This servant is mentioned as early as the middle of the ninth century, when we find the first traces of an extensive hunting service. When the king traveled about with hawks and dogs and horses, the burden of feeding these would fall on the locality where the party might chance to be. In two Mercian charters from this period a release from this obligation is included in the list of immunities.[66] In the Confessor's day, the king's huntsman

---

[62] In 956 Eadwig gave a mansa and a half 'to his beloved, faithful and most famous huntsman, Wulfric by name.' *K. C. D.*, No. 458. Æthelred in 987 gave three mansae and three perticae to his venator Leofwine. *Ibid.*, No. 658. Æthelstan Etheling willed a horse (or a herd of horses: stoð) to his stag-hunter (heah-deor-hunta). *Ibid.*, No. 722. These gifts were doubtless to the more favored among the huntsmen, perhaps to the chiefs of the service. There were also vills dedicated to the chase. Edward in 904 issued a charter from such a "villa venatoria." *Ibid.*, No. 1085.

[63] *Vocab.*, 92: Plecto mihi retia, et pono ea in loco apto, et instigo canes meos ut feras persequantur, usque quo peruenlunt ad retia improuise, et sic inretientur, et ego iugulo eos in retibus.

[64] *Ibid.*, 93: Ego do regi quicquid capio quia sum uenator eius.

[65] An auceps is referred to in Ælfric's *Colloquy* who used the falcon in his profession, though perhaps not generally. There is no evidence that he was anybody's fowler; bird-catching was his means of procuring a livelihood. *Vocab.*, 95.

[66] *K. C. D.*, No. 261, Berhtulf, 848: ...sit liberatum..illud monasterium.... a pastu accipitrorum meorum omnium quam etiam uenatorum omnium, uel a

and falconer were apparently the most important of the lesser officials at court. The *venator*, who a century before received only his daily fare and wear with an occasional 'horse or ring to encourage him in his art,'[67] was a feudal tenant in 1066.[68] It appears that several of these servants retained their holdings and perhaps also their offices even after the Conquest.[69] Their estates were usually small, from half a hide to two hides.

In Berhtulf's charter referred to above, there is also an allusion to the king's horse-thegns.[70] The term is an exceedingly general one; any person having the care of horses in some way or other would be a horse-thegn or *minister equorum*.[71] The dignity of this thegn evidently was in proportion to that of his master. The position of the royal hostlers would therefore be an eminently honorable one. Over them all there seems to have been a *summus minister equorum*, called, however, merely *hors-þegn* in Anglo-Saxon. We read of two such officials in the Chronicle: Ecgulf, who died in 897, and Wulfric, apparently his successor, who seems to have died later in the same year.[72] This official is not mentioned in Eadred's will, in fact, the only notice of such a court official is in the entries of the Chronicle just referred to. It was no doubt the office of the horse-thegn that later developed into the dignity of the marshalship.[73]

There is a servant alluded to in Ine's laws, the *horswealh*, who is generally supposed to have been connected with the service of

---

pastu equorum meorum, siue ministrorum eorum. Similarly, No. 278, Burhred, 855. Cf. Nos. 223, 224, Egbert.

[67] *Vocab.*, 93 : Uestit me bene et pascit, aliquando dat mihi equum, aut armillam, ut libentius artem mean exerceam.

[68] As the holder is nearly always a tenant in chief there can be little doubt that a king's venator or accipitrarius is meant, even where this is not explicitly stated.

[69] *Domesday*, I, 36b : Wlwi uenator tenet de rege Liteltone. Ipse tenuit de rege E. Tunc II hidas. *Ibid.*, I, 50b : Godvinus accipitrarius tenet de rege dimidiam hidam. Isdem tenuit de rege E. See also *ibid.*, I, 139b, 190b et passim.

[70] ...vel a pastu equorum meorum omnium siue ministrorum eorum. An earlier allusion to 'those who lead horses' is found in one of Egbert's grants. *K. C. D.*, No. 236.

[71] Mulio and agaso are translated horse-thegn. *Vocab.*, 33 :24, 119 :34, 356 :11, 440 :32. It is possible that the lowest order of stable servants were known as pabulatores or hors-hierdas. Hors-cniht was also a term used. Says Ælfric, '[Haman] led ᴍordecai...through the city as if he were his hors-cniht.' *Bibl. der ang. Prosa*, III, 99.

[72] It is also possible that they were colleagues.

[73] This subject has been discussed in part in connection with the stallership; see chapter VII. Cf. Stubbs, *C. H.*, I, 383 ; Round, The Officers of Edward the Confessor : *Eng. Hist. Rev.*, XIX, 90.

the king's stables: 'The king's *horswealh*, he who performs his errands, his wergeld shall be two hundred *scillings*.'[74] In the *Quadripartitus*[75] the title is translated *regis stabularius Waliscus;* but this explanation, though accepted by the editors of the Old English codes,[76] cannot be called satisfactory. We should expect most of the work about the royal stables to be performed by serfs. The *horswealh*, however, is not to be classed among the unfree.[77] His wergeld, though exactly equal to that of a common freeman, really indicates a higher rank. Being a Celt, his *wer* would be reckoned only half as great as that of a Saxon of equivalent social position. In his own race, the *horswealh* would stand comparatively high.[78] Furthermore, the fact that these *Wealhs* acted as the king's messengers goes to show that they could not have been bound to the service of the royal stables. It seems more reasonable to think of them as native Celts employed as the king's mounted messengers, carrying royal orders to the different parts of the West Saxon kingdom.[79]

An entry in the Chronicle for 897 records the death of a *Wealh-gerefa* or Welsh-reeve. This title has been variously interpreted: Kemble believes it means a commander of the Welsh serfs at Alfred's court;[80] Earle holds that it refers to a reeve "commissioned to watch the Welsh border."[81] But the probabilities favor neither of these interpretations. Wulfric, the reeve in question, was clearly a man of prominence or he would not have been mentioned in the Chronicle. Primarily, he was the king's marshal: 'The same year Wulfric the king's horse-thegn passed away; he was also *Wealh-gerefa*.'[82] As horse-thegn he must

---

[74] *Laws of Ine*, 33 : Cyninges horswealh, se þe him mæge geærendian, þæs wergield bið cc scil.
[75] Liebermann, *Gesetze*, I, 22.
[76] Thorpe, *Ancient Laws*, Glossary : Horswealh, the Wealh or Briton who had the care of the (king's) horses. Schmid, *Gesetze*, Glossary : horswealh, ein Wäle, der zur Pflege der Pferde bestimmt ist.... Liebermann, *Gesetze*, I, 22 : Von einem [wälschen?] Königsmarschalk [Stallmeister].
[77] Schmid thinks he was a serf: "...vielleicht auch nur überhaupt ein höriger Stallknecht...."
[78] The wergeld of a 'Welshman' possessing one hide was 120 scillings ; of one having half a hide 80; of a landless Wealh 60. *Laws of Ine*, 32.
[79] There was a body of such servants at the Merovingian court called cursores. See Waitz, *D. V. G.*, II, 2, 75.
[80] *Sax. in Eng.*, II, 179.
[81] *Two Saxon Chronicles* (Oxford, 1865), 321.
[82] Two of the manuscripts have Wealh-gefera, which might mean Welsh companion. But the form gerefa in the other three is more probably the correct

have had charge of the royal stables, and being a court-functionary he could scarcely have acted as reeve on the frontier. As *Wealh-gerefa* he must have had charge of certain *Wealhs;* but these need not necessarily have been serfs. In Ine's day a *Wealh* had a wergeld even when landless.[83] To me it seems more reasonable to connect the 'Welsh-reeve' with the *horswealh* and to look upon Wulfric as master of the royal horse and chief of a body of mounted messengers, a service that was or once had been composed of Celts. It must be admitted, however, that this interpretation is also largely a matter of conjecture.

It would appear from certain rather doubtful allusions that the English king had a sword-bearer.[84] Several terms that might be applied to such a servant, such as *armiger, spatarius, wæpen-bora, swyrd-bora,* are found in the glossaries.[85] Bede's account of King Oswin's humility—how he gave his sword to one of his thegns and knelt at Bishop Aidan's feet[86]—permits the inference that the Northumbrian king had such a servant. The term *armiger* is used for one who bore arms for King Edmund in Abbo's Epistle to Dunstan, written toward the close of the tenth century.[87] It is a significant fact that Ælfric in paraphrasing this account translates *armiger,* not with the general term *wæpen-bora,* but with the more specific word *swurd-bora.*[88] This word occurs quite frequently in Anglo-Saxon, especially in the devotional writings of the time.[89] But as these are largely translations, they can hardly be placed among the sources of English institutional history: the terms used may simply represent an effort to express a foreign idea. Still, the continued use of

---

one. If Wulfric were a "conviva regis" of British nationality, we should look for Celtic elements in his name; but Wulfric is Teutonic, root and branch.

[83] It should be remembered that as Alfred reënacted Ine's laws, such must also have been the condition in 897.

[84] The sword-bearer, spatarius, was a well-known official at the Frankish courts. See Waitz, *D. V. G.,* II, 2, 74–75; III, 509.

[85] *Vocab.,* 142:8, 193:17, 332:24.

[86] *H. E.,* III, 14: Porro rex....discinxit se gladio suo, et dedit illum ministro....

[87] This armiger was a decrepit old man who once had related to King Æthelstan the story of Saint Edmund's passion. "Quibus fatebaris...quod eam junior didicisses a quodam sene decrepito, qui eam simpliciter..referebat gloriosissimo regi Anglorum Ethelstano, jurejurando asserens quod eadem die fuisset armiger beati viri, qua pro Christo martyr occubuit." *Memorials of St. Dunstan,* 379.

[88] *Ælfric's Lives,* II, 314.

[89] It occurs several times in the Old English version of Gregory's Dialogues. See *Bibl. der ang. Prosa,* V, 187, 300. It also appears in Ælfric's Homily on Saint Benedict. *Homilies,* II, 168.

swurd-bora where we might expect *wæpen-bora* or some other more general term indicates that the institution was not unknown in England. William of Malmesbury evidently believed that it had existed in Saxon times: he tells us of an *armiger* who was put out to sea in an open boat with the unfortunate Edwin, Æthelstan's brother.[90] But the sword-bearer's office, if it existed at all, could not have been counted among the more important ones at the Old English court.[91]

On the subject of the king's standard-bearer the English sources leave us in much doubt. The war-banner was one of the emblems of Teutonic kingship. It was born before the war-lord when the host was on the march,[92] and it waved above him when the battle was on.[93] Beneath it stood Hygelac the Geat on the field where he fell before the onset of Franks and Frisians.[94] Naturally, the bearer and guardian of the king's ensign was considered an official of great importance. In the earliest days of Norse kingship the 'marksman,' *merkismaþr*, was the highest in dignity among the king's men.[95] In Beowulf we apparently have the name of a banner-bearer, Dæghrefn, a warrior of the Hugs.[96] It is possible that the phrase 'guardian of the standard' used in this case means warrior in general;[97] but that the standard-bearer was known in those days as an important functionary appears from two passages in Bede's history. In the first Germanus,

---

[90] *Gesta Regum*, 156.
[91] In the will of Æthelstan Etheling a bequest is made to the prince's swurð-wita: "And ic geann Ælffnoðe minon swurð-witan ðæs sceardan malswurdes." K. C. D., No. 722; Thorpe, *Diplomatarium*, 566. There seems to be no reason why the second part of the compound should not be connected with bewitan or bewitian, to take care of or watch over. Swurð-wita would then mean sword-keeper. But Thorpe reads swurd-hwita and translates it "sword-furbisher."
[92] This is vividly shown in *Exodus* where the advance of the Egyptian host is described: "Him þær sige-cyning wið þone segn foran, manna þengel mearc-þreate rad" (ll. 172-73). There is, however, some disagreement as to the translation of these lines. On the general subject see Paul, *Grundriss*, II, 2, 126.
[93] When the valkyries came to the host of Hakon the Good to select the worthy ones, they found the most excellent king under the war-banner. C. P. B., I, 263.
[94] *Beow.*, 1202-05.
[95] Later he was superseded by the staller, the king's spokesman, who again had to yield to the chancellor or king's scribe. See Keyser, *Efterladte Skrifter*, II, 80, 82. The standard-bearer seems also to have been a great dignitary among the early Normans. Ordericus Vitalis mentions 'Roger Toni, standard-bearer of Normandy' among the great nobles in 1066. *History of England and Normandy* (London, 1853-56), III, 11.
[96] *Beow.*, 2505: cumbles hyrde.
[97] It appears to be thus used in *Riddle*, No. 41: Ne mæg mec oferswiþan segnberendra ænig ofer eorþan nymþe se ana God.

acting as *signifer*, is described as rallying the Britons.[98] In the second we are told that King Edwin not only had a banner born before him in battle, but also when he traveled about the country in times of peace.[99] `The duties of Edwin's *signifer* were doubtless of a heraldic order. John the Baptist is similarly spoken of in the Blickling Homilies: 'he...was standard-bearer of the heavenly King.'[1] Words meaning banner-bearer frequently occur in the Glossaries and elsewhere,[2] but, as a rule, we cannot affirm that a court-official is meant. The decline of the *signifer* seems to have begun early; he is soon lost in the great troop of thegns that throng the Saxon court. Still, there is no reason to think that his office wholly disappeared.

As to the appearance of the banner nothing definite is known. The term commonly used in describing it is *segen;* but *cumbol,*[3] *tacn, thuf*[4] and other more or less metaphoric terms also occur. The standard is frequently alluded to in Beowulf, and from the language used we should infer that it was highly ornamented,[5] but we are not told how or with what device. It is not improbable that the Old English banner had, as has been suggested,[6] the image of a boar or some other animal as its distinguishing

---

[98] *H. E.*, I, 20: Tum subito Germanus signifer universos admonet et praedicat ut voci suae uno clamore respondeant.
[99] *Ibid.*, II, 16: Tantum vero in regno excellentiae habuit ut non solum in pugna ante illum vexilla gestarentur, sed et tempore pacis equitantem inter civitates sive villas aut provincias suas cum ministris semper antecedere signifer consuesset.
[1] P. 163:22 : He wæs segn-bora þæs ufancundan kyninges.
[2] The Latin terms are draconarius, vexillifer, signifer. The Old English are segnbora, tacnbora, tacnberend. See *Vocab.*, 117:29, 142:10, 225:13, 332:27; *Ælfric's Grammar*, 27. A standard-bearer is alluded to in two spurious charters pretending to be dated in Æthelstan's reign. *K. C. D.*, Nos. 346, 1128. William of Malmesbury uses the word signifier in the sense of leader. *Gesta Regum,* 187. In Abbo's Passion of Saint Edmund, it occurs in the metaphor "signifer in castris aeterni regis." *Memorials of St. Edmund's Abbey,* I, 15.
[3] Cumbol is a very general term; it may mean almost any emblem or even decoration. In the composition eofor-cumbol, it could mean a banner with the picture of a boar on it; but it might also refer to the boar image on the helmet. Thus it is used in *Elene,* 256-59. Earlier in the same poem it is used for the sign that Constantine saw in his vision (l. 76).
[4] The thuf was the particular kind of a banner that Edwin sent before him on his journeys.
[5] A golden banner was placed on the ship that carried Scyld away (47). Hrothgar gave Beowulf a golden standard with an ornamented staff (1020-21). An all-golden banner is found in the Dragon's cave (2767-69).
[6] By Dr. Friedrich Brincker in *Germanische Altertümer in dem angelsächsischen Gedichte Judith* (Hamburg. 1898), 17. Cf. Tacitus, *Germania,* 7; Müllenhoff, *Deutsche Altertumskunde,* IV, 200.

mark.[7] The standard that Harold fought beneath at Hastings was graced with the image of a dragon.[8] A thegn whose duties were to bring up and educate the royal princes is referred to in several of the older sources. The preceptor particularly mentioned is Thunor, *praepositus Ecgberhti Cantwariorum regis*, as Florence calls him.[9] Elsewhere he is spoken of as 'thegn to his [the king's] children.'[10] As Thunor is practically the only one who is known to have occupied such a position, it cannot be positively stated whether the office was regularly filled or not.[11] In Bede's history there seems to be an allusion to a king's almoner. He cannot have been a very important personage, however, as he has no distinctive title either in Latin or in Anglo-Saxon.[12] The Old English king doubtless had his *ostiarius* or door ward, and such a one seems to be mentioned in Beowulf.[13] The cook and the baker do not appear in the English sources before Norman times; but we may safely assume that these useful servants were not wanting at the Anglo-Saxon court.[14] Edward the Confessor had his own mead-maker; the office was doubtless an ancient one.[15] Connected, no doubt,

---

[7] The banner assigned to the tribe of Juda (*Exodus*, 321) bore a golden lion. A raven graced the standard of the Norse invaders. See *A.-S. Chron.*, 878; *Gesta Cnutonis*, II, 9.

[8] Worsaae, *An Account of the Danes and Norwegians in England*, 60: On the often-mentioned Bayeux tapestry is also represented the fall of the English Harald Godvinsön at the battle of Hastings. The king's flag-bearer, or marksman, who, as well as the king, is on foot, bears a flag-staff on which is fixed a figure, probably of cloth, cut in the resemblance of a dragon, which was the royal mark of the Anglo-Saxon king.

[9] I, 259. In one of the later charters he is called princeps. *K. C. D.*, No. 900.

[10] *Saxon Leechdoms*, III, 424: ... se leofestan ðegen to his bearnum.

[11] That there were teachers at the royal court is a well-known fact. Wilfrid and Dunstan were both sent there to be educated. *Hist. York*, I, 4; *Memorials of St. Dunstan*, 11-12. Æthelwald learned many useful things from the wise men at Æthelstan's court. *Chronicon Monasterii de Abingdon*, II, 256. Still earlier, Alfred's court was almost a compulsory educational institution. See Asser in Petrie's *Monumenta*, 486. The early Capetian kings also had their preceptors at court. Luchaire, *Hist. des Inst. Mon.*, I, 165.

[12] Bede calls him the servant "cui suscipiendorum inopum erat cura delegata." *H. E.*, III, 6. Ælfric, in paraphrasing this account speaks of him as 'one of the king's thegns, the one who distributed his alms.' *Lives of Saints*, II, 130.

[13] When the Geats arrived at Heorot, they sat down on a bench outside and waited for an invitation to enter. Soon Wulfgar came out to learn who they were; he bore their message to the king and secured their admission. *Beow.*, 331 ff. The ostiarius is mentioned in the earliest Frankish sources. See Waitz, *D. V. G.*, II, 2, 75.

[14] These were well known at the Frankish court. See *ibid.*, II, 2, 74; Luchaire, *Hist. des Inst. Mon.*, I, 164.

[15] *K. C. D.*, No. 845: paðu mi meodes wrichte....

with the service of the royal kitchen were certain thegns called *praevisores*. Often wealthy subjects would invite the king to their homes when he came into their region; but in such cases the king always wished to make sure that both hunger and thirst would be thoroughly sated and quenched. The *praevisores* were therefore sent ahead to inspect the supplies.[16] The *carnifex* mentioned by Florence of Worcester was probably the king's butcher;[17] strangely enough he is grouped with the great dignitaries of Harthacnut's court. A French monk who was highly skilled in medicine is said to have spent some time at the Confessor's court;[18] it is probable that he was the king's physician.[19] Among the servants of a more purely artisan character may be noted the king's smith,[20] his goldsmith[21] and the *biga* who supplied him with carriages.[22]

There were also certain classes of men on the royal estates who seem to have had no duties either as officials or servants. These were the *convivae regis*,[23] men of prominence who as the king's guests enjoyed royal hospitality for a longer or shorter period.[24] Such were probably the earlier *geneats*. The word *geneat* means primarily a companion and frequently occurs in compounds with

[16] When the holy woman Æthelflæd was preparing a banquet for her royal kinsman Æthelstan, the praevisores found a sufficiency of everything but mead. Knowing the profundity of the royal thirst, they informed her that a greater supply must be prepared. Æthelflæd resorted to prayers and the mead-casks proved equal to the occasion. *Memorials of St. Dunstan*, 17–18.

[17] I, 194: Thrond suum carnificem. Judging from the name we should say the incumbent must have been a Dane. For the meaning of carnifex see Du Cange, *Glossarium*.

[18] *Memorials of St. Edmund's Abbey*, I, 56: ....quidam Baldewinus, ex Franciae partibus gloriosis, monachus....sed et medicina peritus, ex hoc quoque a rege Anglorum cum multa diligentia habitus.

[19] Edward gave him an abbacy, perhaps as a reward. *Ibid.*

[20] The faber regis was evidently a person of some importance. He is given special and prominent mention in one of the earliest sources: "Gif cyninges ambiht-smið oððe laadrinc mannan ofslehð, meduman leodgelde forgelde. *Laws of Æthelbirht*, 7. We read in *Domesday* (I, 36), that a certain smith received half a hide from King Edward.

[21] Asser alludes to Alfred's goldsmiths (aurifices). Petrie's *Monumenta*, 486. In one of Eadred's charters (949) two mansas are given to one of the king's men "uocitato nomine Ælfsige arciselus, ob studium quam mihi auri argentique fabricae solicite deseruit atque decorat..." *K. C. D.*, No. 428. At the time of the Domesday survey, "Teodricus aurifabrus" held lands "de rege Edwardo." *Domesday*, I, 36b.

[22] See *Ibid.*, I, 7, 7b, 8, 12.

[23] C.. Waitz, *D. V. G.*, II, 2, 103–4.

[24] The term conviva regis may also be used in the broad sense of member of the king's household.

such a significance.[25] Perhaps those who came to the court to be educated should also be reckoned among the *convivae*.[26] Among the older we should look for the king's councillor's *(consiliarii)* to whom the sources occasionally allude.[27] The Frenchmen whom Edward brought into his kingdom must be regarded as *convivae regis* at least until they had received official appointments.[28] To classify the members of the king's household, to say which of them were thegns or freemen or serfs, would be an impossibility. We can say only that all these classes were represented. Such terms as *satellites, palatini* and *sodales* are not used with a view to classification, but as general appellations for those in and about the palace who stood nearest the king. *Famulus* is another such inclusive term, but the *famuli* could not have been thegns: Bede carefully distinguishes between the two classes.[29] Florence, following Asser, speaks of the *familiares* and *ministeriales* of Alfred's court.[30] From Bede's account of the aggressions of these *famuli*, we shall have to conclude that they were at least freemen. Serfs were common on the royal estates as elsewhere.[31] That the king held slaves appears both from manumissions[32] and from direct statements in the earlier laws.[33]

---

[25] Later the term came to be applied to one holding land by a particular tenure. See Seebohm, *English Village Community*, 128 ff.

[26] When Dunstan came to court he found a number of his young kinsmen there: "nonnulli propriorum sodalium et palatinorum, tum quam maxime vero consanguineorum suorum,...." *Memorials of St. Dunstan,* 11.

[27] Consiliarius is often used as if a member of the witan is meant, as when Bede tells us that Benedict purchased three estates from "Aldfrido rege ejusque consiliariis," *Opera*, II, 149. But Wilfrid's position at court as "excelsus consiliarius" must be looked on as that of a conviva. *Hist. York*, I, 59; a contemporary account. The consiliarii mentioned in some of Egbert's charters were apparently higher ecclesiastics regularly counted among the witan (*K. C. D.*, Nos. 1031, 1035); but ".Edelfied consiliarius" who signed one of Eadred's charters and the two consiliarii Brihtric and Ælfgar who witnessed one of the Confessor's grants were most likely convivae and not regular officials. Birch, *Cartul.*, No. 876; *K. C. D.*, No. 811.

[28] *Lives of Edward the Confessor*, 399: Cum praedictus...rex repatriaret a Francia, ex eadem gente comitati sunt quam plures non ignobiles viri, quos plurimis honoribus ditatos secum retinuit idem rex, utpote compos totius regni, ordinariosque constituit secretorum consilii sui, et rectores rerum regalis palatii. (An almost contemporary account; written before the death of Queen Edith.)

[29] ...ministri quoque regis ac famuli. *Opera*, II, 219, Epistola ad Ecgberctum, 13.

[30] I, 89.

[31] Queen Æthelfled, wife of Edmund I, in her will gave freedom to half of her serfs. Thorpe, *Diplomatarium*, 519 ff.; Birch, *Cartul.*, No. 1288.

[32] One of Æthelstan's manumissions is extant. See Thorpe, *Diplomatarium*, 622.

[33] In the *Laws of Æthelbirht* there is a clear allusion to female slaves, the king's maids (beowas) who ground the corn (10, 11). The king's esne is mentioned in the *Laws of Wihtræd*, 22.

The only document that gives us any information as to how the king's attendants were classified is Eadred's will.[34] The chamberlains, the butlers and the seneschals form the highest group; the priests rank next to them; the stewards form the third class; all the lower officials are classed together as the following shows: 'and to every one of those who are in my household, be he in what employment he may.' But that there was a still lower group is implied in the concluding words of this same statement: 'unless he be little bound to the throne.'

As to whether the palatines received any wages in the modern sense of the word, we are poorly informed. It is, however, not likely that the king's financial obligations to the great majority of his attendants and servants extended beyond furnishing the necessary shelter, clothing and daily fare. The huntsman in Ælfric's Colloquy received no pay; but the king gave him an occasional gift.[35] These gifts, as we have seen, often took the form of lands. Yet, in the language of Alfred's will, there is a suggestion of fixed payments and a regular pay-day: 'and to those of my serving-men whom I gave fees *(feoh)* at Eastertide, let them give two hundred pounds, and let them divide [the money] among them, to each one as belongs to him, in the manner in which I recently distributed [fees].'[36] Such a custom was the ruling one in Wales[37] and the Northern countries[38] and it would be strange if it was not also general in England.

---

[34] Birch, *Cartul.*, No. 912.
[35] *Vocab.*, 93.
[36] *K. C. D.*, No. 314.
[37] *Ancient Laws of Wales*, 3: Three times in the year the above twenty-four officers are entitled to receive, according to law, their woollen garments from the king and their linen garments from the queen; namely, at Christmas, Easter and Whitsuntide. (See also the pages following where the fees belonging to each office are given.)
[38] The Norse king paid most of his thegns small sums at regular intervals. See *Speculum Regale*, 261 ff.; Keyser, *Efterladte Skrifter*, II, 86-87.

CHAPTER IX.

THE DEVELOPMENT OF THE KING'S HOUSEHOLD IN ENGLAND AND ON THE CONTINENT.

The effort thus far has been principally to determine how the Old English court was organized, what offices composed the royal service, and what functions were assigned to each. There remains the question of the possible origin of this organization: did it originate in England or was it introduced from abroad? The titles borne by the various officials closely resemble those generally used at the Continental courts of that period, and some of the later offices, such as those of the staller and the chancellor, are of unmistakably foreign origin. It seems evident, then, that between the king's household in early England and the neighboring courts on the Continent a close relationship must have existed. It is the purpose of this chapter to trace in outline the development of the Germanic courts in northern and western Europe in order to determine, if possible, to what extent the organization of the Anglo-Saxon court was influenced by Continental custom and what influence, if any, it, in turn, exerted on similar households of a later date.

The early Teutonic household was doubtless a very simple arrangement: the lord of the house, whether mere freeman or mightiest prince, seems to have exercised direct supervision over all the forces in his service. But as wealth and power increased, duties multiplied and the number of servants grew correspondingly. This necessitated some form of divided labor, and several household departments came into being. Of these there were commonly four: a steward *(infertor)* had charge of all that pertained to his master's tables; a butler *(scantio, buticularius)* provided his wine, beer and other beverages; his treasures were in the keeping of a treasurer or chamberlain; a marshal *(comes stabuli)* was in charge of his lord's stables. At times the supervision of the whole service was placed in the hands of a separate official known as the seneschal or *major domus*.[39]

The king, however, was more than a possessor of large estates and other forms of wealth, he was the lord of his people, their leader in war, their judge and protector in peace. As time passed these governing functions of kingship, continuously growing in extent and importance, necessitated the creation of new offices and new departments of service. These were sometimes given to the old household officials and thus the king's personal servants, by taking on new functions, were gradually transformed into public officials; but the general tendency was to give each new department its own responsible head. Thus the royal court developed both on the personal and on the political side.

Under the Merovingian kings the palatine service was divided among eight officials, all of whom, however, were not of equal rank. Lowest, perhaps, stood the master of the horse[40] and the chief butler.[41] On a somewhat higher plane were the *thesaurarius*[42] who kept the king's treasures, including his wardrobe and the like, and the seneschal. This official, who seems to have had the entire household service under his supervision, was also known as the *major domus*. But, after this title had come to mean so much on the political side of the court, the seneschal's title was revived and with it his former general functions.[43] It seems probable that he also supervised the table-service more directly, as the *infertor* is nowhere mentioned in connection with the Merovingian court.[44]

These dignitaries all belonged to the household proper.[45] More purely political were the offices of the *major domus*, the count of

---

[39] For the materials used in this chapter I am largely indebted to the constitutional manuals of Brunner, Keyser, Luchaire, von Maurer, Stubbs, and Waitz. See von Maurer, *Hofverfassung*, 189 ff., for a discussion of the primitive Germanic household.

[40] The comes stabuli. See Waitz, *D. V. G.*, II, 2, 72.

[41] *Ibid.*, 74.

[42] *Ibid.*, 73. He was also called cubicularius, though it may be that the cubicularius was an inferior servant who was sometimes invested with the treasurer's office.

[43] *Ibid.*, 71. Cf. Brunner, *D. R. G.*, II, 104.

[44] Brunner, *D. R. G.*, II, 101.

[45] There were also numerous officials and servants holding subordinate positions. Such were the camerarii who assisted the thesaurar'us; the pincernae who served under the chief butler; the marshals who performed certain duties

the palace and the *referendarius*. Finally, as a Christian ruler, the Frankish king had his own priests, chief among whom was the palatine abbot.[46]

The duty of the count of the palace *(comes palatii)* was to assist the king in his judicial functions, not, however, as a representative or as one who has an independent jurisdiction, but rather as an executive officer who attends to the legal machinery and to the details of the trial.[47] His office was of Germanic origin.[48] That of the *referendarius*, on the other hand, was originally Roman both as to name and functions.[49] The duties of this official corresponded to those of the later chancellor: they related to the keeping and the preparation of royal documents. The scribal work was performed mainly by his assistants who were known as *notarii* and *cancellarii.* Unlike his Carolingian successor, the *referendarius* was a secular dignitary, and had nothing to do with ecclesiastical affairs.[50]

The highest official at the Merovingian court was the *major domus*. Originally he was merely the seneschal or chief servant of the household. 'To his older duties he added others of a more directly political nature: he commanded the king's antrustions, supervised the education of the palatine youths, served as his lord's representative in judicial affairs, acted as peace-officer when quarrels arose among the great lords of the kingdom, sat highest among the king's councillors and even controlled his master's possessions to a great extent.'[51] The history of this official under the later Merovingians is well known. The Carolingian monarchs appointed no mayors and the office disappeared.[52]

Generally speaking, the Carolingian kings and emperors retained the household system of the preceding dynasty.[53] Certain

---

under the orders of the comes stabuli, there were also the cook, the mappaiius whose duty was to hand towels to the king, the spatarius who carried his sword, physicians, minstrels, goldsmiths, door-keepers, couriers and others. See Waitz, *D. V. G.*, II, 2, 73-75; Brunner, *D. R. G.*, II, 101-02.

[46] Waitz, *D. V. G.*, II, 2, 102.
[47] Brunner, *D. R. G.*, II, 108-10; Waitz, *D. V. G.*, II, 2, 76-79.
[48] Waitz, *D. V. G.*, II, 2, 76.
[49] Ibid.
[50] Ibid., 80-82; Brunner, *D. R. G.*, II, 113-14.
[51] Waitz, *D. V. G.*, II, 2, 83 ff.; Brunner, *D. R. G.*, II, 104-08.
[52] It should be added that practically all the higher offices at the Merovingian court, including that of the major domus, could be held by several persons at the same time.
[53] Luchaire, *Hist. des Inst. Mon.*, I, 163.

changes had come about, however, the most important of which was the suppression of the mayorship. The position of the seneschal had declined somewhat: instead of being the chief of the household he was now merely *infertor* or master of the royal tables.[54] The butler, on the other hand, had risen in rank and dignity and had taken his place among the highest officials at court.[55] The palatine count also occupied a more exalted position during the Carolingian period; certain functions of a judicial and notarial character formerly belonging to the *major domus* and the *referendarius* were now exercised by him.[56] The keeper of the king's strongbox was now known as *camerarius* instead of by the older title *thesaurarius;* his assistants bore the title of *cubicularii*.[57] In the notarial office great changes had taken place. The title of *referendarius* had gone into disuse and the chief scribe was now known as chancellor *(cancellarius)* or archchancellor.[58] The office itself had taken on an ecclesiastical character; it was united to that of the archchaplain, and henceforth the chancery and the royal chapel were almost identical.[59] It will readily appear that this consolidation of notarial and clerical offices would tend to transform the rather insignificant *referendarius* into an influential and powerful chancellor.

The confusion that followed the decline of the Carolingian dynasty also extended to the royal household. In the tenth and eleventh centuries the palatine hierarchy in the Frankish kingdom seems to be undergoing constant changes both in relative rank of offices and in the duties assigned to each.[60] Two ruling tendencies, however, are apparent: to change the character of the offices from personal to public, and to feudalize the same by assigning them to certain powerful families.[60] From the very beginning the kings seem to have employed their palace officials in occasional public capacities as judges, ambassadors, military com-

---

[54] Waitz, *D. V. G.,* III, 499–500.
[55] *Ibid.,* 501.
[56] Brunner, *D. R. G.,* II, 110–12.
[57] Waitz, *D. V. G.,* III, 502; Brunner, *D. R. G.,* II, 101.
[58] Waitz, *D. V. G.,* III, 513, note.
[59] *Ibid.,* 516 ff.; Brunner, *D. R. G.,* II, 114–17. This union of offices was largely due to the fact that the royal chapel in Carolingian times came to be used as the chief depository for royal documents; the employment of clerks as scribes led to the same result.
[60] Luchaire, *Hist. des Inst. Mon.,* I, 163 ff.

manders and the like;[61] but now the public functions of these dignitaries become regular and continuous, while their household duties pass into the hands of a lower order of servants.[62] The feudalizing tendency was vigorously resisted by the kings, and the result of their opposition was that in a few centuries the grand offices of the household had been abolished or reduced to honorary dignities.[63]

The household system of the Carolingians was retained both by the early Capetian rulers in France and by the imperial masters of Germany.[64] The palatine count, however, soon disappeared from the French court,[65] thus leaving in control the five historic court-officials: the seneschal, the chamberlain, the chancellor, the constable and the butler. Of these the seneschal was easily the most eminent: he had inherited nearly all the supervising power of the original mayor of the palace, the judicial authority of the palatine count and the duties of steward in the royal kitchen; to these functions was added supreme command of the king's armies.[66] But his royal master soon realized the danger in permitting the concentration of so much power in one official hand, and before the close of the twelfth century the seneschal's office was practically suppressed.[67] His military powers were now entrusted to the constable;[68] but again the subject threatened to become too powerful for his lord, and after 1475 the constable's office was usually left vacant.[69] During the period of his political eminence he had ceased to be a household official, his duties at court being performed by the marshal.[70] The history of the butler and the chamberlain closely resembles that of the seneschal and the constable. As their duties at court came in time to be performed by a lower order of servants, their own offices were reduced to honorary dignities and were finally left vacant or wholly suppressed.[71] The chancellor alone survived into modern times.

[61] Waitz, *D. V. G.*, II, 2, 72 ff.
[62] Luchaire, *Hist. des Inst. Mon.*, I, 171-94, passim.
[63] *Ibid.*, 195-96.
[64] *Ibid.*, 163; Waitz, *D. V. G.*, VI, 327.
[65] *Ibid.*, 170.
[66] *Ibid.*, 178-80.
[67] *Ibid.*, 185.
[68] *Ibid.*, 171.
[69] Viollet, *Histoire des Institutions Politiques*, II, 116-17.
[70] Luchaire, *Hist. des Inst. Mon.*, I, 172.
[71] The camerarius disappeared in the twelfth century (Viollet, *Histoire des Institutions Politiques*, II, 123) and the butler in the fifteenth (*ibid.*, 118, note).

At the imperial court of mediaeval Germany, the household officers did not rise to so great a power as in Capetian France;[72] nor did they entirely lose their character as personal servants of the emperor.[73] The chancellor alone may be said to have attained an influential position.[74] The German monarch preferred to assign public duties to ecclesiastics rather than to the lay members of his household,[75] hence the great importance of the mediaeval chancery. But, in the Empire, as in earlier France, all these dignities finally became mere titles and passed into the hands of certain leading feudal princes.

The last Teutonic court to be organized was that of Norway. As this differed in some respects from the Frankish type, it deserves to be examined somewhat closely.[76] The earliest Norse sources speak of three classes of 'kings-men,' the 'hirdmen,' the 'guests' and the 'house-carles.' Of these the 'hirdmen' composed the king's select guard; they usually served to the number of six or twelve at a time. In the days of Saint Olaf, sixty 'hirdmen' were with the king on his royal estate; half a century later the number was increased to one hundred and twenty. In the twelfth century it seems to have been still greater. The guests served as the outer guards at the royal vill and were frequently employed as the king's messengers, going as such to every part of the realm. Their number was half as great as that of the 'hirdmen.' Like these they were entertained at the king's vill, but sat at his tables only on great festive occasions. The house-carles were the servants who performed the actual labor on the king's manor.[77] Later two other classes appear, the table-servants *(skutilsveinar)* and the candle-bearers *(kertisveinar)*. The former were chosen from among the 'hirdmen' and acted principally (two each day) as his majesty's body-servants; but at great festive gatherings they served the king at his table as bearers of cups and dishes, hence their name. Among the servants at court they ranked the

---

[72] Waltz, *D. V. G.*, VI, 332.
[73] *Ibid.*
[74] *Ibid.*, 336 ff.
[75] *Ibid.*
[76] The following account is summarized from Keyser's study of the Norse Constitution in the Middle Ages, *Efterladte Skrifter*, II. The principal sources are the *Speculum Regale* and the *Hirðskraa* (Court-law) published in *Norges gamle Love*, II.
[77] Keyser, *Efterladte Skrifter*, II, 78–79.

highest.[78] The candle-bearers were pages, sons of the noblest families, who were not yet counted among the kings-men, but were being educated for service at court. Their duty was to hold candles at the king's tables when he feasted with his great lords.[79]

In time four leading officials came to be recognized at court, all being appointed from the 'hirdmen's' class: the marksman (*merkismaþr*), the staller *(stallari)*, the dapifer *(drottseti,* from German *truchsess?)* and the butler *(skenkari)*. The marksman's office seems to have been of great antiquity, at the beginning of the truly historic period his dignity was the highest at court. On sea he defended the forecastle of the king's ship; on land he bore and defended the royal banner.[80] As royal authority grew stronger and a truer kingship developed out of what was once scarcely more than military leadership, the marksman's dignity sank to a somewhat lower plane and the staller took his place at the head of the court. This official was primarily a spokesman: he addressed the popular assemblies on the king's behalf and in turn advised the ruler as to the wishes and requests of the freemen. He was responsible for good order and proper discipline at court, and all disputes that might arise within the household were referred to him for settlement. Incidentally, he had to provide the necessary equipment for the king's journey, and hence may have had supervision of the royal stables.[81] Far below the staller and the standard-bearer both in rank and importance were the *dapifer* and the butler. Both were chosen from among the table-servants and for a long time were household officials merely;[82] but soon after the beginning of the fourteenth century, we find the *dapifer* as the highest official, not only in the king's household, but in the state as well.[83]

The Norse court was also thoroughly organized on the ecclesiastical side. The first Christian rulers had a court-bishop (*hirþ-biskup*) who traveled about with them and assisted in the work

---

[78] Keyser, *Efterladte Skrifter,* II, 79.
[79] *Ibid.,* 79-80. There was also a candle-bearer at the Welsh court.
[80] *Ibid.,* 80.
[81] See *Ibid.,* 80-81; Munch, *N. F. H.,* IV, 1, 612. It will be readily seen that, in a land where the sea was the principal highway, supervision of the king's stables could not have been considered among the important charges.
[82] Keyser, *Efterladte Skrifter,* II, 81.
[83] *Ibid.,* 134.

of conversion. After this had been completed, the bishop seems to have left the court and given place to the household-priests (*hirpprestar*). As elsewhere, the king's chaplain did not remain a spiritual guide merely, but became a public functionary as well; he was the king's notary and perhaps also his treasurer.[84] In time the king's chapel developed into a chancery with a chancellor at its head.[85] In the reign of Magnus Lawmender (1263–80), the chancellor is spoken of as the highest official at court.[86]

Of these officers the marksman and the staller are doubtless of Norse or early Teutonic origin. The standard-bearer seems nowhere else to have held an eminent position in the royal household. It is also difficult to find officials elsewhere that correspond to the Norse staller. Were his office of Frankish origin[87] his functions should have corresponded to those of the Capetian constable, but such is not the case. Much more does he remind us of the early Merovingian seneschal or *major domus*. As no marshal can be found it is probable that at some early date the care of the king's horses passed into the staller's hands. With respect to the table-servants Snorre tells us that in appointing these the king followed the custom of foreign courts.[88] As the steward *(dapifer)* and the butler were chosen from these attendants, it seems probable that these officials were not originally Norse. It may be added that the earliest Norse sources make no mention of a chamberlain or a treasurer.[89]

Turning to the English court, we find but few traces of an organization before the tenth century. The household of the Anglo-Saxon kings in the earliest period was apparently wholly Teutonic, and, so far as we know, it remained so for some time. The king had his thegns or household servants and perhaps a seneschal or *oferealdorman* who had charge of them all; but anything like a systematic distribution of duties or the formation

---

[84] Keyser, *Efterladte Skrifter*, II, 82.
[85] *Ibid.*, 82–83.
[86] *Ibid.*, 82.
[87] Such is Keyser's opinion. See *Efterladte Skrifter*, II, 81, note.
[88] In the *Saga of Olaf the Quiet* (whose reign dates from 1066, when his father fell at Stamford Bridge) Snorre says: 'King Olaf also, after the custom of foreign kings, appointed table servants who were to stand at his tables and serve the dishes to himself and the princely subjects who sat at his table.' (C. 3.)
[89] Cf. the Salic Law (Geffcken), X, 4, where a major, an infertor, a scantio and a mariscalcus are referred to, but no camerarius or thesaurarius.

of a household hierarchy is not apparent. It may seem strange that the close communication existing between England and the Continent ever since the days of Augustine should not have affected the royal surroundings. No doubt it was influential to a certain extent, though it may be that the introduction of foreign elements was for a long time limited to the ecclesiastical side of the court. Moreover, the possibility of influence was not great, for the kings of Kent and Wessex were not mighty emperors like Charlemagne and Otto. An elaborate organization could hardly find room within the cramped limits controlled by the royal lords of the Old English states.

Foreign influences begin to appear in the tenth century, when the Anglo-Saxon kingdom has at last become a unified fact. After the Danish invaders had slain or exiled the rulers of the northern kingdoms the people naturally turned to the only native dynasty remaining, that of Wessex represented by the resourceful Alfred. The unification of England was in a sense the expansion of Wessex. This process, beginning at Wedmore, was practically finished at Brunanburh in the reign of Æthelstan. This event, which in so many respects is a landmark in English history, is also a landmark in the historic development of the English court. It is about this time that the palatine officials first begin to appear prominently in the sources. Their offices no doubt existed at a much earlier period, for Asser speaks of a butler in the reign of Alfred's father;[90] but not before the great age of the Old English monarchy, the age of Æthelstan and his successors, were the chiefs of the royal household counted sufficiently important to be summoned to witness the king's charters, nor are their titles mentioned in the text of any such document issued before this period. If formerly they had appeared at the great council, they had come simply as *ministri;* but they were no longer mere thegns, they were something more. As butlers and chamberlains and seneschals they had advanced to a higher dignity; and yet, they evidently remained household officials only. There is no evidence that their new greatness contained any political elements except, perhaps, membership in the *witenagemot*. The first and apparently the only English court-officials

---

[90] Petrie's *Monumenta*, 469. This 'famous butler' was Alfred's maternal grandfather.

to receive administrative functions were the staller and the chancellor, who seem to have attained their positions at court at almost the same period.

The Anglo-Saxon court of the tenth century resembled in outline that of the Carolingian Franks. The king was his own *major domus;* the functions of the seneschal, the chamberlain and the butler corresponded closely to those of the same officials across the Channel; and the royal chapel had attained a position of considerable influence. But there were also material differences. The marshal was still a servant of low rank and humble position, the chapel had not yet developed into a chancery and no trace can be found of a palatine count. This last official, however, was soon to disappear from the French court, and the chancellorship probably appeared in England before the next century was far advanced. In courtly pomp and display the English king also tried to imitate his Continental brethren. The great number of princes and *ministri* that attended Æthelstan's councils, the splendor of his palatial surroundings, the banquets and the festivals that his courtiers enjoyed, the great retinue that followed him about on his journeys,[91] all these things testify to a magnificence far different from that which characterized the airy lodgings of his famous grandfather, where the wind extinguished the lighted candle on the king's table.[92]

This sudden change in the character and aspect of the Anglo-Saxon court was doubtless due in great measure to the new policy of dynastic alliances entered upon by King Æthelstan. One of the greatest influences in assimilating the different national courts to a common type is the queen.[93] Before the tenth century the Old English kings had nearly always taken wives from among their own people. It is true, Æthelwulf, the son of Egbert, brought a Frankish princess home to Wessex as queen on his return from Rome;[94] but he died a few years later, and, if Asser's account can be trusted, Judith's popularity and influence at Winchester could not have been great.[95] Alfred and Edward the

---

[91] See the lives of the saints of that period.
[92] Petrie's *Monumenta,* 496 (Asser, *Gesta Ælfredi*).
[93] The reign of Otto II, emperor of Germany, furnishes an excellent illustration of this. The Byzantine influence that came in with his queen grew to be a fact of great importance in the following reign.
[94] *A.-S. Chron.*, 855.
[95] Petrie's *Monumenta,* 472.

Elder married English wives. Æthelstan, it seems, was never married, but his four sisters all found husbands on the Continent: Otto the Great, Hugh, the father of Hugh Capet, Louis the Blind, king of Provence, and Charles the Simple, king of the West Franks, each married a sister of the English king.[96] Æthelstan's nephew, Louis d'Outremer, spent fourteen years at the Anglo-Saxon court.[97] It is clear that so many and such close alliances would bring about much communication and many embassies between these allied courts; and the household of the English kings of that period shows unmistakable signs of their influence.

The closing years of the tenth century brought a second wave of Danish invasion, and a few years later an alien dynasty occupied the new English throne. The royal court at Winchester, with its Danish king and his Norse attendants, with the stallership as its highest dignity and with its large corps of armed house-carles guarding the royal person and inspiring the subjects with a prudent respect, now took on a decidedly Norse appearance. But the Danish influence did not long remain the dominant one; in less than a generation it had begun to retreat before a new force from across the Channel.

The first of Æthelstan's successors to seek a wife from abroad was the unfortunate Æthelred. In his reign Emma of Normandy, a woman whose influence can be clearly felt but not measured, came across to England as queen. With her came Norman ideas and men[98] and doubtless also Norman institutions. After her husband's death she became Cnut's consort, and the Normanizing tendency continued.

Edward the Confessor's sojourn in Normandy[99] is also a fact of the utmost importance: it familiarized him with a court organization and with court usages essentially the same as those of the Capetian household.[1] His own court was, to begin with, far from being purely Anglo-Saxon. It continued the organization of the Anglo-Danish household, retaining, it seems, whatever additions had come in with the Danish dynasty. To these were

---

[96] Ramsay, *Found. of Eng.*, I, 288.
[97] *Ibid.*, 289. Other royal exiles also found refuge at the court of this genial monarch.
[98] The year following her arrival in England we find mention of one Hugo, a Frenchman whom Emma had appointed reeve at Exeter. *A.-S. Chron.*, 1003.
[99] Twenty-five years. See Ramsay, *Found. of Eng.*, I, 437.
[1] Stubbs, *C. H.*, I, 372-73.

added an important Norman-French element, the inevitable result of the king's Norman education. Characteristic of his reign is the rise of the chancery, an institution which no doubt was introduced from Normandy, perhaps in Æthelred's reign. When the Saxon line perished, the English court had, like the Continental courts, five high officials, the chancellor, the staller, the seneschal, the chamberlain and the butler.[2] It also had huntsmen and falconers, goldsmiths and wagon-makers, marshals and chaplains, butchers and cup-bearers and other inferior servants, such as would be found at almost any royal court at that time. It differed from those across the Channel, however, in possessing an important military element, the house-carles, and in the circle of duties assigned to some of the higher officials. The Capetian court had no *dapifer,* the English no constable. In a general way the seneschal's office in France seems to have corresponded to the English stallership; but the seneschal also had charge of the royal tables, while the staller probably had the additional duties of chief marshal.

That the Anglo-Saxon court was indebted to the royal households of the Continent for much of its institutional growth is doubtless true; but we must remember that England did not do all the borrowing. The Old English court also had its sphere of influence. The royal households in other parts of Britain and in Scandinavia were nearly all organized later than the court of England, and naturally imitated its organization to a great extent.

In the old Welsh laws[3] there is an extended body of rules for the government of the king's household, many of which betray Saxon influence. The officials, with perhaps a few exceptions, are such as we should expect to find in any Germanic court of that time;[4] hence it seems reasonable to assume that their offices

---

[2] Cf. Round, The Officers of Edward the Confessor: *Eng. Hist. Rev.,* XIX, 90–92.

[3] *Ancient Laws and Institutes of Wales,* 2 ff. It is, of course, difficult to say how far these laws have been modified since the days of Howel (ca., 940), who is supposed to have collected and in part enacted them. But as some of the terms and titles seem derived from the Anglo-Saxon, the organization of the Welsh court in the form given in the laws most probably antedated the Norman Conquest.

[4] Howel's court had a chief of the household, a priest, a steward, a chief falconer, a judge, a marshal, a chamberlain, a bard, a silentiary, a chief huntsman, a meadbrewer, a mediciner, a doorward, a butler, a cook and a candle-bearer. The queen had a separate service, though fewer servants.

were introduced from some Teutonic nation with which the Welsh had come into close contact. The history of Britain, the contiguity of the Welsh and English territories, as well as some of the titles used, point at once to the Anglo-Saxon court as the prototype of the Cymric. The Welsh heir-apparent is called the *edling* (A.-S. *eþeling*); the seneschal is a *dysteyn* (A.-S. *discþegn*); the royal meadbrewer is called a *medyt*.[5] Whether the Welsh kings copied Æthelstan's court, or whether they modified the older Celtic institution by the addition of English elements, I shall not attempt to decide. The latter supposition is, of course, the more probable one.

There are also traces of Saxon influence in the organization of the Norwegian court. The word for household, *hirþ* is evidently the Anglo-Saxon *hired* in Norse form. The term *skutilsveinn*, table-servant, is probably derived directly from Old English *scutel* (Lat. *scutella*), a dish.[6] Whether the institution came in with the term cannot be known; I find no reference of any sort to such a table-service in the English sources. But Snorre affirms that the custom of employing such servants was a foreign one,[7] and it would be strange if the office and the title did not originate at the same court. That the Norwegian kings should have drawn freely on English experience in organizing their households is not to be wondered at. Hakon the Good is said to have spent his childhood and youth at Æthelstan's court.[8] Olaf Trygvesson was baptized (or confirmed) at Æthelred's court.[9] Saint Olaf, who first gave the royal household of Norway a definite organization, was at one time a hostage in Æthelred's hall,[10] and, what is more important, when he became king he surrounded himself with English priests.[11] Thus the royal chapel was likely to be organized along Saxon lines. In view of the fact that the household priest also acted as the king's treas-

---

[5] The Welsh word medd, mead, may be a native term and not derived from Anglo-Saxon medu; but the use of this beverage is so characteristically Teutonic that Old English influence in this matter is very probable.
[6] *Norges gamle Love*, V, Glossary.
[7] *Saga of Olaf the Quiet*, 3.
[8] *Saga of Harold Fairhair*, 40 ff.
[9] *A.-S. Chron.*, 994. Ramsay, *Found. of Eng.*, I, 343.
[10] Ramsay, *Found. of Eng.*, I, 368.
[11] *Adamus*, II, 55: [Olaf] habuit secum multos episcopos et presbyteros ab Anglia, quorum monitu et doctrina ipse cor suum Deo praeparavit subiectumque populum illis ad regendum commisit. For the organization of St. Olaf's court, see Snorre, *Saga of St. Olaf*, 55.

urer[12] his English origin becomes peculiarly significant; the whole fiscal system of the kingdom seems to have originated in the royal chapel. As a king's chaplain in those days usually meant a future chancellor, we should expect to find traces of English influence in the Norse chancery. And it is interesting to note that in the Norwegian laws of the thirteenth century, the terms *kanceler* and *innsigli*[13] appear, identical as far as phonetics would permit, with Old English *canceler* and *innsegl*. That *cancellarius* should have developed similar forms in both these idioms is not surprising; but that both should have practically the same word for seal seems rather strange. Such a term might be derived from *sigillum, sigillare*, or *insigillare; innsegl* and *innsigli* are both from *insigillare*, apparently the least used of the three.[14] There is also a striking similarity between some of the documents emanating from the Norse chancery in the thirteenth century[15] and the Old English writs drawn up by Anglo-Saxon clerks two hundred years before. The charters of the Norwegian kings are usually drawn up in the vulgar idiom and in the form of writs. With the bulls and mandates that regularly arrived from Rome, they have little in common. The formulas used are such as might easily be borrowed from the Confessor's scriptorium. One of King Hakon's grants opens with the following salutation: 'King Hakon Hakon's son sends to Sir Askatl, bishop of Stavanger, N. the archdeacon and all the canons, learned men and landed men,[16] franklins and freeholders, present and future, God's friends and the king's, who may see or hear this letter, God's greetings and his own.'[17] Similar to this, though less elaborate, is the opening sentence of one of Edward's writs: 'King Edward sends to Stigand the archbishop and Ægelmær the bishop and Gyrth the eorl and Toli the shire-reeve, and all his thegns in Norfolk and in Suffolk and all his other wise men (*witan*) throughout all England, learned and lay, friendly greet-

---

[12] Keyser, *Efterladte Skrifter*, II, 82.
[13] *Norges gamle Love*, V, Glossary.
[14] See Du Cange, *Glossarium*.
[15] Norse charters dated before 1200 are exceedingly rare.
[16] The phrase "lærðom oc lendom" means ecclesiastics and tenants on the king's estates.
[17] *Diplomatarium Norvegicum*, I, 1, No. 51 (1226-1254): H[akon] konongr son H[akonar] konongs sendir herra A[skatle] biskupe i Stavangre, N, ærkidiacne oc ollum korsbrøðrum, lærðom oc lendom buandum oc buþægnum, verandum oc viðcomandum ollum guðs vinum oc sinum, þeim er þetta bref sia eða høyra, Q. G. oc. sina. Cf. VIII, 1, Nos. 2 (1170-90), 4 (1170-94), 5 (1202).

ings.'[18] Hakon's charter also has the attestation stated in the same rather informal fashion that we find so often in the Anglo-Saxon writs of the eleventh century. 'And these are the witnesses to this grant: Margaret the queen,.........John the king's court-priest and many other doughty men, learned and lay.'[19] Compare with this the subscriptions to an English document dated 1044: 'And these are the witnesses: Edward the king, and Ælfgyfu the lady.....and Ælfwine the red and many men in adition to them, both learned and lay, within burg and without.'[20] In both formulas the resemblance is too close to be accidental. The charter referred to is by no means exceptional; and further comparison would no doubt disclose many other points of similarity.[21]

As the Norman kings continued the use of the Old English writs,[22] it is possible that this diplomatic form may have come to Norway from the Norman-English chancery. But the probabilities are against this view, as there was very little communication between the Norse and the English court after 1066 compared with what there was before that date. On the other hand we know that the king's chapel in Norway had an Anglo-Saxon origin and that the chaplain acted as royal notary.[23] But even if the Norse chancery did get its formulas from the court of Henry I or of Henry II, their origin would, though indirectly, still be Anglo-Saxon.

The royal court of William the Conqueror was organized on Norman-French lines. The marshal[24] took the place of the staller. The chamberlain's fiscal duties were transferred to the

---
[18] *K. C. D.*, No. 853: Eadward cyng gret Stigand ercebiscop, and Ægelmær biscop, and Gyrð eorl. and Toli scirreue, and ealle his þeines inne Norðfolce and inne Suffolce and ealle his oðra witen ofer eall Ænglande, hadede and leawede, freondlice.

[19] *Diplomatarium Norvegicum*, I, 1, No. 51: En þesser ero vitnis men at þessare giof. Margretta drotneng...... Johan bulsi hirðprestr konongs, oc marger aðrer duganda menn, lærðer oc olærðer. Cf. VIII. 1 No. 2 (1170-90).

[20] *K. C. D.*, No. 773: And þises is to gewitnesse, eadweard cyncg, and ælfgyfu seo hlæfdige.....and ælfwine se reada, and mænig man þærto eacan ge gehadude ge læwede, binnan burgan and butan.

[21] Subscriptions are not very common in the Norse charters, as the seal is used instead.

[22] See Stevenson, An Old English Charter: *Eng. Hist. Rev.*, XI, 731 ff.

[23] Keyser, *Efterladte Skrifter*, II, 82.

[24] Such is his title in *Domesday*. So far as I know, constabularius is used but once in that document and then as a synonym of staller (I, 151). Stubbs gives the Norman court officials as seneschal, cup-bearer, constable, chamberlain and chancellor. *C. H.*, I, 372-73, 380.

treasurer. But on the whole I believe we are inclined to overestimate some of the institutional changes that came in with the Conquest. During the reign of Edward the Confessor the English court seems to have become very nearly assimilated to the type that prevailed across the Channel. And the Conqueror doubtless retained many household customs and usages that were distinctly English. The Chronicler in reviewing William's life tells us that 'three times he bore his crown each year as often as he was in England; at Easter he bore it at Winchester, at Pentecost at Westminster and at midwinter at Gloucester.'[25] At first sight this looks like something of an innovation: a court held regularly at the three great festivals and at three different places, with much parade and the crown on display. 'And then there were with him,' continues the Chronicler, 'all the mighty men of England, archbishops, bishops, abbots, earls, thegns and knights.' We must be careful, however, not to read too much into this. An examination of the sources dealing with Edward's reign will show that the royal court met in festive gatherings with considerable regularity on the great church festivals in the boroughs of Gloucester and Winchester. Evidently what the Chronicler wishes to emphasize is the fact, that after 1066 these gatherings were more formal and pompous, for the Confessor, we are told, lived very plainly.[26]

Like his predecessors, Edward moved his court from place to place, but his movements were more systematic than theirs. A satisfactory itinerary for his reign cannot be made out, but we can at least produce a very suggestive outline.[27] From this it appears that, so far as we know, the king sojourned principally in three leading cities: Gloucester, Winchester and London. He apparently spent the winter months at Gloucester: we find him

---

[25] *A.-S. Chron.*, 1087.
[26] William of Malmesbury, *Gesta Regum*, 271.
[27] 1043. Easter, Winchester. *A.-S. Chron.*, [1042], 1043: *Flor. Wig.*, I, 197. Later in the year we find him at Gloucester where he probably intended to spend the winter; but his lords advised him to descend on the queen's treasures at Winchester, which was done, Nov. 16. *Ibid.*
1044. August, gemot at London. *Flor. Wig.*, I, 199.
1045-1050. No satisfactory information. The king is once in London at a gemot and twice at Sandwich with the fleet. *A. S. Chron.*, 1046, 1047; *Flor. Wig.*, I, 199.
1051. September and later, Gloucester. *Flor. Wig.*, I, 205.
1052. London. The king was present at two assemblies, the latter of which seems to have been held in September. By Christmas he was probably back in

there in September, November, December and January.[28] The two Easter festivals of which we have any account were celebrated at Winchester; at no other time do we find King Edward in that city, except in November, 1043, when he came to raid his mother's treasury. It also appears that London was the favorite place for holding the national assemblies and that these might be called for any date. William was certainly violating no English precedent when he celebrated Christmas at Gloucester and Easter at Winchester. We hear nothing of a Whitsunday celebration in Edward's time. This may have been instituted by the Conqueror to compensate London for the loss of the many meetings of the *witan*.

These festivals were doubtless in obedience to an ancient custom antedating Christianity and by no means limited to the Angles and Saxons.[29] Charters issued on such occasions testify to the character of the assembly that gathered to celebrate with the king. In a life of Saint Oswald, two such banquets are described, the one being an Easter session of the *witenagemot*. 'He himself and all the eminent *primates* and distinguished *duces* and powerful *milites* from all the towns *(castellis)* and strongholds *(oppidis)* and cities and regions, and an infinite multitude came to the king. There came also that prince of bishops, Dun-

---

Gloucester, for we find him there early in January. *A.-S. Chron.*, [1051], 1052; *Flor. Wig.*, I, 209.
    1053. January, Gloucester. *Flor. Wig.*, I, 211. Easter, Winchester. At this festival Godwin died. *Ibid.*; *A.-S. Chron.*, 1053.
    1055. Midlent, London. A witenagemot. Later in the year the army is gathered about the king at Gloucester. *A.-S. Chron.*, 1055; *Flor. Wig.*, I, 212–13.
    1057. Death of Edgar the Etheling at London. Edward was probably there at the time. *A.-S. Chron.*, 1057; *Flor. Wig.*, I, 215.
    1062. The king was probably at Gloucester during the winter months. Two papal legates were waiting at Worcester near that city for a reply which the king had promised to give at the Paschal feast. They went to Worcester on Edward's suggestion. *Flor. Wig.*, I, 220.
    1063. Christmas, Gloucester. *Ibid.*, 221.
    1065. Christmas, Westminster. Dedication of Westminster Abbey. *Ibid.*, 224; *A.-S. Chron.*, 1065.
    [28] The year 1065 is exceptional. Edward's absence from Gloucester finds its explanation in his desire to see the church at Westminster dedicated before death, which he felt was approaching, should take him away.
    [29] The Yule-festival of the northern tribes was celebrated in the middle of January; one of Hakon the Good's first acts in his vain effort to christianize the Norwegians was to move this festival to December 25. Snorre, *Hakon's Saga*, 15. The attempted assassination of Edwin as dated by Bede was on the first day of Easter. *H. E.*, II, 9. Many were present and the gathering has all the appearance of a feast. But the celebration could not have been in honor of

stan with his retinue and also the holy prelate Æthelwold and all the worthies of Albion, all of whom the king received royally, granting them the delights of great joy and blending festivities with merry gladness on that Easter day.'[30] From the nature of the language used we should conclude that the writer was present at the banquet and had his share of the mixed delights.[31]

As the magnates from all over the realm were present at these gatherings,[32] the business of the kingdom would naturally come up for discussion or decision. In other words, they were sessions of the *Witenagemot*.[33] As such they furnished a precedent for the *curia regis* of the Norman kings. Whether there was in Old English times a *curia regis* in the narrower sense, a judicial and administrative body like the one we find in the reign of Henry I and later,[34] is a more difficult question. I know of no evidence for an administrative curia before the Conquest. On the judicial side of the question something can be said, but the evidence even for a judicial curia in Saxon times is far from satisfactory. As we have already seen, the early laws imply that there was a considerable exercise of judicial authority at the king's vill.[35] We also find that the later kings retained the power of punishing or pardoning offenders in their own households. 'If any one fight in the king's house, he shall forfeit all his property and the king shall determine whether or not he shall have his life.' Such

---

Easter, as Christianity was not yet a fact in Northumbria. Either Bede must have been in error or there was a heathen festival falling in the early vernal season which the Christian historian has confused with Easter. In 656, Peada the Mercian king, was treacherously slain "in ipso tempore festi paschalis." *Ibid.*, III, 24. It was on the occasion of such a festival that King Oswald ordered the silver dish to be cut up and given to the poor. *Hist. York*, I, 358. For the Germanic festivals see Müllenhoff, *Deutsche Altertumskunde*, IV, 213 ff.

[30] *Hist. York*, I, 425. (Written in Æthelred's reign.) The second festival is merely alluded to, but all the worthies of the region were present. "Cum esset omnis dignitas hujusce regionis cum rege in Paschali festivitate contigit ....ut quidam inclytus miles regis obiret. *Ibid.*, 427.

[31] There was a banquet at Easter in 1043 when Edward was crowned, and there was also much feasting at the Easter celebration at Winchester when Godwin died. See *A.-S. Chron.*, 1043, 1053.

[32] On the fourth day of Christmas, 1064, Gospatric, a Northumbrian nobleman, was murdered "in curia regis" by order of the queen, perhaps on Tostig's instigation. The fact that this Northumbrian was present would lead us to infer that the occasion was a general gathering of the aristocracy. *Flor. Wig.*, I, 223.

[33] Cf. Stubbs, *C. H.*, I, 138; Kemble, *Sax. in Eng.*, II, 191.

[34] See Stubbs, *C. H.*, I, 407.

[35] *Laws of Æthelbirht*, 2; *Laws of Hlotar and Eadric*, 7, 16.

was Ine's law,[36] and Alfred's code has a similar chapter.[37] The royal authority in this matter is further extended in the laws of Edmund,[38] Æthelred[39] and Cnut.[40] In direct line with this is the judicial authority of the *Huskarlesteffne* as described by Sveno. If this gemot was ever a reality in England, as it evidently was, we should look upon it as one of the possible sources of the later *curia regis*.[41] Its jurisdiction was, indeed, limited to the membership of the corps, but that would not prevent it from developing and spreading.[42] And there are also indications that the king sometimes exercised judicial authority in cases where the litigants were not necessarily members of the royal household.[43]

It will not do to make any extravagant claims for the Anglo-Saxon *curia* as a part of the national government. If it existed at all as such, it must have been in a rather undeveloped form. All we are justified in affirming is that the principle of curial jurisdiction seems to have been established to some extent, and that the practice of applying the laws in the king's own court was familiar to the nation. It will thus be seen that William the Conqueror could with comparative ease fit his own system into that of the Saxon kings. It may have been radically different in theory, but if it amounted to the same thing in practice there would be no great opposition to its permanent establishment. Perhaps there was, after all, not such a great difference between the system of national administration (if such a term may be used) that the Conqueror found in England and the system that he brought with him from Normandy. In many respects the

---

[36] C. 6.
[37] C. 7.
[38] II, 4 : Eac ic cyðe, þæt ic nelle socne habban to minum hirede þone, þe mannes blod geate.
[39] VI, 36 : And gif mordwyrhtan oððe man-sworan oððe æbære man-slagan to þam geþristian, þæt hi on þæs cyninges neaweste gewunian ær þam þe hi habban bote agunnen.....þone plihte hi heora æhton butan hit friðbenan sindan.
[40] II, 59 : Gif hwa on cynincges hirede gefeohte, þolige þæs lifes buton se cynincg him geahrian wylle.
[41] I find the same conclusion stated in Holberg's work: *Dansk Rigslovgivning*, 93.
[42] Such was actually the case in Denmark. 'Persons who did not belong to the royal household would voluntarily submit their differences to the king's household court for settlement ;' and in this way the tribunal of the housecarles developed into a system of popular courts. *Ibid*.
[43] See Zinkeisen, Anglo Saxon Courts of Law : *Political Science Quarterly*, X, 132-35.

Confessor's reign was a transitional one. The palatine organization was rapidly taking on a Norman appearance. English feudalism was coming more and more to resemble the Continental type. Men from across the Channel were influential in directing the policies of the English church. It seems more than probable that the Normans did not introduce so many innovations as has formerly been supposed; that some of the principal changes attributed to them date from the closing years of the Anglo-Saxon period.

INDEX.

Abbots, admitted to the royal council, 102; of the Merovingian court, 187.
Absentee-thegn, duties of, 99.
Accipitrarius, 175–76.
Adzurus, king's *dapifer*, 135.
Æfic, high-reeve, 115.
Æfic, seneschal of the ethelings, 135.
Ælfheah, seneschal, 134.
Ælfredus, *strator regius*, 150.
Ælfsige, *discifer*, 134.
Ælfstan, staller, 151.
Ælfwine, king's priest, 139, 141.
Ælmere, Æthelstan Etheling's seneschal, 135.
Æschere, cup-bearer at Heorot, 126.
Æsgarus (Asgærus), staller or *dapifer*, 135; great wealth of, 149; mentioned, 151.
Æthelflæd's banquet in honor of King Æthelstan, 126.
Æthelred, perhaps the first English king who used a seal, 145; Norman influence at the court of, 195.
Æthelsie, chamberlain, 129.
Æthelstan, king's priest, 138–39.
Æthelstan's policy as to the *witan*, 102; as to dynastic alliances, 195.
Æthelthryth, queen of the East Angles, 118–19.
Æthelweard, high-reeve, 114.
Alanus, *dapifer*, 135.
Aldhun, king's reeve, 108.
Alfred's court, thegns at, 98; ecclesiastics numerous at, 138; contrasted with Æthelstan's, 194.
Almoner, king's, 181.
Alneredus, marshal, 150. See Ælfredus.
Aluric, chamberlain, 129.
Anglo-Saxon court in the reign of Alfred, 98, 138; in the tenth century, 125, 139–40, 194; in the eleventh century, 195–96; foreign influences at, 193–96; as an influence affecting other courts, 196 ff.
Antrustions of the Frankish court, 187.

Archchancellor of the Frankish court, 188.
Archicapellanus (*summus capellanus*), Frankish, 142.
Armiger, king's, 178–79.

Baker, king's, 181.
Banner, king's, appearance of, 180–81.
Bear-sarks, of the Norse court, 157–58.
Bebbanburh, importance of, 114.
Bed-thegn, king's, 128.
Beorn, Cnut's nephew, slain by Swegen, 165–66.
Beornstan, king's priest, 138–39.
Beor-sccalc, Old English cup-bearer, 125.
Berctfrith, king's prefect, military leader, 109; declares the decision of the *witan*, 112–13.
Bertha, queen of Kent, 137.
Beverages served at royal banquets, 126–27.
Biga, king's wagon-maker, 182, 196.
Biographies of kings and saints, 66, 70–71.
Bishops at the early Anglo-Saxon courts, 102.
Björn, Norwegian staller, **147–48.**
Bondig, staller, 151–52.
Brorda, prefect, 110.
Burcniht, 128.
Bur-thegn (bower-thegn), keeper of the king's chamber, 128; keeper of the king's documents, 133, 143.
Butcher (*carnifex*), 182.
Buticularius, 185. See butler.
Butler, an officer of the early Teutonic household, 124, 185; mentioned in Eadred's will, 125; earlier allusions to, 93, 125–26; duties of, 126–28; a prominent official in the tenth century, 136, 140, 172; at the Frankish courts, 186, 188, 189; at the Norse court, 191–92; at the Old English court, 193, 194, 196.
Byrele (cup-bearer), 125–26.

206 INDEX.

Camerarius, 128–29, 188. See chamberlain.
Canceler, 198. See chancellor.
Candle-bearers at the Norse court, 190.
Capellanus, 138. See priest.
Capetian court, 189.
Carolingian court, 187–88.
Carnifex. See butcher.
Cefi, *ealdorbisceop* at Edwin's court, 101–02.
Cellerarius, keeper of provisions, 132.
Chamberlain, an early Teutonic official, 124, 185; keeper of the king's wardrobe, 128; terms used for, 128–29; usually had colleagues, 129; ordinary functions of, 129–30; acted as royal treasurer, 130, 132–33, 199; one of the chiefs of the household service, 136, 193–94; at the Frankish court, 188, 189.
Chancellor, mentioned, 141, in the reign of Edward the Confessor, 144; duties of, 144; conclusions regarding, 145, 193–94, 196; at the Frankish court, 188–89; at the Norse court, 192, 198.
Chancery, mentioned, 132; writs and formulas of, 132, 198–99; uncertainty as to first appearance of, in England, 143; opinions of earlier students regarding, 143–44; probably introduced from Normandy in Æthelred's reign, 145, 196; at the Frankish court, 187–90; at the Norse court, 192, 198; at the Norman-English court, 199.
Chapel, royal, reward for service in, 140–42; developed into a chancery, 142–43, 194; at the Carolingian court, 188; at the Norse court, 192, 198–99.
Chaplain, king's, 137–43. See priest.
Charters, Old English, 64–65, 96, 109, 132, 142, 198–99; Norse, 198–99.
Christianity, effect of, on Old English institutions, 94.
Classification of thegns in Cnut's laws, 102; of court servants in Eadred's will, 125–184; of kingsmen in Norway, 190.
Cnut's guard, 71, 159–71; thegns, 102; priests, 139, 141; court, 146; invading host, 156–58.
Comes, 77, 84–86. See gesith.
Comes palatii of the Merovingian court, 187.

Comes stabuli, not the equivalent of staller, 146–47; an early Teutonic official, 185–86.
Comitatus in Anglian and Eddic poetry, 67, 77–78, 92; earliest princely household among the Teutons, 76; decline of, 81; nature of, 82–84; members of, how rewarded, 86–87; developed into a landed aristocracy, 87, 95–98; in its later form composed of thegns, 89 ff; of Woden, 94; of Jom, 154–56; of housecarles, 170.
Consiliarii, 183.
Conviva regis, 182–83.
Constable, Frankish, mentioned, 186; office of, suppressed, 189.
Constabularius, 151.
Continental influence on the Old English court, 193–96.
Cook, king's, 181.
Councillors, king's, 183.
Count of the palace, at the Merovingian court, 186; duties of, 187; disappears from the Capetian court, 189; no trace of, in the English sources, 194.
Court poetry, Old English, 122; Norse, 146–147, 153.
Cubicularius, 128–29. See chamberlain.
Cumbol, banner, 180.
Cup-bearers at the English court, 125–28, 196; at the Norse court, 190.
Curia regis, the, may have existed as a judicial body before 1066, 202–04.
Custos cubile, 128. See chamberlain.
Cuthred, *pessesor*, 123.
Cynehelm, crown, not worn by the queen, 118.

Danelaw, possibility of high-reeves in, 116; no house-carles in, 164.
Danish dynasty, influence of, 146, 195.
Danish sources, 71–72.
Dapifer, 134–35, 172, 191–92, 196. See seneschal.
Deor, *scop*, 122.
Discifer (*discoforus*), 134, 173. See seneschal.
Discþegn (dish-thegn), 133, 197. See seneschal.
Domesday, 71.
Dooms, Old English, 65–66.
Doorward, king's, 181.
Drihten, warlord, 77.

INDEX.

Drott (*drottinn, drottning*), 76–77.
Drottseti, Norse seneschal, 191.
Duduc, king's priest, 141.
Dux, significance of term in the ninth century, 111.
Dynastic alliances in the tenth and eleventh centuries, 194–95.
Dysteyn, Welsh seneschal, 197.

Eadbald, king's prefect, 110.
Eadnoth, staller, 150, 151.
Eadred's will, 125.
Eadsie, king's priest, 141.
Eadsige, king's reeve, 114.
Eadwold, king's priest, 139.
Ealdorbisceop, chief priest at Edwin's court, 101.
Ealdorman, not necessarily a shire-official, 105–06; in the North-people's Law, 114; mentioned in Eadred's will, 125.
Ealdred, seneschal, 134.
Ealhstan, king's priest, 139.
Eastmund, *pedisecus*, 123.
Ecclesiastics at the Old English court, 137 ff.; at the Frankish court, 187–89; at the imperial court, 190; at the Norse court, 191–92.
Ecgulf, horse-thegn, 150, 176.
Eddas, 68, 153.
Edling, derived from Anglo-Saxon eðeling, 197.
Edmund Etheling, seneschals of, 118.
Edmund's household, members of, dwelt in different shires, 99.
Ednod, *dapifer*, 135.
Edward the Confessor, chaplains of, 140–41; house-carles of, 168–71; educated in Normandy, 195–96; court of, 196; festivities at court of, 200; itinerary of, 200–01.
Edward the Elder's attitude toward ecclesiastics, 96, 138–39.
Edwin, king of Northumbria, household of 94–95.
Ellif (Eglaf), chief of the vikings at London, 155–56.
Emele, prefect, 110.
Eorl, as described in the earlier poetry, 69, 77–78, 92; privileges of, 79; leader of a comitatus, 80–81, 86–87; becomes known as gesith, 82.
Eorlcund, 90.
Esme, prefect, 110.
Etheling, equivalent of princeps, 66; of *edling*, 197.

Falconer, king's, 176.
Familiares (*famuli*), 183.
Feorm, king's, 174.
Festivals celebrated at the English and Norman-English courts, 200–01.
Five-hide theory, 101.
Fore-oath, employed at the gemot of house-carles, 167.

Gazophylacium, king's treasury, 133.
Geneat, service owed by, 98; definition of term, 182–83.
Gerefa, king's, 104 ff. See reeve.
Gesith, original meaning of term, 82; a member of some *comitatus*, 82–84; becomes a land-owner, 85–86; receives gifts from his lord, 86–87; conclusions regarding, 87–88.
Gesiþcund, 85, 86, 90.
Gesiþræden, 84.
Giso, king's priest, 141.
Godric, son of Godmannus, king's priest, 141.
Godwin's trial, 166–67.
Goldsmith, king's, 182.
Grimbald, king's priest, 138.
Grimkell, Norse court bishop, 148.
Guests (*Gestir*) of the Norse court, 173, 174, 190.
Gwesdva, food-rent, due to the Welsh king, 174.
Gwestai, servants at the Welsh court, 174.

Haligdom, king's treasures, 131, 133.
Hall-thegn, 93.
Heafod-weard, nature of, 98.
Heah-gerefa, 113 ff. See high-reeve.
Heca, king's priest, 141.
Heming, chief of the vikings at Slesswick, 155–56.
Here, a term used in the Chronicle for the guard of house-carles, 165–67.
Hereman, king's priest, 141.
High-reeve, earliest mention of, in the sources, 113–14; significance of term as used in the tenth century documents, 114–15; conclusions regarding, 116.
Hirð, term derived from Anglo-Saxon *hired*, 197.
Hirðbiskup, chief priest at the Norse court, 191–92.
Hirðmenn, royal guard at the Norse court, 173; number of, 190; rank at court, 191.

INDEX.

Hirðprestar, household priests of the Norse king, 192.
Hirðskraa, Norse court law, 148.
Hirðstefna, gemot of the hirðmenn, 165–66.
Historians, modern, 73–75.
Histories, chronicles, and biographies, 70–73.
Hoard, king's, character of, 130–31; guarded by the chamberlain, 133.
Hoarder (*hordere*), significance of the term as used in the sources, 131–32; not a court official, 132.
Homilies, Anglo-Saxon, 70.
Hornklofi, Harold Fairhair's minstrel, 157.
Horse-thegn, not the equivalent of staller, 146; one of the lesser court officials, 150; office of, 176, 178.
Horswealh, not of the royal stable service, 176–77; conclusions regarding, 177–78.
Hospites, servants at the Welsh court, 175.
House-carle-gemot. See *huskarle steffne*.
House-carles, Cnut's guard of, 71, 152–71, 196; earliest appearance of, 152; meaning of term, 153; Munch's opinion regarding, 156; of Norse origin, 157–58; guild of, when established in England, 158–59; laws governing, 159–63; were mercenary troops, 163–64; gemot of, 165–67; number of, 167–68; final fate of guild of, 168–69; summary of conclusions regarding, 170–71; of the Norse court, 190.
Hrægel-weard (rail-thegn), keeper of the king's wardrobe, 128.
Hugelinus (Hugo), chamberlain, 129, 133.
Hundred, opinions of Adams, Hildebrand, and Steenstrup regarding 106–07; not the equivalent of *regio*, 107.
Huskarlesteffne, gemot of house-carles for settling disputes arising within the guild, 159; evidence for, in the Chronicle, 165–67; probably continued in the *curia regis,* 203.

Imperial household, 189–90.
Infertor, seneschal, 185–86, 188.
Influence of the Old English court on the court of Wales, 196–97; of Norway, 197–99; of the Norman Conqueror, 199 ff.

Itinerary of Edward the Confessor, 200–01.

John, king's priest, 138.
Jomvikings, 154–57.

Kanceler, Norse, 198.
Kertisveinar, candle-bearers at the court of Norway, 190.
King's council, 101–03. See *witenagemot*.
King's daughters, position of, at court, 118.
King's household, 63, 70, 91–92, 94, 99, 100–103, 108, 125–27, 137, 139–40, 146, 165–66, 172–74, 186–88, 191 ff. *et passim*. See Alfred, Æthelstan, Anglo-Saxon, Capetian, Carolingian, Cnut, Edmund, Edward the Confessor, Edwin, Merovingian, Norman-English, Northumbrian and Saint Olaf.
King's vill, 108, 190.
Kola, king's high-reeve, 114–15.
Kynsige, king's priest, 141.

Land-dues of thegns and geneats, 98–100.
Laws, Old English, 65–66, 69–70; Norse, 148, 162.
Lay of Righ, quoted, 77–78.
Lesser officials and servants of the king's household, 172 ff.; steward, 172–75; huntsmen and falconers, 175–76; horse thegns and 'horswealhs', 176–178; sword-bearers, 178–79; standard-bearers, 179–80; preceptors, almoners, door-wards, cooks, bakers, mead-makers, *praerisores,* butchers, physicians, smiths, goldsmiths and wagon-makers, 181–82. See also p. 196.
Leofric, king's priest and chancellor, 141, 144.
Lifing (Leofing), staller, 135, 151.
Litsmen, naval troops, 168–69.
Liudhard, queen's chaplain, 137.

Magister calicum, chief butler, 126.
Major domus, Merovingian, 111, 112, 118–19, 186–88, 192; officer corresponding most nearly to, in England, 118–19, 149, 194.

INDEX.

Markgraf, Carolingian, *heah-gerefa* corresponding to, 116.
Marksman of the Norse court, 179, 191-92.
Marshal, Teutonic, 124, 185 : Danish, 148 ; Old English, 176, 194 ; Merovingian, 186 ; Norman, 199.
Massacre of Danes in 1015, 155-56.
Master of the horse, 136. See marshal.
Mayor of the palace. See *major domus*.
Meadmaker, king's, 181.
Medyt, derivation of term, 197.
Merkismaðr, See marksman.
Merovingian court, 186-88.
Messenger service, king's, 99-100, 177.
Minister, Latin equivalent of thegn, 93 ; continuity of service of, 95 ; mentioned, 97, 124 ; privileges of, 102-03, 193-94.
Minister equorum, 176. See horse-thegn.
Ministeriales, 183.
Ministrel, king's. See *scop*.
Monasteries as royal treasuries, 130.

'Nithing', originally a Norse term, 165-66.
Norman-English court, 199-200.
Norse court, 157, 190-92, 197-99.
Norse sources, 68, 72-73.
Northumbrian court, 94, 101-02, 137, 140.
Notary (*notarius*), subordinate to chancellor, 144 ; at the Merovingian court, 187 ; chaplain of the Norse king acted as, 192.

Oferealdorman, chief of Queen Æthelthryth's court, 119, 192.
Osgod Clapa, staller, 148, 151-52.
Oslac, king's butler, 126.
Ostiarius, doorward, 181.
Osulf, high-reeve, 114.
Owini, Queen Æthelthryth's *major domus*, 118.

Palatini, 183.
Patrician, 118.
Paulinus, queen's chaplain, 137.
Pedes sessor (pessesor), 123.
Pedisecus (pedisequus), 123-24.
Physician, king's, 182.
Poetic sources, 67-68.
Praefectus, 104, 107, 110, 113. See reeve.

Praepositus, 104, 181.
Praevisores, 182.
Preceptor, king's, 181.
Prefect, 104 ff. See reeve.
Presbyter, 138-41. See priest.
Priest, king's, in Kent and Northumbria, 137 ; at Alfred's court, 138 ; in the tenth century, 138-39 ; admitted to the *witan,* 138 ; position of, 139-40 ; rewards of, 140-41 ; functions of, 142-43.
Princeps, 66, 87, 113, 119.
Princes, royal, position of, at court, 118.

Queen's household, 95, 118-19.

Rædesmann, king's, 119.
Reeve, king's, in the eighth century, 104, 107 ; as a fiscal agent, 107-08 ; as a judicial assistant, 108 ; as a military chief, 108-09 ; official tenure of, 110-11 ; held a lucrative position, 111-12 ; analogous to the Merovingian *major domus,* 112-13, 119 ; mentioned, 115.
Redfrid, king's reeve, 108.
Referendarius, chief notary of the Merovingian kings, 187-88.
Regenbaldus, king's priest and chancellor, 141, 144-45.
Regio, not a territorial hundred, 106-07.
Relationship between eorl and gesith, 82-83 ; between king and thegn, 95.
Rewards and privileges of gesiths, 86-87 ; of king's thegns, 95-97, 101-102 ; of the king's high officials, 111, 134, 193 ; of the king's priests, 138, 140-42 ; of the house-carles, 162-64 ; of the palace servants, 184.
Rodbertus, marshal, 151-52.
Roger, marshal, 150.
Roulf (Radulfus), staller, 135, 149, 151-52.
Runic inscriptions, 83, 120.

Sagas, Norse, 72-73.
Saint Olaf's court, 190, 197.
Satellites of Alfred's court, 98, 183.
Scald, a professional historian, 72-73.
Scandinavian court customs, 162.
Scantio, butler, 185.
Scir. See shire.
Scirman of the Laws of Ine not necessarily a shire-reeve, 105 ; a manager of a large estate, 107.

INDEX.

Scirgerefa, sheriff, 104–05.
Scop, king's minstrel, history of, 121–22; conclusions regarding, 123.
Scriniarius, Ælfric's translation of, 143.
Scutel (*scutella*), 197.
Seal, when first used in England, 144–45; use of, in the Norse chancery, 198.
Segen, banner, 180.
Seneschal, an early Teutonic official, 124; earliest mention of, 125, 134; dignity of, 134–35, 193; duties of, 135–36, 173, 194, 196; Merovingian, 186.
Sequipedas. See *pedisecus.*
Serfs on royal estates, 177, 183.
Shire, no evidence for, before the reign of Alfred, 105–06.
Sighvat the Poet, Cnut's minstrel, 147.
Signifer. See standard-bearer.
Skenkari, Norse butler, 191.
Skutilsveinar, table-servants at the Norse court, 190.
Slaves on royal estates, 183.
Smith, king's, 182.
Sources, dscussion of, 64–73, 152–53.
Spatarius, king's sword-bearer, 178.
Speculum Regale, description of Norse court system in, 99.
Stabilitor (*stabulator*), 147, 151.
Stallari, Norse staller, earliest appearance of, 147; duties of, in the thirteenth century, 149, 191, mentioned, 169; rank of, at court, 148, 191.
Staller, mentioned, 135; earlier opinions regarding, 146–47; of Norse origin, 147–48, 185; found in the reigns of Cnut, Edward, and Harold, 148–151, 195; functions of, 149–50, 194, 196, 199.
Standard-bearer, king's, 179–80.
Steward, mentioned in Eadred's will, 125; equivalent of *hordere*, 132; sometimes translated *dapifer*, 172–73; office of, possibly analogous to that of the Norse guests and the Welsh *gwestai*, 173–74; duties of, 174–75.
Stigand, king's priest, 139, 141.
Stir (Steorra), king's *nœdesmann*, 119.
Strator regius, 150.
Sunder-note, special service owed by the king's thegns, 97–98.
Swyrd-bora, king's sword-bearer, 178.

Table-servants at the Norse court, 190–92, 197.
Tacn, standard, 180.
Tata, king's priest, 139.
Thegn, etymology of term, 89–90; significance of the term in the earliest sources, 90–93.
Thegns, successors of the gesiths in the royal comitatus, 87–88; called *ministri* in the Latin sources, 93; number of, at the English courts of the seventh and eighth centuries, 94–95; position of, a permanent one, 95; grants of lands to, 96–97; duties of, 97–99; not always at court, 97–99; privileges of, 99–102; at the Norse court, 99; under the Danish kings, 102–03; mention of, 183.
Thesaurarius, king's treasurer, came to England with the Normans, 132; at the Merovingian court, 186; called *camerarius* at the Carolingian court, 188.
'Thingamannalith', host of house-carles. See 'Thingamenn.'
'Thingamenn', probable origin of the term, 154; corps of, when established, 155, 158–59; mentioned in Morkinskinna, 169.
Thored, staller, 152.
Thorkil, leader of the vikings in England, 155–56.
Thuf, royal standard, 180.
'Thulr', the sage at the king's court, 120.
Thunor, preceptor, 181.
'Thyle', 120–21. See 'Thulr'.
Titstan, chamberlain, 129.
Tofig, staller, 152.
Treasurer, king's, mentioned, 130; chamberlain acting as, 132–33, 135; chaplain at the Norse court, acting as, 192, 197–98; at the Norman-English court, 132, 199–200.
Treasury, king's, 130–33.

Ulf, king's priest, 141.
Ulf, Norse staller, 169.
Unferth, 'thyle', 120.

Venator regis, 175–76.

INDEX.

Wæpen-bora, king's armour-bearer, 178-79.
Wages of royal servants. See rewards and privileges.
Wagon-maker, king's, 196. See *biga*.
Walter, queen's chaplain, 141.
Wealh-gerefa, probable significance of term, 177-78.
Welsh court, 196-97.
Wenesi, chamberlain, 129.
Werulf, king's priest, 138-39.
Widsith, king's minstrel, 86, 92, 122.
William, king's priest, 141.
William's court, customs at, 200-01.

Winchester, royal treasury located at, 131.
Winstan, chamberlain, 129.
Witenagemot, ministri members of, 102, 193; acting with *here* at Godwin's trial, 166; sessions of, at the great festivals, 201-02.
Wolf-coats, 158. See bear-sarks.
Writs, Old English, 149, 198-99.
Wulfheard, prefect, 109, 111.
Wulfhelm, seneschal, 134.
Wulfric, Welsh-reeve, 177.

Yfingus, *dapifer*, 135.